Aspects of the Modern European Mind

John Cruickshank

PROFESSOR OF FRENCH
AT THE UNIVERSITY OF SUSSEX

LONGMANS

LONGMANS, GREEN AND CO LTD
London and Harlow

*Associated companies, branches and representatives
throughout the world*

© Longmans, Green & Co Ltd 1969
First published 1969

*Printed in Great Britain by Richard Clay (The Chaucer Press), Ltd.,
Bungay, Suffolk*

Editor's Foreword

'Study problems in preference to periods' was the excellent advice given by Lord Acton in his inaugural lecture at Cambridge. To accept it is one thing, to put it into practice is another. In fact, in both schools and universities the teaching of history, in depth, is often hindered by certain difficulties of a technical nature, chiefly to do with the availability of sources. In this respect, history tends to be badly off in comparison with literature or the sciences. The historical equivalents of set texts, readings or experiments, in which the student is encouraged to use his own mind, are the so-called 'special periods'. If these are to be fruitful, the student must be encouraged to deal in his own way with the problems raised by historical documents and the historiography of the issues in question and he must be made aware of the wider perspectives of history. Thus, if the enclosure movement of the sixteenth century is studied, the student might examine the historiographical explanations stretching from More's *Utopia* and Cobbett to Beresford's *Lost Villages of England*. At the same time he might also be dealing with selected documents raising important problems. Finally he might be encouraged to realize the problems of peasantries at other periods of time, including Russia and China in the nineteenth and twentieth centuries. In this particular instance, thanks to Tawney and Power, *Tudor Economic Documents*, the history teacher is comparatively well off. For other special periods the situation is much more difficult. If, however, the study of history is to encourage the development of the critical faculties as well as the memory, this approach offers the best hope. The object of this series is to go some way towards meeting these difficulties.

The general plan of each volume in the series will be similar, with a threefold approach from aspects of historiography, documents and editorial consideration of wider issues, though the structure and balance between the three aspects may vary.

A broad view is being taken of the limits of history. Political history will not be excluded, but a good deal of emphasis will be placed on economic, intellectual and social history. The idea has in fact grown out of the experience of a group of historians at the University of Sussex, where the student is encouraged to investigate the frontier areas between his own and related disciplines.

H. F. KEARNEY

Contents

I

A Fourfold Revolution

A society or culture that has reached a certain level of sophistication tends to become introspective and experiences a desire to account for its present character. It does so primarily by scrutinizing its past and isolating those factors which appear to have influenced it most. Many things encourage us in the view that if we can uncover the earlier sources of some of our current ideas we shall both know ourselves better and be in a position to evaluate more rigorously the beliefs and assumptions by which we live. The modern temper of Western Europe – since we all participate in it and are formed by it – naturally prompts us to attempt this kind of appraisal, however complex the whole operation may turn out to be. Nevertheless, before we can contemplate embarking on such a task, we need to have various documents at our disposal; the main purpose of the following pages is to provide some of this material.

The choice of significant material immediately gives rise to two problems. First, the particular direction in which we look towards the past, and the texts we choose, must be governed by our prior assessment of what we think to be the distinctive features of the present age. As a result, the choice I myself have made here derives from my own particular reading of our contemporary sensibility and will be far from obtaining complete and general agreement. But at least I have included various writings which express ideas that are anathema to me yet which, I believe, have had an important formative influence on certain modern attitudes and ways of thought. Again, in attempting to find a starting point for what is most distinctive in current patterns of thought and feeling, we can easily begin on a process of almost infinite regress. One historian will date the modern period from the outbreak of the First World War, another will trace its origin to the early nineteenth century, a third may settle on the French Revolution, yet another on the break-up of medieval society, and so on. I myself have chosen a period, roughly corresponding to the reign of Queen Victoria (1837–1901), in the course of which a very important revolution took place in our conception of man – and therefore in our conception of ourselves.

In his *Eminent Victorians*, published in 1918, Lytton Strachey wrote with critical insight about four Victorian notables: Cardinal Manning, Florence Nightingale, Dr Arnold and General Gordon. Undoubtedly, these were all eminent figures in their own day (despite Strachey's ironical use of the adjective) yet it is equally true that they no longer possess for us the directness and relevance which they had for their contemporaries. On the other hand, we certainly find in the same period figures who speak to us with continuing authority and whose voice has virtually become our own. Such 'prophets of our age' as Sir Charles Lyell, Charles Darwin, Karl Marx and Sigmund Freud disconcerted more contemporaries than they persuaded, yet they have now largely determined, for good or ill, some of our main assumptions about man and society. Their influence has been so pervasive that schoolchildren are now taught, as a matter of course, geological and biological theories which Lyell and Darwin sought to document adequately and fought hard to render acceptable. Again, many of those who teach these children are guided in their work by Freud's account of the nature of adolescent behaviour and development. Even at a much less self-aware level, and often without invoking the names of Marx or Freud, many of our contemporaries naturally include in their day-to-day vocabulary such terms as 'class struggle', 'capitalism', 'repression' or 'neurosis'.

It would no doubt be rather arbitrary to locate the origins of our contemporary outlook in the second half of the nineteenth century simply because certain phrases associated with that period have become common intellectual coin. The truth is, however, that Lyell, Darwin, Marx and Freud represent a new starting point primarily because all of them were at once destroyers and creators. They attacked, in different ways and on different grounds, the foundations of their own age, and in doing so they laid the foundations of ours. Each, in his own particular sphere, radically altered the existing conception of man, and in doing so he added a new dimension to our view of ourselves. In addition, though the doctrine propounded by each of them was anticipated in part at least by earlier theorists, all four systematized, and won increasing assent to, those doctrines which we rightly associate primarily with their names.

The geological researches and observations of Lyell had the primary effect of producing evidence which completely changed previously widespread ideas about the age of the earth and the existence of life on its surface. He showed, particularly in his *Principles of Geology*, how steadily working physical laws had brought about geological change over an enormous period of time and were still active. Into this picture of natural forces moulding organic life over immense epochs was also introduced the idea of progressive development. *The Antiquity of Man* related the history of human beings to this idea of progress. Thus Lyell revolutionized our view of the earth's history, and of man's place within that history, at a time when the *Encyclopedia Britannica* was still discussing, on the basis of the Book of Genesis, whether the earth was created in 4305 or 4000 B.C. And while Lyell did so much to discredit the literal truth of the Old Testament (without wishing to discredit the fundamental truth of Christianity), he was also helping to relate man more closely to the rest of the animal creation.

The revolutionary theory of Darwin, as set out in *The Origin of Species* and *The Descent of Man*, had the effect of showing man to be an integral part of the animal world. Man emerged from Darwin's researches as different from the 'lower' animals only, though importantly, through the fact that he had proved more successful in the struggle for existence and more adaptable to the law of natural selection. Here again was an account of human beings, backed up by a great mass of scientific evidence, which was to have almost incalculable consequences for many previous religious, moral and political ideas.

In the case of Marx, the new dimension which emerged was economic and historical rather than geological or biological. Such works as the *Communist Manifesto* (with Engels), *A Contribution to the Critique of Political Economy* and *Capital* emphasized the materialist infrastructure of life and the phenomenon of historical inevitability. A picture of economic man emerged, a creature controlled by historical process and economic forces. Nevertheless, Marx also argued that, with a right understanding of these forces, man could learn to control and plan them for his own betterment and in the interests of social justice.

Finally, a quite different dimension to our view of man in which personality is shown to be the product of laws located in the individual's unconscious and his early infantile life was added by Freud. In such works as *Studies on Hysteria* (with Breuer), *The Interpretation of Dreams* and *Introductory Lectures on Psychoanalysis*, unconscious forces are presented as playing both a complex and a determining role in each individual's attitudes and behaviour. Later, Freud was to apply his theories more widely, if not always successfully, to art and to more general social questions in *The Future of an Illusion, Civilization and its Discontents* and other publications. Thus the determining dimension of unconscious life was added to the dimensions of geological time, biological status and economico-historical dependence already revealed.

All this amounts to a scientifically based (though no longer always scientifically accurate) reappraisal which led to the death of many previous concepts and the birth of a radically new view of man's past, his present and his potentialities in the future. It is obvious enough, I think, that all has not been gain. In so far as we live in a period no less violent, sceptical and neurotic than earlier ages, we may well ask both how far we have accurately interpreted these revolutionaries, how far some of their doctrines are in themselves of value to us, and how far we have succeeded in applying their discoveries in a genuinely liberating and beneficial way.

FURTHER READING

Some of the points raised above are discussed at much more length in J. Barzun, *Darwin, Marx, Wagner: Critique of a Heritage*, Secker & Warburg, 1942; and S. E. Hyman, *The Tangled Bank: Darwin, Marx, Frazer and Freud as Imaginative Writers*, New York, Atheneum, 1962.

1 Lyell

Although called to the bar in 1825, Sir Charles Lyell (1797–1875) devoted himself wholly to the study of geology from 1827 onwards. A number of his theories were anticipated by a fellow-Scot, James Hutton (1726–97), but Hutton's views did not influence more than a few specialists. At the beginning of the nineteenth century, many geologists still favoured the so-called 'catastrophic theory' which explained geological change, on a relatively minute time-scale, in terms of floods and disasters of a quite enormous magnitude unknown in more recent history. It was argued that such catastrophes killed off all the existing fauna at a given period and that the earth was subsequently repopulated, on each occasion, by a new creation. Between 1830 and 1833 Lyell published his three-volume 'Principles of Geology', a work which was widely read in intellectual circles and proved to be very influential. Lyell argued (e.g. passage (a) below) that geological formations were mistakenly ascribed to tremendous convulsions and disasters. He insisted that the natural

*forces causing geological change have remained the same throughout time but
that they have operated over a vastly longer period than most people, and most
biblical scholars, previously believed. He did not consider his conclusions to be
incompatible with belief in a supernatural creative power (see passage (b)
below). In his second main work, 'The Antiquity of Man' (1863), Lyell
used geological evidence to support his claim that man appeared much earlier
on the earth than most people assumed (see passage (c) below) and in the same
book he expressed his close agreement with Darwin's theory concerning the
origin of species.*

(a) From *Principles of Geology*, I, ch. 5

If we reflect on the history of the progress of geology . . . we perceive
that there have been great fluctuations of opinion respecting the nature
of the causes to which all former changes of the earth's surface are
referable. The first observers conceived the monuments which the
geologist endeavours to decipher to relate to an original state of the
earth, or to a period when there were causes in activity, distinct, in
kind and degree, from those now constituting the economy of nature.
These views were gradually modified, and some of them entirely
abandoned in proportion as observations were multiplied, and the signs
of former mutations were skilfully interpreted. Many appearances,
which had for a long time been regarded as indicating mysterious and
extraordinary agency, were finally recognized as the necessary result of
the laws now governing the material world; and the discovery of this
unlooked-for conformity has at length induced some philosophers to
infer, that, during the ages contemplated in geology, there has never
been any interruption to the agency of the same uniform laws of
change. The same assemblage of general causes, they conceive, may
have been sufficient to produce, by their various combinations, the
endless diversity of effects, of which the shell of the earth has preserved
the memorials; and, consistently with these principles, the recurrence
of analogous changes is expected by them in time to come . . .

   As a belief in the want of conformity in the causes by which the
earth's crust has been modified in ancient and modern periods was, for
a long time, universally prevalent, and that, too, amongst men who
were convinced that the order of nature had been uniform for the last
several thousand years, every circumstance which could have influenced
their minds and given an undue bias to their opinions deserves particular attention. Now the reader may easily satisfy himself, that, however undeviating the course of nature may have been from the earliest

epochs, it was impossible for the first cultivators of geology to come to such a conclusion, so long as they were under a delusion as to the age of the world, and the date of the first creation of animate things. . . . Even when they conceded that the earth had been peopled with animate beings at an earlier period than was at first supposed, they had no conception that the quantity of time bore so great a proportion to the historical era as is now generally conceded. How fatal every error as to the quantity of time must prove to the introduction of rational views concerning the state of things in former ages, may be conceived by supposing the annals of the civil and military transactions of a great nation to be perused under the impression that they occurred in a period of one hundred instead of two thousand years. Such a portion of history would immediately assume the air of a romance; the events would seem devoid of credibility, and inconsistent with the present course of human affairs. A crowd of incidents would follow each other in thick succession. Armies and fleets would appear to be assembled only to be destroyed, and cities built merely to fall in ruins. There would be the most violent transitions from foreign or intestine war to periods of profound peace, and the works effected during the years of disorder or tranquillity would appear alike superhuman in magnitude.

He who would study the monuments of the natural world under the influence of a similar infatuation, must draw a no less exaggerated picture of the energy and violence of causes, and must experience the same insurmountable difficulty in reconciling the former and present state of nature. . . .

One consequence of undervaluing greatly the quantity of past time, is the apparent coincidence which it occasions of events necessarily disconnected, or which are so unusual, that it would be inconsistent with all calculation of chances to suppose them to happen at one and the same time. When the unlooked-for association of such rare phenomena is witnessed in the present course of nature, it scarcely ever fails to excite a suspicion of the preternatural in those minds which are not firmly convinced of the uniform agency of secondary causes; – as if the death of some individual in whose fate they are interested happens to be accompanied by the appearance of a luminous meteor, or a comet, or the shock of an earthquake. It would be only necessary to multiply such coincidences indefinitely, and the mind of every philosopher would be disturbed. Now it would be difficult to exaggerate the number of physical events, many of them most rare and unconnected in their nature, which were imagined by the Woodwardian[1] hypothesis to have happened in the course of a few months: and numerous other examples might be found of popular geological theories, which require us to imagine that a long succession of events happened in a brief and almost momentary period.

Another liability to error, very nearly allied to the former, arises from the frequent contact of geological monuments referring to very distant periods of time. We often behold, at one glance, the effects of causes which have acted at times incalculably remote, and yet there may be no striking circumstances to mark the occurrence of a great chasm in the chronological series of Nature's archives. In the vast interval of time which may really have elapsed between the results of operations thus compared, the physical condition of the earth may, by slow and insensible modifications, have become entirely altered; one or more races of organic beings may have passed away, and yet have left behind, in the particular region under contemplation, no trace of their existence.

To a mind unconscious of these intermediate events, the passage from one state of things to another must appear so violent, that the idea of revolutions in the system inevitably suggests itself. The imagination is as much perplexed by the deception, as it might be if two distant points in space were suddenly brought into immediate proximity.

(b) From *Principles of Geology*, III, ch. 18 (end)

If, in tracing back the earth's history, we arrive at the monuments of events which may have happened millions of ages before our times, and if we still find no decided evidence of a commencement, yet the arguments from analogy in support of the probability of beginning remain unshaken; and if the past duration of the earth be finite, then the aggregate of geological epochs, however numerous, must constitute a mere moment of the past, a mere infinitesimal portion of eternity.

[1] John Woodward (1665–1728) published *An Essay toward a Natural History of the Earth* in 1695. He recognized the existence of various strata in the earth's crust and recognized fossils to be the 'real spoils of once living animals'. However, he was one of those theorists who, as Lyell says above, was 'under a delusion as to the age of the world and the date of the first creation of animate things'. Woodward was a proponent of the so-called 'diluvial theory', conceiving 'the whole terrestrial globe to have been taken to pieces and dissolved at the flood, and the strata to have settled down from this promiscuous mass as any earthy sediment from a fluid'. He explained the disposition of fossils within the strata by claiming that 'marine shells are lodged in the strata according to the order of their gravity, the heavier shells in stone, the lighter in chalk, and so of the rest'. J.C.

It has been argued, that, as the different states of the earth's surface, and the different species by which it has been inhabited, have all had their origin, and many of them their termination, so the entire series may have commenced at a certain period. It has also been urged, that, as we admit the creation of man to have occurred at a comparatively modern epoch – as we concede the astonishing fact of the first introduction of a moral and intellectual being – so also we may conceive the first creation of the planet itself.

I am far from denying the weight of this reasoning from analogy; but, although it may strengthen our conviction, that the present system of change has not gone on from eternity, it cannot warrant us in presuming that we shall be permitted to behold the signs of the earth's origin, or the evidences of the first introduction into it of organic beings. We aspire in vain to assign limits to the works of creation in *space*, whether we examine the starry heavens, or that world of minute animalcules which is revealed to us by the microscope. We are prepared, therefore, to find that in *time* also the confines of the universe lie beyond the reach of mortal ken. But in whatever direction we pursue our researches, whether in time or space, we discover everywhere the clear proofs of a Creative Intelligence, and of His foresight, wisdom and power.

As geologists, we learn that it is not only the present condition of the globe which has been suited to the accommodation of myriads of living creatures, but that many former states also have been adapted to the organization and habits of prior races of beings. The disposition of the seas, continents, and islands, and the climates, have varied; the species likewise have been changed; and yet they have all been so modelled, on types analogous to those of existing plants and animals, as to indicate, throughout, a perfect harmony of design and unity of purpose. To assume that the evidence of the beginning or end of so vast a scheme lies within the reach of our philosophical inquiries, or even of our speculations, appears to be inconsistent with a just estimate of the relations which subsist between the finite powers of man and the attributes of an Infinite and Eternal Being.

(c) From *The Geological Evidence of the Antiquity of Man*, 1863 edition, ch. 20

When speaking in a former work[1] of the distinct races of mankind, I remarked that, 'if all the leading varieties of the human family sprang

[1] *Principles of Geology.*

originally from a single pair' (a doctrine, to which then, as now, I could see no valid objection) 'a much greater lapse of time was required for the slow and gradual formation of such races as the Caucasian, Mongolian, and Negro, than was embraced in any of the popular systems of chronology'.

In confirmation of the high antiquity of two of these, I referred to pictures on the walls of ancient temples in Egypt, in which, a thousand years or more before the Christian era, 'the Negro and Caucasian physiognomies were portrayed as faithfully, and in as strong contrast, as if the likenesses of these races had been taken yesterday'. In relation to the same subject, I dwelt on the slight modification which the Negro has undergone, after having been transported from the tropics, and settled for more than two centuries in the temperate climate of Virginia. I therefore concluded that, 'if the various races were all descended from a single pair, we must allow for a vast series of antecedent ages, in the course of which the long-continued influence of external circumstances gave rise to peculiarities increased in many successive generations, and at length fixed by hereditary transmission'.

So long as physiologists continued to believe that Man had not existed on the earth above six thousand years, they might, with good reason, withhold their assent from the doctrine of a unity of origin of so many distinct races; but the difficulty becomes less and less, exactly in proportion as we enlarge our ideas of the lapse of time during which different communities may have spread slowly, and become isolated, each exposed for ages to a peculiar set of conditions, whether of temperature, or food, or danger, or ways of living. The law of the geometrical rate of increase of population which causes it always to press hard on the means of subsistence, would ensure the migration, in various directions, of offshoots from the society first formed abandoning the area where they had multiplied. But when they had gradually penetrated to remote regions by land or water – drifted sometimes by storms and currents in canoes to an unknown shore – barriers of mountains, deserts, or seas, which oppose no obstacle to mutual intercourse between civilised nations, would ensure the complete isolation for tens or thousands of centuries of tribes in a primitive state of barbarism.

Some modern ethnologists, in accordance with the philosophers of antiquity, have assumed that men at first fed on the fruits of the earth, before even a stone implement or the simplest form of canoe had been invented. They may, it is said, have begun their career in some fertile island in the tropics, where the warmth of the air was such that no clothing was needed, and where there were no wild beasts to endanger their safety. But as soon as their numbers increased, they would be forced to migrate into regions less secure and blessed with a less genial climate. Contests would soon arise for the possession of the most fertile lands, where game or pasture abounded, and their energies and inventive powers would be called forth, so that, at length, they would make progress in the arts.

But as ethnologists have failed, as yet, to trace back the history of any one race to the area where it originated, some zoologists of eminence have declared their belief, that the different races, whether they be three, five, twenty, or a much greater number ... have all been primordial creations, having from the first been stamped with the characteristic features, mental and bodily, by which they are now distinguished, except where intermarriage has given rise to mixed or hybrid races. Were we to admit, say they, a unity of origin of such strongly marked varieties as the Negro and European, differing as they do in colour and bodily construction, each fitted for distinct climates, and exhibiting some marked peculiarities in their osteological, and even in some details of cranial and cerebral conformation, as well as in their average intellectual endowments – if, in spite of the fact that all these attributes have been faithfully handed down unaltered for hundreds of generations, we are to believe that, in the course of time, they have all diverged from one common stock, how shall we resist the arguments of the transmutationist, who contends that all closely allied species of animals and plants have in like manner sprung from a common parentage, albeit that for the last three or four thousand years they may have been persistent in character? Where are we to stop, unless we make our stand at once on the independent creation of those distinct human races, the history of which is better known to us than that of any of the inferior animals?

So long as Geology had not lifted up a part of the veil which formerly concealed from the naturalist the history of the changes which the animate creation had undergone in times immediately antecedent to the Recent period, it was easy to treat these questions as too transcendental, or as lying too far beyond the domain of positive science to require serious discussion. But it is no longer possible to restrain curiosity from attempting to pry into the relations which connect the present state of the animal and vegetable worlds, as well as of the various races of mankind, with the state of the fauna and flora which immediately preceded.

FURTHER READING

Two studies of Lyell that appeared within twenty years of his death still make interesting reading: K. M. Lyell, *Life, Letters and Journals of Sir Charles Lyell, Bart* (1881), and T. G. Bonney, *Charles Lyell and Modern Geology*, Cassell, 1895.

The religious and scientific significance of nineteenth-century geology, and much else besides, is discussed and accompanied by an extremely full bibliography in C. C. Gillispie, *Genesis and Geology*, Harper Torchbooks, 1959.

2 Darwin

Charles Darwin (1809–82) made two false starts in life before he found his scientific vocation. He began, as a student, with two years of unsuccessful medical studies at Edinburgh University and then, his father having decided that he should become a clergyman, he read classics and mathematics at Cambridge (receiving an undistinguished pass B.A. in 1831). Of this latter period Darwin tells us in his 'Autobiography':

In order to pass the B.A. examination, it was also necessary to get up Paley's *Evidences of Christianity*, and his *Moral Philosophy*. This was done in a thorough manner, and I am convinced that I could have written out the whole of the *Evidences* with perfect correctness, but not of course in the clear language of Paley. The logic of this book and, as I may add, of his *Natural Theology*, gave me as much delight as did Euclid. The careful study of these works, without attempting to learn any part by rote, was the only part of the academical course which, as I then felt, and as I still believe, was of the least use to me in the education of my mind. I did not at that time trouble myself about Paley's premises; and taking these on trust, I was charmed and convinced by the long line of argumentation.

Considering the effect on traditional Christian theology of Darwin's own subsequent work, it is one of those frequent ironies in the history of thought that he should have learned logical deduction and demonstration from Paley's 'Evidences'.

Shortly after leaving Cambridge, and initially against his father's wishes, Darwin joined H.M.S. 'Beagle' as naturalist to an expedition which was to circumnavigate the world. A Captain Fitzroy was in command of the 'Beagle' with instructions from the Admiralty to survey, in particular, the coasts of Patagonia, Tierra del Fuego, Chile and Peru, and to visit certain Pacific islands. The expedition set out in December 1831 and eventually returned home in October 1836. In 1839 Darwin published a very readable account of his experiences in 'The Voyage of the Beagle.'

It was during the 'Beagle' expedition that Darwin made his main contribution to geology by explaining the origin and nature of coral reefs (he later wrote up his observations and expanded his theories in 'The Structure and Distribution of Coral Reefs', published in 1842). In effect, Darwin showed that these atolls had not resulted from a special act of creation but were the result of age-old processes brought about by innumerable generations of tiny creatures responding to the changing circumstances of their environment. Also, he emphasized, as Lyell had done, that these processes were still going on before the observer's eyes.

The most important feature of Darwin's voyage on board the 'Beagle' was the fact that he came to disbelieve in the so-called 'fixity of species'. According to this view, the many forms of organic life had been made separate and diverse by an initial creative act at the beginning of time. During the expedition Darwin observed many facts which he judged to be irreconcilable with the doctrine of fixed species and, although he still had no adequate theory with which to replace this doctrine, this represents the starting point from which his theory of evolutionary development through a process of natural selection was eventually to develop (see passages (a) and (b) below). The first breakthrough (see also passage (a) below) was the result of a chance reading of Malthus's 'An Essay on the Principle of Population' (1798). One of the main points made by Malthus was that the reproductive rate of most living organisms is normally much higher than the productive capacity of their food supply; indeed, that population tends to increase by geometrical progression while food production grows by arithmetical progression. Two consequences follow: first, there is a natural, competitive situation where the obtaining of food is concerned (Malthus wrote: 'During the lapse of many thousand years there might not be a single period when the mass of people could be said to be free from distress for want of food'); second, there is a high death-rate, and a weeding out of the less successful or the unfortunate, by such factors as poverty, disease, vice, war. On this basis, Darwin was able to explain his first principle – of evolutionary change – by his second principle – of natural selection, and he later described his own theory (in his Introduction to the 'Origin of Species') as 'the doctrine of Malthus applied to the whole animal and vegetable kingdoms'.

It is this doctrine which we find set out, with a mass of supporting evidence, in the 'Origin of Species by Natural Selection or The Preservation of Favoured Races in the Struggle for Life' (1859). Some of Darwin's own comments on his theory are set out in passages (c) and (d) below. It has to be said, of course, that Darwin was not the first thinker to put forward the evolutionary hypothesis. Quite apart from the independent and closely similar views of his contemporary, Alfred Russell Wallace, some idea of evolution is present in the writings of Buffon (1707–88), Darwin's grandfather, Erasmus Darwin (1751–1802), Lamarck (1744–1829) and others. But whereas most of these thinkers arrived at their views more by deductive logic than by scientific observation, Darwin worked primarily with an enormous mass of carefully checked scientific evidence. This is not the place to analyse the continuing scientific value of Darwin's work. But it should be said, briefly, that he failed to account for the facts of inheritance or for those variations that appear to arise spontaneously in the passage from one generation to another. These problems lead us into the sphere of genetics and some of the most valuable basic work in this science was done by the Austrian abbé, Gregor Mendel (1822–84), who had read the 'Origin of Species' but whose own experiments on inheritance (through the breeding of peas) only attracted serious attention at the beginning of this century.

A subject notably absent from the 'Origin of Species' was any consideration of man's place in the evolutionary scheme of things; man as a product of the forces of natural selection. This omission was repaired twelve years after the first publication of the 'Origin' by the publication, in 1871, of Darwin's 'The Descent of Man and Selection in Relation to Sex'. Curiously enough, this work caused much less outcry than the 'Origin' despite the implications of the chapters dealing with man's physical, mental, moral and social nature (see passages (e), (f) and (g) below).

(a) From the *Autobiography*

During the voyage of the *Beagle* I had been deeply impressed by discovering in the Pampean formation great fossil animals covered with armour like that on the existing armadillos; secondly, by the manner in which closely allied animals replace one another in proceeding southwards over the Continent; and thirdly, by the South American character of most of the productions of the Galapagos archipelago, and more especially by the manner in which they differ slightly on each island of the group; none of the islands appearing to be very ancient in a geological sense.

It was evident that such facts as these, as well as many others, could only be explained on the supposition that species gradually become modified; and the subject haunted me. But it was equally evident that neither the action of the surrounding conditions, nor the will of the organisms (especially in the case of plants) could account for the innumerable cases in which organisms of every kind are beautifully adapted to their habits of life – for instance, a wood-pecker or a tree-frog to climb trees, or a seed for dispersal by hooks or plumes. I had always been much struck by such adaptations, and until these could be explained it seemed to me almost useless to endeavour to prove by indirect evidence that species have been modified.

After my return to England it appeared to me that by following the example of Lyell in Geology, and by collecting all facts which bore in any way on the variation of animals and plants under domestication and nature, some light might perhaps be thrown on the whole subject. My first note-book was opened in July 1837. I worked on true Baconian principles, and without any theory collected facts on a wholesale scale, more especially without respect to domesticated productions, by printed enquiries, by conversation with skilful breeders and gardeners, and by extensive reading. When I see the list of books of all kinds which I read and abstracted, including whole series of Journals and Transactions, I am surprised at my industry. I soon perceived that selection was the keystone of man's success in making useful races of animals and plants. But how selection could be applied to organisms living in a state of nature remained for some time a mystery to me.

In October 1838, that is, fifteen months after I had begun my systematic enquiry, I happened to read for amusement Malthus on *Population*, and being well prepared to appreciate the struggle for existence which everywhere goes on from long-continued observation of the habits of animals and plants, it at once struck me that under these circumstances favourable variations would tend to be preserved and unfavourable ones to be destroyed. The result of this would be the formation of new species. Here, then, I had at last got a theory by which to work; but I was so anxious to avoid prejudice, that I determined not for some time to write even the briefest sketch of it. In June 1842 I first allowed myself the satisfaction of writing a very brief abstract of my theory in pencil in 35 pages; and this was enlarged during the summer of 1844 into one of 230 pages, which I had fairly copied out and still possess.

(b) From the preliminary Essay of 1844[1]

Shall we then allow that the three distinct species of rhinoceros which separately inhabit Java and Sumatra and the neighbouring mainland of Malacca were created, male and female, out of the inorganic materials of these countries? Without any adequate cause, as far as our reason serves, shall we say that they were merely, from living near each other, created very like each other, so as to form a genus dissimilar from the African section, some of the species of which sections inhabit very similar and some very dissimilar stations? Shall we say that without any apparent cause they are created on the same generic type with the woolly rhinoceros of Siberia and of the other species which formerly inhabited the same division of the world: that they were created less and less closely related, but still with interbranching affinities, with all the other living and extinct mammalia? That without any apparent adequate cause their short necks should contain the same number of vertebrae with the giraffe; that their thick legs should be built on the same plan as those of the antelope, of the mouse, of the hand of the monkey, of the wing of the bat, and of the fin of the porpoise. . . . That in the jaws of each when young there should exist small teeth which never come to the surface. That in possessing these useless abortive teeth, and other characters, these three rhinoceroses in their embryonic state should much more closely resemble other mammals than they do when mature. And lastly, that in a still earlier period of life, their arteries should run and branch as in a fish, to carry the blood to gills which do not exist. . . .

I repeat, shall we then say that a pair, or a gravid female, of each of these three species of rhinoceros, were separately created with deceptive appearances of true relationship, with the stamp of inutility on some parts, and of conversion in other parts, out of the inorganic elements of Java, Sumatra and Malacca? or have they descended, like our domestic races, from the same parent stock? For my own part I could no more admit the former proposition than I could admit that the planets move in their courses, and that a stone falls to the ground, not through the intervention of the secondary and appointed law of gravity, but from the direct volition of the Creator.

---

[1] This is the essay referred to at the end of passage *(a)*.

(c) From *The Origin of Species*, ch. 6

To suppose that the eye with all its inimitable contrivances for adjusting the focus to different distances, for admitting different amounts of light, and for the correction of spherical and chromatic aberration, could have been formed by natural selection, seems, I freely confess, absurd in the highest degree. When it was first said that the sun stood still and the world turned round, the common sense of mankind declared the doctrine false; but the old saying of *Vox populi, vox Dei*, as every philosopher knows, cannot be trusted in science. Reason tells me, that if numerous gradations from a simple and imperfect eye to one complex and perfect can be shown to exist, each grade being useful to its possessor, as is certainly the case; if further, the eye ever varies and the variations be inherited, as is likewise certainly the case; and if such variations should be useful to any animal under changing conditions of life, then the difficulty of believing that a perfect and complex eye could be formed by natural selection, though insuperable by our imagination, should not be considered as subversive of the theory. How a nerve comes to be sensitive to light, hardly concerns us more than how life itself originated; but I may remark that, as some of the lowest organisms, in which nerves cannot be detected, are capable of perceiving light, it does not seem impossible that certain sensitive elements in their sarcode should become aggregated and developed into nerves, endowed with this special sensibility. . . .

It is scarcely possible to avoid comparing the eye with a telescope. We know that this instrument has been perfected by the long-continued efforts of the highest human intellects; and we naturally infer that the eye has been formed by a somewhat analogous process. But may not this inference be presumptuous? Have we any right to assume that the Creator works by intellectual powers like those of man? If we must compare the eye to an optical instrument, we ought in imagination to take a thick layer of transparent tissue, with spaces filled with fluid, and with a nerve sensitive to light beneath, and then suppose every part of this layer to be continually changing slowly in density, so as to separate into layers of different densities and thicknesses, placed at different distances from each other, and with the surfaces of each layer slowly changing in form. Further we must suppose that there is a power, represented by natural selection or the survival of the fittest, always intently watching each slight alteration in the transparent layers; and carefully preserving each which, under varied circumstances, in any way or in any degree, tends to produce a distincter image. We must suppose each new state of the instrument to be multiplied by the million; each to be preserved until a better one is produced, and then the old ones to be all destroyed. In living bodies, variation will cause the slight alterations, generation will multiply them almost infinitely, and natural selection will pick out with unerring skill each improvement. Let this process go on for millions of years; and during each year on millions of individuals of many kinds; and may we not believe that a living optical instrument might thus be formed as superior to one of glass, as the works of the Creator are to those of man.

(*d*) From *The Origin of Species*, ch. 15

It can hardly be supposed that a false theory would explain, in so satisfactory a manner as does the theory of natural selection, the several large classes of facts above specified. It has recently been objected that this is an unsafe method of arguing – but it is a method used in judging of the common events or life, and has often been used by the greatest natural philosophers. The undulatory theory of light has thus been arrived at; and the belief in the revolution of the earth on its own axis was until lately supported by hardly any direct evidence. It is no valid objection that science as yet throws no light on the far higher problem of the essence or origin of life. Who can explain what is the essence of the attraction of gravity? No one now objects to following out the results consequent on this unknown element of attraction; notwithstanding that Leibnitz formerly accused Newton of introducing 'occult qualities and miracles into philosophy'.

I see no good reason why the views given in this volume should shock the religious feelings of anyone. It is satisfactory, as showing how transient such impressions are, to remember that the greatest discovery ever made by man, namely, the law of the attraction of gravity, was also attacked by Leibnitz, 'as subversive of natural, and inferentially of revealed, religion'. A celebrated author and divine has written to me that 'he has gradually learnt to see that it is just as noble a conception of the Deity to believe that He created a few original forms capable of self-development into other and needful forms, as to believe that He required a fresh act of creation to supply the voids caused by the action of His laws'.

Why, it may be asked, until recently did nearly all the most eminent living naturalists and geologists disbelieve in the mutability of species.

It cannot be asserted that organic beings in a state of nature are subject to no variation; it cannot be proved that the amount of variation in the course of long ages is a limited quantity; no clear distinction has been, or can be, drawn between species and well-marked varieties. It cannot be maintained that species when intercrossed are invariably sterile, and varieties invariably fertile; or that sterility is a special endowment and sign of creation. The belief that species were immutable productions was almost unavoidable as long as the history of the world was thought to be of short duration; and now that we have acquired some idea of the lapse of time, we are too apt to assume, without proof, that the geological record is so perfect that it would have afforded us plain evidence of the mutation of species, if they had undergone mutation.

But the chief cause of our natural unwillingness to admit that one species has given birth to other and distinct species, is that we are always slow in admitting great changes of which we do not see the steps. The difficulty is the same as that felt by so many geologists, when Lyell first insisted that long lines of inland cliffs had been formed, and great valleys excavated, by the agencies which we see still at work. The mind cannot possibly grasp the full meaning of the term of even a million years; it cannot add up and perceive the full effects of many slight variations, accumulated during an almost infinite number of generations. . . .

The noble science of Geology loses glory from the extreme imperfection of the record. The crust of the earth with its imbedded remains must not be looked at as a well-filled museum, but as a poor collection made at hazard and at rare intervals. The accumulation of each great fossiliferous formation will be recognised as having depended on an unusual concurrence of favourable circumstances, and the blank intervals between the successive stages as having been of vast duration. But we shall be able to gauge with some security the duration of these intervals by a comparison of the preceding and succeeding organic forms. We must be cautious in attempting to correlate as strictly contemporaneous two formations, which do not include many identical species, by the general succession of the forms of life. As species are produced and exterminated by slowly acting and still existing causes, and not by miraculous acts of creation; and as the most important of all causes of organic change is one which is almost independent of altered and perhaps suddenly altered physical conditions, namely, the mutual relation of organism to organism, – the improvement of one organism entailing the improvement or the extermination of others; it follows,

that the amount of organic change in the fossils of consecutive formations probably serves as a fair measure of the relative, though not actual
lapse of time. A number of species, however, keeping in a body might
remain for a long period unchanged, whilst within the same period,
several of these species by migrating into new countries and coming into
competition with foreign associates, might become modified; so that
we must not overrate the accuracy of organic change as a measure of
time. ...

It is interesting to contemplate a tangled bank, clothed with many
plants of many kinds, with birds singing on the bushes, with various
insects flitting about, and with worms crawling through the damp
earth, and to reflect that these elaborately constructed forms, so different from each other, and dependent upon each other in so complex
a manner, have all been produced by laws acting around us. These
laws, taken in the largest sense, being Growth with Reproduction;
Inheritance which is almost implied by reproduction; Variability from
the indirect and direct action of the conditions of life, and from use
and disuse: a Ratio of Increase so high as to lead to a Struggle for Life,
and as a consequence to Natural Selection, entailing Divergence of
Character and the Extinction of less-improved forms. Thus, from the
war of nature, from famine and death, the most exalted object which
we are capable of conceiving, namely, the production of the higher
animals, directly follows. There is grandeur in this view of life, with its
several powers, having been originally breathed by the Creator into a
few forms or into one; and that, whilst this planet has gone cycling on
according to the fixed law of gravity, from so simple a beginning
endless forms most beautiful and most wonderful have been, and are
being evolved.

(e) From *The Descent of Man*, ch. 1

It is notorious that man is constructed on the same general type or
model as other animals. All the bones in his skeleton can be compared
with corresponding bones in a monkey, bat, or seal. So it is with his
muscles, nerves, blood-vessels and internal viscera. The brain, the most
important of all the organs, follows the same law, as shewn by Huxley
and other anatomists. ... The homological construction of the whole
frame in the members of the same class is intelligible, if we admit their
descent from a common progenitor, together with their subsequent
adaptation to diversified conditions. On any other view, the similarity
of pattern between the hand of a man or monkey, the foot of a horse,

the flipper of a seal, the wing of a bat, etc., is utterly inexplicable. It is no scientific explanation to assume that they have all been formed on the same ideal plan. With respect to development, we can clearly understand, on the principle of variations supervening at a rather late embryonic period, and being inherited at a corresponding period, how it is that the embryos of wonderfully different forms should still retain, more or less perfectly, the structure of their common progenitor. No other explanation has ever been given of the marvellous fact that the embryos of a man, dog, seal, bat, reptile, etc., can at first hardly be distinguished from each other. In order to understand the existence of rudimentary organs, we have only to suppose that a former progenitor possessed the parts in question in a perfect state, and that under changed habits of life they became greatly reduced, either from simple disuse, or through the natural selection of those individuals which were least encumbered with a superfluous part, aided by the other means previously indicated.

Thus we can understand how it has come to pass that man and all other vertebrate animals have been constructed on the same general model, why they pass through the same early stages of development, and why they retain certain rudiments in common. Consequently we ought frankly to admit their community of descent. ... This conclusion is greatly strengthened, if we look to the members of the whole animal series, and consider the evidence derived from their affinities or classification, their geographical distribution and geological succession.

(f) From *The Descent of Man*, ch. 3

We have seen in the last two chapters that man bears in his bodily structure clear traces of his descent from some lower form; but it may be urged that, as man differs so greatly in his mental power from all other animals, there must be some error in this conclusion. No doubt the difference in this respect is enormous, even if we compare the mind of one of the lowest savages, who has no words to express any number higher than four, and who uses hardly any abstract terms for common objects or for the affections, with that of the most highly organized ape. The difference would, no doubt, still remain immense, even if one of the higher apes had been improved or civilized as much as a dog has been in comparison with its parent-form, the wolf or jackal. The Fuegians rank amongst the lowest barbarians; but I was continually struck with surprise how closely the three natives on board

H.M.S. 'Beagle', who had lived some years in England and could talk a little English, resembled us in disposition and in most of our mental faculties. If no organic being except man had possessed any mental power, or if his powers had been of a wholly different nature from those of the lower animals, then we should never have been able to convince ourselves that our high faculties had been gradually developed. But it can be shewn that there is no fundamental difference of this kind. We must also admit that there is a much wider interval in mental powers between one of the lowest fishes, as a lamprey or lancelet, and one of the higher apes, than between an ape and man; yet this interval is filled up by numberless gradations. . . .

Several writers, more especially Professor Max Müller, have lately insisted that the use of language implies the power of forming general concepts; and that as no animals are supposed to possess this power, an impassable barrier is formed between them and man. With respect to animals, I have already endeavoured to shew that they have this power, at least in a rude and incipient degree. As far as concerns infants of from ten to eleven months old, and deaf-mutes, it seems to me incredible, that they should be able to connect certain sounds with certain general ideas as quickly as they do, unless such ideas were already formed in their minds. The same remark may be extended to the more intelligent animals; as Mr Leslie Stephen observes, 'A dog frames a general concept of cats or sheep, and knows the corresponding words as well as a philosopher. And the capacity to understand is as good a proof of vocal intelligence, though in an inferior degree, as the capacity to speak.'

Why the organs now used for speech should have been originally perfected for this purpose, rather than any other organs, it is not difficult to see. Ants have considerable powers of intercommunication by means of their antennae, as shewn by Huber, who devotes a whole chapter to their language. We might have used our fingers as efficient instruments, for a person with practice can report to a deaf man every word of speech rapidly delivered at a public meeting; but the loss of our hands whilst thus employed, would have been a serious inconvenience. As all the higher mammals possess vocal organs, constructed on the same general plan as ours, and used as a means of communication, it was obviously probable that these same organs would be still further developed if the power of communication had to be improved; and this has been effected by the aid of adjoining and well adapted parts, namely the tongue and lips. The fact of the higher apes not using their vocal organs for speech, no doubt depends on their intelligence not having been sufficiently advanced. The possession by them of organs, which with long-continued practice might have been used for speech, although not thus used, is paralleled by the case of many birds which possess organs fitted for singing, though they never sing. Thus the nightingale and crow have vocal organs similarly constructed, these being used by the former for diversified song, and by the latter only for croaking. If it be asked why apes have not had their intellects developed to the same degree as that of man, general causes only can be assigned in answer, and it is unreasonable to expect anything more definite, considering our ignorance with respect to the successive stages of development through which each creation has passed.

(*g*) From *The Descent of Man*, ch. 4

The following proposition seems to be in a high degree probable – namely, that any animal whatever, endowed with well-marked social instincts, the parental and filial affections being here included, would inevitably acquire a moral sense or conscience, as soon as its intellectual powers had become as well, or nearly as well developed, as in man. For, *firstly*, the social instincts lead an animal to take pleasure in the society of its fellows, to feel a certain amount of sympathy with them, and to perform various services for them. The services may be of a definite and evidently instinctive nature; or there may be only a wish and readiness, as with most of the higher social animals, to aid their fellows in certain general ways. But these feelings and services are by no means extended to all the individuals of the same species, only to those of the same association. *Secondly*, as soon as the mental faculties had become highly developed, images of all past actions and motives would be incessantly passing through the brain of each individual; and that feeling of dissatisfaction, or even misery, which invariably results, as we shall hereafter see, from any unsatisfied instinct, would arise, as often as it was perceived that the enduring and always present social instinct had yielded to some other instinct, at the time stronger, but neither enduring in its nature, nor leaving behind it a very vivid impression. It is clear that many instinctive desires, such as that of hunger, are in their nature of short duration; and after being satisfied, are not readily or vividly recalled. *Thirdly*, after the power of language had been acquired, and the wishes of the community could be expressed, the common opinion how each member ought to act for the public good would naturally become in a paramount degree the guide to action. But it should be borne in mind that however great the weight we may attribute to public opinion, our regard for the approbation and disapprobation of our fellows depends on sympathy, which, as we shall see, forms an essential part of the social instinct, and is indeed its foundation-stone. *Lastly*, habit in the individual would ultimately play a very important part in guiding the conduct of each member; for the social instinct, together with sympathy, is, like any other instinct, greatly strengthened by habit, and so consequently would be obedience to the wishes and judgement of the community. . . .

. . . the difference in mind between man and the higher animals, great as it is, certainly is one of degree and not of kind.

FURTHER READING

Apart from Darwin's major works, the following is well worth reading: F. Darwin, ed, *The Autobiography of Charles Darwin, and Selected Letters*, New York, Dover, 1958. The simplest exposition of Darwin's ideas is: B. Farrington, *What Darwin Really Said*, Macdonald, 1966. Other useful books include: G. Himmelfarb, *Darwin and the Darwinian Revolution*, Chatto & Windus, 1959; S. A. Barnett, ed., *A Century of Darwin*, Heinemann, 1958; Sir Gavin de Beer, *Charles Darwin: Evolution by Natural Selection*, Nelson, 1963.

3 Marx

Although he came of a long line of Jewish rabbis, Karl Marx (1818–83) was the son of a lawyer. He was born in the Rhineland and brought up by a father who had become a Protestant for social reasons. At an early age the young Marx himself rejected all religious faith. After a brief spell as a student in Bonn, Marx studied law and developed his interests in philology, theology and philosophy at the University of Berlin. He came under the influence of Hegelian philosophy, in particular, being impressed by Hegel's dialectical system though rejecting the abstract and idealistic elements in his thought (see passage (d) below). The rejection of Hegelian orthodoxy was accelerated by his contact with the 'left-wing' Hegelians, and particularly by the materialist thought of Ludwig Feuerbach (1804–72). Yet here again, although Marx admired Feuerbach's critique of religion and used his materialism to turn Hegelianism 'on its head' (as he himself put it) he nevertheless considered that Feuerbach emphasized the social nature of man at the expense of his historical reality. Marx's historical materialism is set out in passages (a) and (b) below, with its contention that human history is governed by economic laws and cannot be altered by individuals inspired by an abstract ideal.

After completing his doctorate at Berlin, Marx became chief editor of the radical 'Rheinische Zeitung' in 1842. The paper was suppressed in 1843 because of its left-wing militancy and atheistic opposition to the Prussian government. In the same year Marx married and went to Paris to study socialism at the fountain-head. Here he met Engels (1820–95) and a crucial and lifelong friendship developed between the two men. Later, Engels was largely responsible for relieving Marx and his family from dire poverty. It was also in Paris that Marx met Proudhon and Bakunin. Expelled from France at the request of the Prussian government in 1845, he went to Brussels and two years later, on behalf of the Communist League, he and Engels drew up the 'Communist Manifesto' (published in 1848). Something of the vigour and militancy of this pamphlet can be seen in passage (g) below, even though it received little attention when it first appeared. It was also during this time that Marx wrote 'The Holy Family' (posthumously published) and 'The Poverty of Philosophy' (1847).

In 1848 Marx took some part in the revolutions in France and Germany but in 1849 was expelled from Prussia. From then on he lived in London, writing, lecturing and agitating. He died there in 1883 and Engels pronounced a funeral oration by his graveside which included the following passage:

> *Just as Darwin discovered the law of evolution in organic matter, so Marx discovered the law of evolution in human history; he discovered the simple fact . . . that mankind must first of all eat and drink, have shelter and clothing, before it can pursue politics, religion, art, science, etc.*

It was also during this period in England that Marx published his 'Contribution to a Critique of Political Economy' (1859) and the first volume of his major work, 'Capital' (1867). The second and third volumes were published by Engels in 1885 and 1893–4. The manuscripts of a planned fourth volume were first published as 'Theories of Surplus Value' between 1905 and 1910. Incidentally, it is of some interest and significance that Marx wished to dedicate the first volume of 'Capital' to Darwin, though the latter declined this honour.

As with so many 'original' thinkers, most of Marx's ideas had previously been adumbrated by other writers: we find historical materialism in d'Holbach; the dictatorship of the proletariat in Babeuf and Blanqui; the idea of alienation in Hegel; the labour theory of value in Locke and Adam Smith; the theory of exploitation and of surplus value in Fourier and others. However, Marx's originality and power as a thinker lie in the manner in which he welded these ideas together into a coherent and systematic whole. Some indication of his methodology is contained in passage (c) below, while his accounts of the

*development of capitalism, alienation under capitalism, the class-struggle and
the relationship between social evolution and political revolution are contained
respectively in passages* (e), (f), (g) *and* (h).

*In some ways, it is Marx's economic theory which has lasted least well.
Nevertheless, his theory of surplus value had a widespread influence and it
seemed useful to include part of his exposition in passage* (i) *below. Surplus
value is the profit which the capitalist makes, through the labourer's work,
over and above the wages received by the labourer for that work – and this
is the basis of one of Marx's several miscalculations. He believed, in a way that
modern industrialized society has proved to be false, that the more labour
(i.e. variable capital) and the less machinery (i.e. constant capital) employed,
the greater would be the capitalist's profit.*

(a) From *Capital*, I

Darwin has aroused our interest in the history of natural technology,
i.e. in the formation of the organs of plants and animals, as instruments
of production for sustaining life. Does not the history of the productive
organs of man, of organs that are the material basis of all social organization, deserve equal attention? And would not such a history be easier to
compile, since, as Vico says, human history differs from natural history
in this respect, that we have made the former, but not the latter?
Technology discloses man's mode of dealing with Nature, the process
of production by which he sustains his life, and by which also his
social relations, and the mental conceptions that flow from them, are
formed. Any history of religion even, that fails to take account of this
material basis, is uncritical. It is, in practice, much easier to discover by
analysis the earthly core of the misty creations of religion, than, con-
versely, to infer from the actual relations of life at any period the corresponding 'spiritualized' forms of those relations. But the latter
method is the only materialistic, and therefore the only scientific one.
The inadequacy of the abstract materialism of natural science, which
leaves out of consideration the historical process, is at once evident
from the abstract and ideological conceptions of its spokesmen, whenever they venture beyond the bounds of their own specialism.

(b) From *A Contribution to the Critique of Political Economy*, Preface

The general conclusion at which I arrived and which, once reached,
continued to serve as the guiding thread in my studies, may be formulated briefly as follows: In the social production which men carry

on they enter into definite relations that are indispensable and independent of their will; these relations of production correspond to a definite stage of development of their material powers of production. The totality of these relations of production constitutes the economic structure of society – the real foundation, on which legal and political superstructures arise and to which definite forms of social consciousness correspond. The mode of production of material life determines the general character of the social, political, and spiritual processes of life. It is not the consciousness of men that determines their being, but, on the contrary, their social being determines their consciousness. At a certain stage of their development, the material forces of production in society come in conflict with the existing relations of production, or – what is but a legal expression for the same thing – with the property relations within which they had been at work before. From forms of development of the forces of production these relations turn into their fetters. Then occurs a period of social revolution. With the change of the economic foundation the entire immense superstructure is more or less rapidly transformed. In considering such transformations, the distinction should always be made between the material transformation of the economic conditions of production which can be determined with the precision of natural science, and the legal, political, religious, aesthetic or philosophical – in short, ideological – forms in which men become conscious of this conflict and fight it out. Just as our opinion of an individual is not based on what he thinks of himself, so can we not judge of such a period of transformation by its own consciousness; on the contrary, this consciousness must rather be explained from the contradictions of material life, from the existing conflict between the social forces of production and the relations of production. No social order ever disappears before all the productive forces for which there is room in it have been developed; and new, higher relations of production never appear before the material conditions of their existence have matured in the womb of the old society. Therefore, mankind always sets itself only such problems as it can solve; since, on closer examination, it will always be found that the problem itself arises only when the material conditions necessary for its solution already exist or are at least in the process of formation. In broad outline we can designate the Asiatic, the ancient, the feudal, and the modern bourgeois modes of production as progressive epochs in the economic formation of society. The bourgeois relations of production are the last antagonistic form of the social process of production; not in the sense of individual antagonisms, but of conflict arising from conditions surrounding the life of individuals in society. At the same time the productive forces developing in the womb of bourgeois society create the material conditions for the solution of that antagonism. With this social formation, therefore, the prehistory of human society comes to an end.

(c) From *The German Ideology*

In direct contrast to German philosophy, which transcends from heaven to earth, here we ascend from earth to heaven. That is to say, we do not set out from what men say, imagine, or conceive, nor from what has been said, thought, imagined, or conceived of men, in order to arrive at men in the flesh. We begin with real, active men, and from their real life-process show the development of the ideological reflexes and echoes of this life-process. The phantoms of the human brain also are necessary sublimates of men's material life-process, which can be empirically established and which is bound to material preconditions. Morality, religion, metaphysics, and other ideologies, and their corresponding forms of consciousness, no longer retain therefore their appearance of autonomous existence. They have no history, no development; it is men, who, in developing their material production and their material intercourse, change, along with this their real existence, their thinking and the products of their thinking. Life is not determined by consciousness, but consciousness by life. Those who adopt the first method of approach begin with consciousness, regarded as the living individual; those who adopt the second, which corresponds with real life, begin with the real living individuals themselves, and consider consciousness only as *their* consciousness.

This method of approach is not without presuppositions, but it begins with the real presuppositions and does not abandon them for a moment. Its premises are men, not in some imaginary condition of fulfilment or stability, but in their actual, empirically observable process of development under determinate conditions. As soon as this active life-process is delineated, history ceases to be a collection of dead facts as it is with the empiricists (themselves still abstract), or an illusory activity of illusory subjects, as with the idealists.

Where speculation ends – in real life – real, positive science, the representation of the practical activity and the practical process of men, begins. Phrase-making about consciousness ceases, and real knowledge has to take its place. When reality is depicted, philosophy as an independent activity loses its medium of existence. At the most its place can only be taken by a conspectus of the general results, which are derived from the consideration of the historical development of men. In themselves and detached from real history, these abstractions have not the least value. They can only serve to facilitate the arrangement of historical material, and to indicate the sequence of its separate layers. They do not in the least provide, as does philosophy, a recipe or schema, according to which the epochs of history can rightly be distinguished. On the contrary, the difficulties only begin when we set about the consideration and arrangement of the material, whether of a past epoch or of the present, and the representation of reality.

(*d*) From the *Theses on Feuerbach*

The philosophers have only *interpreted* the world in different ways; the point is to change it.

(*e*) From *Capital*, I

Private property, as the antithesis to social, collective property, exists only where the means of labour and external conditions of labour belong to private individuals. But according as these private individuals are labourers or not labourers, private property has a different character. The innumerable shades that it at first sight presents correspond to the intermediate stages lying between these two extremes. The private property of the labourer in his means of production is the foundation of petty industry, and petty industry is an essential condition for the development of social production and of the free individuality of the labourer himself. Of course, this petty mode of production exists also under slavery, serfdom, and other states of dependence. But it flourishes, it lets loose its whole energy, it attains its full classical form, only where the labourer is the private owner of the means of labour which he uses; the peasant of the land which he cultivates; the artisan of the tool which he handles as a virtuoso. This mode of production presupposes parcelling out of the soil, and of the other means of production. As it excludes the concentration of these means of production, so also it excludes cooperation, division of labour within each separate process of production, the control over, and the productive application of, the forces of Nature by society, and the free development of the social productive powers. It is only compatible with a primitive and limited society and system of production. To perpetuate it would be, as Pecqueur rightly says, 'to decree universal mediocrity'. At a certain

28

stage of development it brings forth the material agencies for its own dissolution. From that moment new forces and new passions spring up in the bosom of society; but the old social organization fetters them and keeps them down. It must be annihilated; it is annihilated. Its annihilation, the transformation of the individualized and scattered means of production into socially concentrated ones, of the pigmy property of the many into the huge property of the few, the expropriation of the great mass of people from the soil, from the means of subsistence, and from the means of labour, this fearful and painful expropriation of the mass of the people forms the prelude to the history of capital. It comprises a series of forcible measures, of which we have passed in review only those that have been epoch-making as methods of the primitive accumulation of capital. The expropriation of the immediate producers was accomplished with merciless vandalism, and under the stimulus of the most infamous, sordid, petty, and odious passions. Self-earned private property that is based, so to say, on the fusing together of the isolated, independent, labouring-individual with the conditions of his labour, is supplanted by capitalist private property, which rests on exploitation by the nominally free labour of others.

As soon as this process of transformation has sufficiently decomposed the old society from top to bottom, as soon as the labourers are turned into proletarians, and their means of labour into capital, as soon as the capitalist mode of production stands on its own feet, then the further socialization of labour and further transformation of the land and other means of production into socially exploited and, therefore, common means of production, as well as the further expropriation of private proprietors, take a new form. That which is now to be expropriated is no longer the labourer working for himself, but the capitalist exploiting many labourers. This expropriation is accomplished by the action of the immanent laws of capitalist production itself, by the centralization of capital. One capitalist always kills many. Hand in hand with this centralization, this expropriation of many capitalists by few, develop, on an ever-extending scale, the cooperative form of the labour process, the conscious application of science, the planned exploitation of the earth, the transformation of the instruments of labour into instruments which can only be used in cooperative work, the economizing of all means of production by their use as the means or production of combined, socialized labour, the entanglement of all peoples in the net of the world-market, and with this, the international character of the capitalist system. Along with the constantly diminishing number of the magnates of capital, who usurp and monopolize all the advantages of this process of transformation, grows the mass of misery, oppression, slavery, degradation, and exploitation; but with this too grows the revolt of the working-class, a class always increasing in numbers, and disciplined, united, organized by the mechanism of the process of capitalist production itself. The monopoly of capital becomes a fetter upon the mode of production, which has sprung up and flourished along with, and under it. Centralization of the means of production and socialization of labour at last reach a point where they become incompatible with their capitalist integument. This integument is burst asunder. The knell of capitalist private property sounds. The expropriators are expropriated.

The capitalist mode of appropriation, the result of the capitalist mode of production, produces capitalist private property. This is the first negation of individual private property, as founded on the labour of the proprietor. But capitalist production begets, with the inexorability of a law of Nature, its own negation. It is the negation of negation. This does not re-establish private property for the producer, but gives him individual property based on the acquisitions of the capitalist era: i.e. on cooperation and the possession in common of the land and of the means of production which are produced by labour.

The transformation of scattered private property, arising from individual labour, into capitalist private property is, of course, a process incomparably more protracted, violent, and difficult, than the transformation of capitalist private property, which already is in fact based upon socialized production, into socialized property. In the former case, we had the expropriation of the mass of the people by a few usurpers; in the latter, we have the expropriation of a few usurpers by the mass of the people.

(*f*) From *Economic and Philosophical Manuscripts*

In what does this alienation of labour consist? First, that the work is *external* to the worker, that it is not a part of his nature, that consequently he does not fulfil himself in his work but denies himself, has a feeling of misery, not of well-being, does not develop freely a physical and mental energy, but is physically exhausted and mentally debased. The workers therefore feels himself at home only during his leisure, whereas at work he feels homeless. His work is not voluntary but imposed, *forced labour*. It is not the satisfaction of a need, but only a *means* for satisfying other needs. Its alien character is clearly shown by the fact that as soon as there is no physical or other compulsion it is avoided like the plague. Finally, the alienated character of work for the worker appears in the fact that it is not his work but work for someone else, that in work he does not belong to himself but to another person.

Just as in religion the spontaneous activity of human fantasy, of the human brain and heart, reacts independently, that is, as an alien activity of gods or devils, upon the individual, so the activity of the worker is not his spontaneous activity. It is another's activity, and a loss of his own spontaneity. . . .

The more the worker expends himself in work, the more powerful becomes the world of objects which he creates in face of himself, and the poorer he himself becomes in his inner life, the less he belongs to himself. It is just the same as in religion. The more of himself man attributes to God, the less he has left in himself. The worker puts his life into the object, and his life then belongs no longer to him but to the object. The greater his activity, therefore, the less he possesses. What is embodied in the product of his labour is no longer his. The greater this product is, therefore, the more he himself is diminished. The *alienation* of the worker in his product means not only that his labour becomes an object, takes on its own existence, but that it exists outside him, independently, and alien to him, and that it stands opposed to him as an autonomous power. The life which he has given to the object sets itself against him as an alien and hostile force. . . .

The object produced by labour, its product, now stands opposed to it as an *alien being*, as a *power independent* of the producer. The product of labour is labour which has been embodied in an object, and turned into a physical thing; this product is an *objectification* of labour. The performance of work is at the same time its objectification. This performance of work appears, in the sphere of political economy, as a vitiation of the worker, objectification as a *loss* and as *servitude to the object*, and appropriation as *alienation*.

(g) From *The Communist Manifesto*

The history of all hitherto existing society is the history of class struggles. Freeman and slave, patrician and plebeian, lord and serf, guild-master and journeyman, in a word, oppressor and oppressed, stood in constant opposition to one another, carried on an uninterrupted, now hidden, now open fight, a fight that each time ended either in a revolutionary reconstitution of society at large, or in the common ruin of the contending classes.

In the earlier epochs of history, we find almost everywhere a complicated arrangement of society into various orders, a manifold gradation of social rank. In ancient Rome we have patricians, knights, plebeians, slaves; in the Middle Ages, feudal lords, vassals, guild-masters, journeymen, apprentices, serfs; in almost all of these classes, again, subordinate gradations.

The modern bourgeois society that has sprouted from the ruins of feudal society has not done away with class antagonisms. It has but established new classes, new conditions of oppression, new forms of struggle in place of the old ones.

Our epoch, the epoch of the bourgeoisie, possesses, however, this distinctive feature: it has simplified the class antagonisms. Society as a whole is more and more splitting up into two great hostile camps, into two great classes directly facing each other – bourgeoisie and proletariat.

(h) From *The Poverty of Philosophy*

An oppressed class is a vital condition of every society based on class antagonism. The emancipation of the oppressed class therefore necessarily involves the creation of a new society. For an oppressed class to be able to emancipate itself, it is essential that the existing forces of production and the existing social relations should be incapable of continuing to exist side by side. Of all the instruments of production, the greatest productive force is the revolutionary class itself. The organization of the revolutionary elements as a class presupposes that all the productive forces which could develop within the old society are in existence.

Does this mean that the downfall of the old society will be followed by a new class domination, expressing itself in a new political power? No. The condition for the emancipation of the working class is the abolition of all classes, just as the condition for the emancipation of the third estate, of the bourgeois order, was the abolition of all estates and orders.

The working class, in the course of its development, will substitute for the old civil society an association which will exclude classes and their antagonism, and there will no longer be any political power, properly so-called, since political power is precisely the official expression of the antagonism in civil society.

In the meantime, the antagonism between the proletariat and the bourgeoisie is a class struggle, whose most complete expression is a total revolution. Is it astonishing, moreover, that a society founded on the *opposition* of classes should end in a brutal *contradiction*, in a hand-to-hand struggle, as its last act?

Let us not say that the social movement excludes a political movement. There is no political movement which is not at the same time social. It is only in an order of things where there are no longer classes and class antagonism that *social evolution* will cease to involve *political revolution*. Until then, the last word of social science, on the eve of every general reconstruction of society, will always be:

Le combat ou la mort; la lutte sanguinaire ou le néant.

C'est ainsi que la question est invinciblement posée.

George Sand

(i) From *Capital*, I

As regards the means of production, what is really consumed is their use-value, and the consumption of this use-value by labour results in the product. There is no consumption of their value, and it would therefore be inaccurate to say that it is reproduced. It is rather preserved; not by reason of any operation it undergoes itself in the process, but because the article in which it originally exists vanishes, it is true, but vanishes into some other article. Hence in the value of the product there is a reappearance of the value of the means of production, but there is strictly speaking no reproduction of that value. That which is produced is a new use-value in which the old exchange-value reappears.

It is otherwise with the subjective factor of the labour-process, with labour-power in action. While the labourer, by virtue of his labour being of a specialized kind that has a special object, preserves and transfers to the product the value of the means of production, he at the same time, by the mere act of working, creates each instant an additional or new value. Suppose the process of production to be stopped just when the workman has produced an equivalent for the value of his own labour-power, when, for example, by six hours' labour, he has added a value of three shillings. This value is the surplus of the total value of the product over the portion of its value that is due to the means of production. It is the only original bit of value formed during this process, the only portion of the value of the product created by this process. Of course, we do not forget that this new value only replaces the money advanced by the capitalist in the purchase of the labour-power and spent by the labourer on the necessities of life. With regard to the money spent, the new value is merely a reproduction; but nevertheless it is an actual and not, as in the case of the value of the means of production, only an apparent reproduction. The substitution of one value for another, is here effected by the creation of new value. . . .

By our explanation of the different parts played by the various factors of the labour-process in the formation of the product's value, we have in fact disclosed the characters of the different functions allotted to the different elements of capital in the process of expanding its own value. The surplus of the total value of the product over the sum of the values of its constituent factors is the surplus of the expanded capital over the capital originally advanced. The means of production on the one hand, labour-power on the other, are merely the different modes of existence which the value of the original capital assumed when from being money it was transformed into the various factors of the labour-process. That part of capital then which is represented by the means of production, by the raw material, auxiliary material and the instruments of labour, does not in the process of production undergo any quantitative alteration of value. I therefore call it the constant part of capital, or more shortly, *constant capital*.

On the other hand, that part of capital represented by labour-power does, in the process of production, undergo an alteration of value. It both reproduces the equivalent of its own value, and also produces an excess, a surplus-value, which may itself vary, may be more or less according to circumstances. This part of capital is continually being transformed from a constant into a variable magnitude. I therefore call it the variable part of capital, or shortly, *variable capital*. The same elements of capital which, from the point of view of the labour-process, present themselves respectively as the objective and subjective factors, as means of production and labour-power, present themselves, from the point of view of the process of creating surplus-value, as constant and variable capital. . . .

John Stuart Mill says in his Principles of Political Economy: 'It is questionable if all the mechanical inventions yet made have lighted the day's toil of any human being.' That is, however, by no means the aim of the capitalistic application of machinery. Like every other increase in the productiveness of labour, machinery is intended to cheapen commodities, and, by shortening that portion of the working day in which the labourer works for himself, to lengthen the other portion that he gives without an equivalent to the capitalist. In short, it is a means for producing surplus-value.

FURTHER READING

Selections, with comments, from Marx, Lenin, Trotsky, Stalin, etc., are contained in S. Hook, ed., *Marx and the Marxists*, Van Nostrand (Anvil Original), 1955. Writings by Marx alone are selected and introduced by T. B. Bottomore and M. Rubel, eds, *Karl Marx: Selected Writings in Sociology and Social Philosophy*, Penguin, 1963, and R. Freedman, ed., *Marx on Economics*, Penguin, 1962. R. N. Carew Hunt gives a general account of communism in *The Theory and Practice of Communism*, Penguin, 1963. Useful biographies of Marx are: Sir Isaiah Berlin, *Karl Marx: his Life and Environment*, Oxford University Press, 1948, and E. H. Carr, *Karl Marx: a Study of Fanaticism*, Dent, 1934. Among the many analyses of Marxist ideas mention should be made of: E. Burns, *What is Marxism?*, Gollancz, 1939; Max Eastman, *Marxism: is it a Science?*, Allen & Unwin, 1941; K. R. Popper, *The Open Society and its Enemies*, 2 vols, Routledge & Kegan Paul, vol. 2, 1945; R. Tucker, *Philosophy and Myth in Karl Marx*, Cambridge University Press, 1964.

4 Freud

The work of Sigmund Freud (1856–1939) continues to be a subject of controversy and, inevitably, some of his attackers and defenders have displayed equal ignorance and naïveté. It is inaccurate to accuse him of 'reducing everything to sex', just as it is foolish and misleading not to distinguish between what he presented as fact and what he offered as hypothesis. To have no part of Freud is an untenable intellectual position, but equally, as one of his most penetrating commentators has reminded us,[1] it is foolish to treat psychoanalysis as a cult, and more particularly as a cult which has 'its canonical literature, its apocryphas, its orthodoxies and heterodoxies, its inquisitors and its apostolic succession'.

Freud was born in Freiburg, lived in Vienna between 1860 and 1938, and died in England the following year. As a young doctor he concentrated on the treatment of nervous ailments and quickly found that the procedures laid down in the textbooks brought no real cure. For a period he came under the

[1] R. Dalbiez, *Psychoanalytical Method and the Doctrine of Freud*, 2 vols, Longmans, 1941.

influence of several French doctors and psychologists who were using hypnosis, sometimes with striking results, in this sphere. In Paris, between 1885–6, he studied Charcot's treatment of hysteria. He co-operated particularly with Charcot's pupil, Janet, learning a considerable amount about the split mind and dissociated personality that can accompany mental disorders. In 1889 Freud made contact with Bernheim who had a practice in Nancy. Bernheim put his patients into a state of hypnotic somnambulism and found that on regaining consciousness they quite genuinely denied any knowledge of the hypnotic experience. Nevertheless, with careful and repeated questioning, the experience was always remembered and reproduced. This 'talking out' or 'free association' method was being used in Vienna by Josef Breuer who treated cases of hysteria with the aid of hypnosis. Freud and Breuer co-operated for a period and produced clear evidence, in their 'Studies on Hysteria' (1895), of the mental mechanisms underlying these disorders (see passage (a) below). Further study brought Freud to two major conclusions: (i) '. . . that mental processes are essentially unconscious, and that those which are conscious are merely isolated acts and part of the whole psychic entity' and (ii) '. . . that impulses, which can only be described as sexual in both the narrower and the wider sense, play a peculiarly large part, never before sufficiently appreciated, in the causation of nervous and mental disorders'. The conclusion (i) above eventually led Freud to posit a tripartite structure of personality – id, ego and superego – which is set out in his own words in passage (b) below. The reveal- ing role for the unconscious life of slips of the tongue or pen, misreading or mishearing, forgetting names, etc., was emphasized in 'The Psycopathology of Everyday Life' (1901) and later in the 'Introductory Lectures on Psycho- Analysis' (1916–17) – see passage (c) below. As regards conclusion (ii) above, Freud had already reached it in some considerable measure during his work with Breuer and it was a major cause of disagreement between them, as it was later to be between Freud and Jung. Freud's study of his patients' dreams added further evidence of the truth of the 'sexual hypothesis' – not least through his investigation of such things as censorship, dream distortion, etc. – and led to the publication of one of his major works, 'The Interpretation of Dreams' (1900). A brief indication of his work in this sphere is contained in passage (d) below, while passage (e) contains part of one of his most famous sexual theories – the so-called 'Oedipus complex'.

Freud's capacity for work and his total written output were both enormous. Apart from his clinical studies of hysteria, his dynamic psychology of un- conscious life, his interpretation of dreams and his general sexual theories (particularly in their relationship to infancy), he produced a general theory and classification of neuroses (hysteria, anxiety, obsession, depression, paranoia and sexual immaturity). Significantly, he himself defined psychoanalysis as 'a strict and universal application of determinism to mental life' and there is evidence in this phrase, as in much of his work, of the nineteenth-century scientific determinist presuppositions underlying his thought. But apart from his clinical activities, Freud also propounded various 'philosophical' theories concerned with the nature of man (the two basic instincts of eroticism and death), the origin of conscience and the psychological and social significance of morality and religion. These speculations are much less securely grounded and have even been questioned by some of Freud's most enthusiastic successors. The main 'philosophical' works are 'Totem and Taboo' (1912–13), 'Beyond the Pleasure Principle' (1920), 'The Future of an Illusion' (1927), 'Civilization and its Discontents' (1930) and 'Moses and Monotheism' (1939). The latter contains a most illuminating section on anti-semitism, part of which is quoted in passage (f) below. Freud also claimed that psychoanalysis can reveal much about the nature of artistic creation and indeed that 'sexual impulses have contributed invaluably to the highest cultural, artistic and social achievements of the human mind'.

(a) From 'Preliminary Communication' in Breuer and Freud's joint *Studies on Hysteria*

A chance observation has led us, over a number of years, to investigate a great variety of different forms and symptoms of hysteria, with a view to discovering their precipitating cause – the event which provoked the first occurrence, often many years earlier, of the phenomenon in question. In the great majority of cases it is not possible to establish the point of origin by a simple interrogation of the patient, however thoroughly it may be carried out. This is in part because what is in question is often some experience which the patient dislikes discussing; but principally because he is genuinely unable to recollect it and often has no suspicion of the causal connection between the precipitating event and the pathological phenomenon. As a rule it is necessary to hypnotize the patient and to arouse his memories under hypnosis of the time at which the symptom made its first appearance; when this has been done, it becomes possible to demonstrate the connection in the clearest and most convincing fashion.

This method of examination has in a large number of cases produced results which seem to be of value alike from a theoretical and a practical point of view.

They are valuable theoretically because they have taught us that external events determine the pathology of hysteria to an extent far

ASPECTS OF THE MODERN EUROPEAN MIND

greater than is known and recognized. It is of course obvious that in cases of 'traumatic' hysteria what provokes the symptoms is the accident. The causal connection is equally evident in hysterical attacks when it is possible to gather from the patient's utterances that in each attack he is hallucinating the same event which provoked the first one. The situation is more obscure in the case of other phenomena.

Our experiences have shown us, however, that the most various symptoms, which are ostensibly spontaneous and, as one might say, idiopathic products of hysteria, are just as strictly related to the precipitating trauma as the phenomena to which we have just alluded and which exhibit the connection quite clearly. The symptoms which we have been able to trace back to precipitating factors of this sort include neuralgias and anaesthesias of very various kinds, many of which had persisted for years, contractures and paralyses, hysterical attacks and epileptoid convulsions, which every observer regarded as true epilepsy, *petit mal* and disorders in the nature of *tic*, chronic vomiting and anorexia, carried to the pitch of rejection of all nourishment, various forms of disturbance of vision, constantly recurrent visual hallucinations, etc. The disproportion between the many years' duration of the hysterical symptom and the single occurrence which provoked it is what we are accustomed invariably to find in traumatic neuroses. Quite frequently it is some event in childhood that sets up a more or less severe symptom which persists during the years that follow.

The connection is often so clear that it is quite evident how it was that the precipitating event produced this particular phenomenon rather than any other. In that case the symptom has quite obviously been determined by the precipitating cause. We may take as a very commonplace instance a painful emotion arising during a meal but suppressed at the time, and then producing nausea and vomiting which persists for months in the form of hysterical vomiting . . . .

In other cases the connection is not so simple. It consists only in what might be called a 'symbolic' relation between the precipitating cause and the pathological phenomenon – a relation such as healthy people form in dreams. For instance, a neuralgia may follow upon mental pain or vomiting upon a feeling of moral disgust. We have studied patients who used to make the most copious use of this sort of symbolization. In still other cases it is not possible to understand at first sight how they can be determined in the manner we have suggested. It is precisely the typical hysterical symptoms which fall into this class, such as hemi-anaesthesia, contraction of the field of vision, epileptiform convulsions, and so on. An explanation of our views on this group must be reserved for a fuller discussion of the subject.

Observations such as these seem to us to establish an analogy between the pathogenesis of common hysteria and that of traumatic neuroses, and to justify an extension of the concept of traumatic hysteria. In traumatic neuroses the operative cause of the illness is not the trifling physical injury but the affect of fright – the psychical trauma. In an analogous manner, our investigations reveal, for many, if not for most, hysterical symptoms, precipitating causes which can only be described as psychical traumas. Any experience which calls up distressing affects – such as those of fright, anxiety, shame or physical pain – may operate as a trauma of this kind; and whether it in fact does so depends naturally enough on the susceptibility of the person affected (as well as on another condition which will be mentioned later). In the case of common hysteria it not infrequently happens that, instead of a single, major trauma, we find a number of partial traumas forming a *group* of provoking causes. These have only been able to exercise a traumatic effect by summation and they belong together in so far as they are in part components of a single story of suffering. There are other cases in which an apparently trivial circumstance combines with the actually operative event or occurs at a time of peculiar susceptibility to stimulation and in this way attains the dignity of a trauma which it would not otherwise have possessed but which thenceforward persists.

But the causal relation between the determining physical trauma and the hysterical phenomena is not of a kind implying that the trauma merely acts like an *agent provocateur* in releasing the symptom, which thereafter leads an independent existence. We must presume rather that the physical trauma – or more precisely the memory of the trauma – acts like a foreign body which long after its entry must continue to be regarded as an agent that is still at work; and we find the evidence for this in a highly remarkable phenomenon which at the same time lends an important *practical* interest to our findings.

For we found, to our great surprise at first, that *each individual hysterical symptom immediately and permanently disappeared when we had succeeded in bringing clearly to light the memory of the event by which it was provoked and in arousing its accompanying affect, and when the patient had described that event in the greatest possible detail and had put the affect into words.* Recollection without affect almost invariably produces no result. The physical process which originally took place must be repeated as vividly as possible; it must be brought back to its *status nascendi* and then given verbal utterance. Where what we are dealing with are phenomena involving stimuli (spasms, neuralgias and hallucinations) these re-appear once again with the fullest intensity and then vanish for ever. Failures of function, such as paralyses and anaesthesias, vanish in the same way, though, of course, without the temporary intensification being discernible.

(b) From *An Outline of Psycho-Analysis*

We assume that mental life is the function of an apparatus to which we ascribe the characteristics of being extended in space and of being made up of several portions – which we imagine, that is, as resembling a tele-scope or microscope or something of the kind. Notwithstanding some earlier attempts in the same direction, the consistent working-out of a conception such as this is a scientific novelty.

We have arrived at our knowledge of this psychical apparatus by studying the individual development of human beings. To the oldest of these psychical provinces or agencies we give the name of *id*. It contains everything that is inherited, that is present at birth, that is laid down in the constitution – above all, therefore, the instincts, which originate from the somatic organization and which find a first psychical expression here (in the id) in forms unknown to us.

Under the influence of the real external world around us, one portion of the id has undergone a special development. From what was origin-ally a cortical layer, equipped with the organs for receiving stimuli and with arrangements for acting as a protective shield against stimuli, a special organization has arisen which henceforward acts as an inter-mediary between the id and the external world. To this region of our mind we have given the name of *ego*.

Here are the principal characteristics of the ego. In consequence of the pre-established connection between sense perception and muscular action, the ego has voluntary movement at its command. It has the task of self-preservation. As regards *external* events, it performs that task by becoming aware of stimuli, by storing up experiences about them (in the memory), by avoiding excessively strong stimuli (through flight), by dealing with moderate stimuli (through adaptation) and finally by learning to bring about expedient changes in the external world to its own advantage (through activity). As regards *internal* events, in relation to the id, it performs that task by gaining control over the demands of the instincts, by deciding whether they are to be allowed satisfaction, by postponing that satisfaction to times and circumstances favourable in the external world or by suppressing their excitations entirely. It is guided in its activity by consideration of the tensions produced by stimuli, whether these tensions are present in it or introduced into it. The raising of these tensions is in general felt as *unpleasure* and their lowering as *pleasure*. It is probable, however, that what is felt as pleasure or unpleasure is not the *absolute* height of this tension but something in the rhythm of the changes in it. The ego strives after pleasure and seeks to avoid unpleasure. An increase in unpleasure that is expected and foreseen is met by a *signal of anxiety*; the occasion of such an increase, whether it threatens from without or within, is known as a *danger*. From time to time the ego gives up its connection with the external world and withdraws into the state of sleep, in which it makes far-reaching changes in its organization. It is to be inferred from the state of sleep that this organization consists in a particular distribution of mental energy.

The long period of childhood, during which the growing human being lives in dependence on his parents, leaves behind it as a precipitate the formation in his ego of a special agency in which this parental influence is prolonged. It has received the name of *super-ego*. In so far as this super-ego is differentiated from the ego or is opposed to it, it constitutes a third power which the ego must take into account.

An action by the ego is as it should be if it satisfies simultaneously the demands of the id, of the super-ego and of reality – that is to say, if it is able to reconcile their demands with one another. The details of the relation between the ego and the super-ego become completely intelligible when they are traced back to the child's attitude to its parents. This parental influence of course includes in its operation not only the personality of the actual parents but also the family, racial and national traditions handed on through them, as well as the demands of the immediate social milieu which they represent. In the same way, the super-ego, in the course of an individual's development, receives contributions from later successors and substitutes of his parents, such as teachers and models in public life of admired social ideals. It will be observed that, for all their fundamental difference, the id and the super-ego have one thing in common: they both represent the influences of the past – the id the influence of heredity, the super-ego the influence, essentially, of what is taken over from other people – whereas the ego is principally determined by the individual's own experience, that is by accidental and contemporary events.

(c) From *Introductory Lectures on Psycho-Analysis*

Let us still keep to the examples of slips of the tongue and review a larger number of such manifestations. We then find whole categories of cases in which the intention, the meaning, of the slip is quite obvious, particularly so in those instances in which the opposite of what was intended is said. The President says in his opening speech: 'I declare the session *closed*.' That is surely not ambiguous. The meaning and intention of this slip is that he wants to close the session. One might well say, 'he said so himself'; we only take him at his word. Please do not interrupt me with the objection that this is impossible, that we know quite well that he wished to open the session, not to close it, and that he himself whom we have just recognized as the best judge of his intention will affirm that he meant to open it. In doing so you forget that we agreed to consider the error by itself; its relation to the intention which it disturbs will be discussed later. *You* would be guilty of an error in logic, by which you would conveniently dispose of the whole problem under discussion, which in English is called 'begging the question'.

In other cases, where the form of the slip is not exactly the opposite of what is intended, a contradictory sense may still often come to expression. 'I am not *inclined* (*geneigt*) to appreciate my predecessor's merits.' 'Inclined' is not the opposite of 'in a position to' (*geeignet*), but it is an open confession of a thought in sharpest contradiction to the speaker's duty to meet the situation gracefully.

In still other cases the slip simply adds a second meaning to the one intended. The sentence then sounds like a contraction, an abbreviation, a condensation of several sentences into one. Thus the determined lady who said: 'He may eat and drink whatever *I* choose.' That is as if she had said: 'He can eat and drink what he chooses, but what does it matter what he chooses? It is for me to do the choosing!' Slips of the tongue often give this impression of abbreviation; for instance, when a professor of anatomy at the end of his lecture on the nasal cavities asks whether his class has thoroughly understood it and, after a general reply in the affirmative, goes on to say: 'I can hardly believe that that is so, since persons who can thoroughly understand the nasal cavities can be counted, even in a city of millions, on *one finger* . . . I mean, on the fingers of one hand.' The abbreviated sentence has its own meaning: it says that there is only one person who understands the subject. . . .

Psycho-physiological factors such as excitement, absent-mindedness, distraction of attention, obviously provide very little in the way of explanation. They are mere phrases; they are screens, and we should not be deterred from looking behind them. The question is rather what has here called forth the excitement or the particular diversion of attention. The influence of sound-values, resemblances between words, and common associations connecting certain words, must also be recognized as important. They facilitate the slip by pointing out a path for it to take. But if there is a path before me does it necessarily follow that I must go along it? I also require a motive to determining my choice and, further, some force to propel me forward. These sound-values and word associations are, therefore, just like the bodily conditions, the facilitating causes of slips of the tongue, and cannot provide the real explanation of them. Consider for a moment the enormous majority of cases in which the words I am using in my speech are not deranged on account of sound-resemblance to other words, intimate associations with opposite meanings, or with expressions in common use. It yet remains to suppose, with the philosopher Wundt, that a slip of the tongue arises when the tendency to associations gains an ascendance over the original intention owing to bodily fatigue. This would be quite plausible if experience did not controvert it by the fact that in a number of cases the bodily, and in another large group the associative, predisposing causes are absent.

Particularly interesting to me, however, is your next question, namely, by what means the two mutually disturbing tendencies may be ascertained. You probably do not suspect how portentous this question is. You will agree that one of these tendencies, the one which is interfered with, is always unmistakable; the person who commits the slip knows it and acknowledges it. Doubt and hesitation only arise in regard to the other, what we have called the interfering, tendency. Now we have already heard, and you will certainly not have forgotten, that in a certain number of cases this other tendency is equally plain. It is evident in the result of the slip if only we have the courage to let the slip speak for itself. The President who said the opposite of what he meant – it is clear that he wishes to open the session, but equally clear that he would also like to close it. That is so plain that it needs no interpreting. But in the other cases, in which the interfering tendency merely distorts the original without itself coming to full expression, – how can the interfering tendency be detected in the distortion?

In one group of cases by a very safe and simple method, by the same method, that is, by which we establish the tendency that is interfered with. We enquire of the speaker, who tells us then and there; after making the slip he restores the word he originally intended. 'O, it may *stad* – no, it may *take* another month.' Well, the interfering tendency may be likewise supplied by him. We say, 'Now why did you first say stad?' He replies, 'I meant to say it was a sad business'; and in the other case in which 'refilled' was said, the speaker informs you that he first meant to say it was a filthy business, but controlled himself and substituted another expression. The discovery of the disturbing tendency is here as definitely established as that of the disturbed tendency. It is not without intention that I have selected as examples cases which owe neither their origin nor their explanation to me or to any supporter of mine. Still, in both these cases, a certain intervention was necessary in order to produce the explanation. One had to ask the speaker why he made the slip, what explanation he could give. Without that he might have passed it by without seeking to explain it. Being asked, however, he gave as his answer the first idea that occurred to him. And see now, this little intervention and the result of it constitute already a psycho-analysis, a prototype of every psycho-analytic investigation that we may undertake further. . . .

That errors have a meaning we may certainly set down as established by our efforts up to this point, and may take this conclusion as a basis for our further investigations. Let me once more emphasize the fact that we do not maintain – and for our purposes do not need to maintain – that every single mistake which occurs has a meaning, although I think that probable. It is enough for us to prove that such a meaning is relatively frequent in the various forms of errors. In this respect, by the way, the various forms show certain differences. Some cases of slips of the tongue, slips of the pen, and so on, may be the effect of a purely physiological cause, though I cannot believe this possible of those errors which depend upon forgetfulness (forgetting of names or intentions, mislaying, and so on); losing possessions is in all probability to be recognized as unintentional in some cases; altogether our conceptions are only to a certain extent applicable to the mistakes which occur in daily life. These limitations should be borne in mind by you when we proceed on the assumption that errors are mental acts arising from the mutual interference of two intentions.

(d) From *Five Lectures on Psycho-Analysis*

You must distinguish the *manifest content of the dream*, as you vaguely recollect it in the morning and laboriously (and, as it seems, arbitrarily) clothe it in words, and the *latent dream-thoughts*, which you must suppose were present in the unconscious. The distortion in dreams is the same process that you have already come to know in investigating the formation of hysterical symptoms. It indicates, too, that the same interplay of mental forces is at work in the formation of dreams as in that of symptoms. The manifest content of the dream is the distorted substitute for the unconscious dream-thoughts and this distortion is the work of the ego's forces of defence – of resistances. In waking life these resistances altogether prevent the repressed wishes of the unconscious from entering consciousness; and during the lowered state of sleep they are at least strong enough to oblige them to adopt a veil of disguise. Thereafter, the dreamer can no more understand the meaning of his dreams than the hysteric can understand the connexion and significance of his symptoms.

You can convince yourself that there are such things as latent dream-thoughts and that the relation between them and the manifest content of the dream is really as I have described it, if you carry out an analysis of dreams, the technique of which is the same as that of psycho-analysis. You entirely disregard the apparent connexions between the elements in the manifest dream and collect the ideas that occur to you in connexion with each separate element of the dream by free association according to the psychoanalytic rule of procedure. From this material you arrive at the latent dream-thoughts, just as you arrived at the patient's hidden complexes from his associations to his symptoms and memories. The latent dream-thoughts which have been reached in this way will at once show you how completely justified we have been in tracing back adults' dreams to children's dreams. The true meaning of the dream, which has now taken the place of its manifest content, is always clearly intelligible; it has its starting-point in experiences of the previous day, and proves to be a fulfilment of unsatisfied wishes. The manifest dream, which you know from memory when you wake up, can therefore only be described as a *disguised* fulfilment of *repressed* wishes.

You can also obtain a view, by a kind of synthetic work, of the process which has brought about the distortion of the unconscious dream-thoughts into the manifest content of the dream. We call this process the 'dream-work'. It deserves our closest theoretical interest, since we are able to study in it, as nowhere else, what unsuspected psychical processes can occur in the unconscious, or rather, to put it more accurately, *between* two separate psychical systems like the conscious and unconscious. Among these freshly discovered psychical processes those of *condensation* and *displacement* are especially noticeable. The dream-work is a special case of the effects produced by two different mental groupings on each other – that is, of the consequences of mental splitting; and it seems identical in all essentials with the process of distortion which transforms the repressed complexes into symptoms where there is unsuccessful repression.

You will also learn with astonishment from the analysis of dreams (and most convincingly from that of your own) what an unsuspectedly great part is played in human developments by impressions and experiences of early childhood. In dream-life the child that is in man pursues its existence, as it were, and retains all its characteristics and wishful impulses, even such as have become unserviceable in later life. There will be brought home to you with irresistible force the many developments, repressions, sublimations, and reaction-formations, by means of which a child with a quite other innate endowment grows into what we call a normal man, the bearer, and in part the victim, of the civilization that has been so painfully acquired.

I should like you to notice, too, that the analysis of dreams has shown us that the unconscious makes use of a particular symbolism, especially for representing sexual complexes. This symbolism varies partly from individual to individual; but partly it is laid down in a typical form and seems to coincide with the symbolism which, as we suspect, underlies our myths and fairy tales. It seems not impossible that these creations of the popular mind might find an explanation through the help of dreams.

(e) From *Introductory Lectures on Psycho-Analysis*

At about the time when the mother becomes the love-object, the mental operation of repression has already begun in the child and has withdrawn from him the knowledge of some part of his sexual aims. Now with this choice of the mother as love-object is connected all that which, under the name of '*the Oedipus complex*', has become of such great importance in the psycho-analytic explanation of the neuroses, and which has had a perhaps equally important share in causing the opposition against psycho-analysis. . . .

You all know the Greek myth of King Oedipus, whose destiny it was to slay his father and to wed his mother, who did all in his power to avoid the fate prophesied by the oracle, and who in self-punishment blinded himself when he discovered that in ignorance he had committed both these crimes. I trust that many of you have yourselves experienced the profound effect of the tragic drama fashioned by Sophocles from this story. The Attic poet's work portrays the gradual discovery of the deed of Oedipus, long since accomplished, and brings it slowly to light by skilfully prolonged enquiry, constantly fed by new evidence; it has thus a certain resemblance to the course of a psychoanalysis. In the dialogue the deluded mother-wife, Jocasta, resists the continuation of the enquiry; she points out that many people in their dreams have mated with their mothers, but that dreams are of no account. To us dreams are of much account, especially typical dreams which occur in many people; we have no doubt that the dream Jocasta speaks of is intimately related to the shocking and terrible story of the myth. . . .

There is no possible doubt that one of the most important sources of the sense of guilt which so often torments neurotic people is to be found in the Oedipus complex. More than this: in 1913, under the title of *Totem und Tabu*, I published a study of the earliest forms of religion and morality in which I expressed a suspicion that perhaps the sense of guilt of mankind as a whole, which is the ultimate source of religion and morality, was acquired in the beginnings of history through the Oedipus complex. . . .

It should also be remarked that long before the time of psychoanalysis the two criminal offences of Oedipus were recognized as the true expressions of unbridled instinct. Among the works of the Encyclopaedist Diderot you will find the famous dialogue, *Le Neveu de Rameau*, which was translated into German by no less a person than Goethe. There you may read these remarkable words: *Si le petit sauvage était abandonné à lui-même, qu'il conserva toute son imbécillité et qu'il réunit au peu de raison de l'enfant au berceau la violence des passions de l'homme de trente ans, il tordrait le cou à son père et coucherait avec sa mère.*

(f) From *Moses and Monotheism*

A phenomenon of such intensity and permanence as the people's hatred of the Jews must of course have more than one ground. It is possible to find a whole number of grounds, some of them clearly derived from reality, which call for no interpretation, and others, lying deeper and derived from hidden sources, which might be regarded as the specific reasons. Of the former, the reproach of being aliens is perhaps the weakest, since in many places dominated by anti-semitism today the Jews are among the oldest portions of the population or had even been there before the present inhabitants. This applies, for instance, to the city of Cologne, to which the Jews came with the Romans, before it was occupied by the Germans. Other grounds for hating the Jews are stronger – thus, the circumstances that they live for the most part as minorities among other peoples, for the communal feeling of groups requires, in order to complete it, hostility towards some extraneous minority, and the numerical weakness of this excluded minority encourages its suppression. There are, however, two other characteristics of the Jews which are quite unforgivable. First is the fact that in some respects they are different from their 'host' nations. They are not fundamentally different, for they are not Asiatics of a foreign race, as their enemies maintain, but composed for the most part of remnants of the Mediterranean peoples and heirs of the Mediterranean civilization. But they are none the less different, often in an indefinable way different, especially from the Nordic peoples, and the intolerance of groups is often, strangely enough, exhibited more strongly against small differences than against fundamental ones. The other point has a still greater effect: namely, that they defy all oppression, that the most cruel persecutions have not succeeded in exterminating them, and, indeed, that on the contrary they show a capacity for holding their own in commercial life and, where they are admitted, for making valuable contributions to every form of cultural activity.

The deeper motives for hatred of the Jews are rooted in the remotest past ages; they operate from the unconscious of the peoples, and I am prepared to find that at first they will not seem credible. I venture to assert that jealousy of the people which declared itself the first-born, favourite child of God the Father, has not yet been surmounted among other peoples even today; it is as though they had thought there was truth in the claim. Further, among the customs by which the Jews made themselves separate, that of circumcision had made a disagreeable, uncanny impression, which is to be explained, no doubt, by its recalling the dreaded castration and along with it a portion of the primaeval past which is gladly forgotten. And finally, as the latest motive in this series, we must not forget that all those peoples who excel today in their hatred of Jews became Christians only in late historic times, often driven to it by bloody coercion. It might be said that they are all 'mis-baptized'. They have been left, under a thin veneer of Christianity, what their ancestors were, who worshipped a barbarous polytheism. They have not got over a grudge against the new religion which was imposed on them; but they have displaced the grudge on to the source from which Christianity reached them. The fact that the Gospels tell a story which is set among Jews, and in fact deals only with Jews, has made this displacement easy for them. Their hatred of Jews is at bottom a hatred of Christians, and we need not be surprised that in the German National-Socialist revolution this intimate relation between the two monotheist religions finds such a clear expression in the hostile treatment of both of them.

FURTHER READING

The classic life of Freud is: E. Jones, *The Life and Work of Sigmund Freud*, Chatto & Windus, 1953–57; abridged, 1962; Penguin, 1964 (abr.). Apart from his own *Introductory Lectures on Psycho-Analysis*, Allen & Unwin, 1961, and *Two Short Accounts of Psycho-Analysis*, Penguin, 1962, the clearest exposition of his ideas, is D. Stafford-Clark, *What Freud Really Said*, Macdonald, 1965. Other expositions of his thought include: R. Dalbiez, *Psychoanalytical Method and the Doctrine of Freud* (2 vols), Longmans, 1941; P. Rieff, *Freud: the Mind of the Moralist*, Gollancz, 1960; L. Trilling, *Freud and the Crisis of our Culture*, Boston, Beacon Press, 1955; H. Marcuse, *Eros and Civilization: a Philosophical Inquiry into Freud*, new edn, Beacon Press, 1960; R. S. Lee, *Freud and Christianity*, Penguin, 1967. Wider implications are studied by N. O. Brown, *Life against Death*, Routledge & Kegan Paul, 1959; and later developments in psychoanalysis (e.g. Horney, Fromm, etc.) by J. A. C. Brown, *Freud and the Post-Freudians*, Penguin, 1964. F. J. Hoffman has written on *Freudianism and the Literary Mind*, New York, Evergreen Books, 1959; the case against Freud is put by A. Salter, *The Case against Psychoanalysis*, rev. edn, New York, Citadel Press, 1963.

II
Other Major Figures

One can scarcely expect to find general agreement on the essential writers and thinkers to be included under this rubric. The choice must finally be a personal one and will therefore be open to the various objections (also personal), and the canvassing of alternative or additional names, which accompany the appearance of any anthology. Granted more space, I should certainly have wished to include Bergson and Croce, among others, in this particular section on 'Other Major Figures'. Similarly, a case could be made out for adding Sorel, Lévy-Bruhl, Schleiermacher, Feuerbach and others to later sections. Nevertheless, I believe that all the thinkers included here have made significant contributions to the growth of modern European intellectual life. The 'further reading' suggested at various points should take the reader beyond these particular names to other influential writers who have not been included but whose work deserves to be read. As with any anthology or book of readings, the present volume is offered as a starting point and a stimulus, not as a closed and completed whole.

One other general point should be made. The general grouping of authors throughout this volume as a whole is inevitably somewhat artificial. The main headings are a convenient and reasonably coherent method of presentation but they do not necessarily correspond to a clearly definable intellectual reality. Thus there are passages from Kierkegaard and Dostoevsky, for example, that are highly relevant to the section on religious thinkers (Part V) just as several passages quoted from Marx (Part I) can be related to some of the sociological extracts (Part IV). In a similar way some of the quotations from Nietzsche and Spengler which follow ought to be re-examined in the light of the later selections from Mussolini and Hitler (Part III). In a word, this is a volume which needs to be worked at by the reader and to be read in both a critical and synthesizing spirit.

5 Hegel

It is easier to summarize the relatively uneventful life of Georg Wilhelm Friedrich Hegel (1770–1831) than to give a concise account of his philosophy. He was born in Stuttgart and obtained his first post as an academic philosopher at Jena in 1801. The Battle of Jena (1806), in which Napoleon crushed the Prussian army, interrupted Hegel's university career and he edited a newspaper and directed the Nuremberg 'gymnasium' before occupying chairs of philosophy at Heidelberg (1816–18) and Berlin (1818–31). The chief works published in his lifetime were 'The Phenomenology of Mind' ('Die Phaenomenologie des Geistes', 1807), 'Logic' ('Wissenschaft der Logik', 1812–16), 'Encyclopedia of the Philosophical Sciences' ('Encyclopaedie der philosophischen Wissenschaften im Grundrisse', 1817), and 'The Philosophy of Right' ('Grundlinien der Philosophie des Rechts', 1820). After his death his lectures on the philosophy of religion, the history of philosophy, aesthetics and history were all separately published on the basis of notes taken by his students.

Hegel's thought dominated much nineteenth-century speculation and was revived at the beginning of the twentieth century by Dilthey in Germany and Croce in Italy. More recently still the spread of communism has sustained the study of Hegel's 'Logic' and his political ideas. Hegelianism is also important because of the different ways in which Kierkegaard and Marx defined their own ideas in opposition to it.

Hegel conceived all reality in primarily historical terms. Everything has a rhythmic evolution involving fruition, death and renewal. This is the dialectical pattern which infuses all his thought and which he defined succinctly on one occasion only (see passage (a) below). At some stage before a dialectical synthesis is achieved, thesis and antithesis coexist. This coexistence, in human consciousness, gives rise to the sense of alienation – 'the contrite consciousness' – on which Marx was later to draw (see passage (b); also pp. 30–1). Related to his concept of a dialectical reality is Hegel's argument that reality is rational – indeed that only the rational is real. This doctrine had immense consequences for his view of history. Passage (c) gives a brief glimpse of the way in which he argued that history is the working out of a rationality which, through dialectical sublimation, supersedes the seemingly irrational and ultimately spiritualizes evil. The logic of this position finally leads Hegel to assert (no doubt an alarming assertion in view of subsequent European history) that the highest embodiment of reason is the (Prussian?) state (see passage (d)).

(*a*) From *Encyclopedia of the Philosophical Sciences*

There are three aspects in every thought which is logically real or true: the abstract or rational form, which says what something is; the dialectical negation, which says what something is not; the speculative – concrete comprehension: A is also that which it is not, A is non-A. These three aspects do not constitute three parts of logic, but are moments of everything that is logically real or true. They belong to every philosophical Concept. Every Concept is rational, is abstractly opposed to another, and is united in comprehension together with its opposites. *This is the definition of dialectic.*

(*b*) From *The Phenomenology of Mind*

In Scepticism Consciousness learns in truth, that it is divided against itself. And from this experience there is born a new Type of Consciousness, wherein are linked the two thoughts which Scepticism had kept asunder. The thoughtless self-ignorance of Scepticism must pass away; for in fact the two attitudes of Scepticism express One Consciousness. This new Type of Consciousness is therefore explicitly aware of its own doubleness. It regards itself on the one hand as the Deliverer, changeless and self-possessed; on the other hand it regards itself as the absolutely confounded and contrary ... and the CONTRITE CONSCIOUSNESS is this awareness of the Self as the Divided Nature, wherein is only conflict. This Contrite and Broken Consciousness, just because the conflict of its Nature is known as belonging to one person, must forever, in each of its two forms, have the other also present to it. Whenever, in either form, it seems to have come to victory and unity, it finds no rest there, but is forthwith driven over to the other. Its true home-coming, its true reconciliation with itself, will, however, display to us the law of the Spirit, as he will appear when, having come to life, he has entered the world of his manifestation. For it already belongs to the Contrite Consciousness to be one undivided soul in the midst of its doubleness. It is in fact the very gazing of one Self into another; it is both these selves; it has no nature save in so far as it unites the two. But thus far it knows not yet this its own real essence; it has not entered into possession of this unity.

(*c*) From *Introduction to the Philosophy of History*

That development of the thinking spirit, which has resulted from the revelation of the Divine Being as its original basis, must ultimately advance to the *intellectual* comprehension of what was presented in the first instance, to *feeling* and *imagination*. The time must eventually come for understanding that rich product of active Reason, which the History of the World offers to us. It was for a while the fashion to profess admiration for the wisdom of God, as displayed in animals, plants, and isolated occurrences. But, if it be allowed that Providence manifests itself in such objects and forms of existence, why not also in Universal History? This is deemed too great a matter to be thus regarded. But Divine Wisdom, *i.e.* Reason, is one and the same in the great as in the little; and we must not imagine God to be too weak to exercise his wisdom on the grand scale. Out intellectual striving aims at realising the conviction that what was *intended* by eternal wisdom, is actually *accomplished* in the domain of existent, active Spirit, as well as in that of mere Nature. Our mode of treating the subject is, in this aspect, a Theodicaea, – a justification of the ways of God, – which Leibnitz attempted metaphysically, in his method, *i.e.* in indefinite abstract categories, – so that the ill that is found in the World may be comprehended, and the thinking Spirit reconciled with the fact of the existence of evil. Indeed, nowhere is such a harmonising view more pressingly demanded than in Universal History; and it can be attained only by recognizing the *positive* existence, in which that negative element is a subordinate, and vanquished nullity. On the one hand, the ultimate design of the World must be perceived; and, on the other hand, the fact that this design has been actually realised in it, and that evil has not been able permanently to assert a competing position. But this conviction involves much more than the mere belief in a superintending 'νοῦς' or in 'Providence'. 'Reason', whose sovereignty over the World has been maintained, is as indefinite a term as 'Providence', supposing the term to be used by those who are unable to characterise it distinctly, – to shew wherein it consists, so as to enable us to decide whether a thing is rational or irrational. An adequate definition of Reason is the first desideratum; and whatever boast may be made of strict adherence to it in explaining phenomena, – without such a definition we get no farther than mere words.

(*d*) From *Introduction to the Philosophy of History*

What is the material in which the Ideal of Reason is wrought out? The primary answer would be, – Personality itself – human desires – Subjectivity generally. In human knowledge and volition, as its material element, Reason attains positive existence. We have considered subjective volition where it has an object which is the truth and essence of a reality, viz. where it constitutes a great world-historical passion. As a subjective will, occupied with limited passions, it is dependent, and can gratify its desires only within the limits of this dependence. But the subjective will has also a substantial life – a reality, – in which it moves in the region of essential being and has the *essential* itself as the object of its existence. This essential being is the union of the *subjective* with the *rational* Will: it is the moral Whole, the State, which is that form of reality in which the individual has and enjoys his freedom; but on the condition of his recognition, believing in and willing that which is common to the Whole. And this must not be understood as if the subjective will of the social unit attained its gratification and enjoyment through that common Will; as if this were a means provided for its benefit; as if the individual, in his relations to other individuals, thus limited his freedom, in order that this universal limitation – the mutual constraint of all – might secure a small space of liberty for each. Rather, we affirm, are Law, Morality, Government, and they alone, the positive reality and completion of Freedom. Freedom of a low and limited order, is mere caprice; which finds its exercise in the sphere of particular and limited desires.

Subjective volition – Passion – is that which sets men in activity, that which effects 'practical' realization. The Idea is the inner spring of action; the State is the actually existing, realised moral life. For it is the Unity of the universal, essential Will, with that of the individual; and this is 'Morality'. The Individual living in this unity has a moral life; possesses a value that consists in this substantiality alone. Sophocles in his Antigone, says, 'The divine commands are not of yesterday, nor of today; no, they have an infinite existence, and no one could say whence they came.' The laws of morality are not accidental, but are the essentially Rational. It is the very object of the State that what is essential in the practical activity of men, and in their dispositions, should be duly recognised; that it should have a manifest existence, and maintain its position. It is the absolute interest of Reason that this moral Whole should exist; and herein lies the justification and merit of heroes who have founded states, – however rude these may have been. In the history of the World, only those peoples can come under our notice which form a state. For it must be understood that this latter is the realization of Freedom, *i.e.* of the absolute final aim, and that it exists for its own sake. It must be further understood that all the worth which the human being possesses – all spiritual reality, he possesses only through the State. For his spiritual reality consists in this, that his own essence – Reason – is objectively present to him, that it possesses objective immediate existence for him. Thus only is he fully conscious; thus only is he a partaker of morality – of a just and moral social and political life. For Truth is the Unity of the universal and subjective Will; and the Universal is to be found in the State, in its laws, its universal and rational arrangements. The State is the Divine Idea as it exists on Earth.

FURTHER READING

General introductions to Hegel's thought include: G. R. G. Mure, *The Philosophy of Hegel*, Oxford University Press, 1965; W. Kaufmann, *Hegel: Reinterpretation, Texts and Commentary*, Doubleday, 1965; J. N. Findlay, *Hegel: a re-examination*, Allen & Unwin, 1958. Certain specific questions are discussed in D. C. Travis, ed., *A Hegel Symposium*, University of Texas, 1962; and Hegel's thought is seen against the wider nineteenth-century intellectual background in H. Marcuse, *Reason and Revolution: Hegel and the Rise of Social Theory*, New York, Humanities Press, 1963, and K. Löwth, *From Hegel to Nietzsche: the Revolution in Nineteenth-Century Thought*, Constable, 1964.

6 Kierkegaard

Although born during the Napoleonic era, Søren Kierkegaard (1813–55) has had a remarkably strong influence on both the secular and religious thinking of our own times. During his life he was little known outside his native Denmark (he was born in Copenhagen) and his wider recognition as a major thinker dates from the beginning of the present century. Though physically deformed through falling from a tree in childhood, Kierkegaard was also witty and highly intelligent and these gifts brought him both devoted friends and implacable enemies. His father was an upright and God-fearing man filled with guilt and remorse because he had desperately cursed God as a boy of twelve and because he had seduced a servant girl (later Søren's mother) round about the time of his first wife's death in 1796. The father interpreted this death, together with the deaths of two daughters in 1819 and 1821 and also, much later, in 1834–6, the deaths of his second wife and three more children, as divine punishment for his sins. This sense of family guilt, with its overtones of Greek tragedy, is said to be one of the reasons why Kierkegaard himself felt unable to marry Regine

Olson to whom he became engaged in 1840. He also believed that his own spiritual destiny required the sacrifice of his love (cf. his own allusions to this struggle in his comments on Abraham's willingness to sacrifice Isaac in 'Fear and Trembling').

The affair with Regine occurred at a point where Kierkegaard's life had changed considerably. After a period which he himself described as being 'on the path to perdition', he became reconciled with his father. In the year of the latter's death (1838) he noted in his 'Journal': 'If Christ is to come and take up his abode in me, it must happen according to the title of today's Gospel . . . Christ came in through locked doors,' and again: 'I mean to labour to achieve a far more inward relation to Christianity; hitherto I have fought for its truth while in a sense standing outside it.' Ten years later he found in the 1848 revolutions confirmation of his diagnosis of his times (cf. 'The Present Age') and wrote in his 'Journal': 'I must speak out – Lord give thy grace.'

Kierkegaard's first major works did not appear until 1843, but he then wrote steadily until his death at the age of forty-two: 'Either/Or' (1843), 'Fear and Trembling' (1843), 'Philosophical Fragments' (1844), 'The Concept of Dread' (1844), 'Stages on Life's Way' (1845), 'Concluding Unscientific Postcript' (1846), 'The Present Age' (1846), 'The Works of Love' (1847), 'The Point of View for my Work as an Author' (1848), 'The Sickness unto Death' (1849), 'Training in Christianity' (1850), 'The Attack on "Christendom"' (1854–5). To this list should be added a whole series of 'Edifying Discourses' and several volumes making up the 'Journal'.

Both as a religious and a philosophical thinker, Kirkegaard rejected rational systematization and took as his starting point the category of the particular existing individual (see passages (a) and (b) below). He was completely opposed to a Hegelianism which claimed to have 'rationalized' Christianity, held that rational 'proofs' of God are impossible, and insisted that only an 'inward relationship' with God is meaningful (passage (c)). In his first work, 'Either/Or', he argued that all individuals face an ineluctable choice between Christ and the world, though no logical compulsion can act on this choice. Those who opt for the world, and who thus live on either the 'aesthetic' or 'ethical' levels (which Kierkegaard distinguishes from the 'religious' level) experience despair whether or not they are conscious of the fact (see passage (d) below). Mass pressures and collectivist aims, by removing individual responsibility, create a sense of existential dread which only the 'leap' of faith can cure. The quality of faith, as Kierkegaard conceives it, is indicated in passage (e), while passage (f) shows the rigorous and demanding interpretation of Christianity which led him, particularly towards the end of his life, to attack the established Church in Denmark as a mockery.

(a) From *Concluding Unscientific Postscript*, Bk 2, pt 1, ch. 2

In the construction of a logical system, it is necessary first and foremost to take care not to include in it anything which is subject to an existential dialectic, anything which is, only because it exists or has existed, and not simply because it is. From this it follows quite simply that Hegel's unparalleled discovery, the subject of so unparalleled an admiration, namely, the introduction of movement into logic, is a sheer confusion of logical science; to say nothing of the absence, on every other page, of even so much as an effort on Hegel's part to persuade the reader that it is there. And it is surely strange to make movement fundamental in a sphere where movement is unthinkable; and to make movement explain logic, when as a matter of fact logic cannot explain movement. . . .

An existential system cannot be formulated. Does this mean that no such system exists? By no means; nor is this implied in our assertion. Reality itself is a system – for God; but it cannot be a system for any existing spirit. System and finality correspond to one another, but existence is precisely the opposite of finality. It may be seen, from a purely abstract point of view, that system and existence are incapable of being thought together; because in order to think existence at all, systematic thought must think it as abrogated, and hence as not existing. Existence separates, and holds the various moments of existence discretely apart; the systematic thought consists of the finality which brings them together. . . .

Two ways, in general, are open for an existing individual: *Either* he can do his utmost to forget that he is an existing individual, by which he becomes a comic figure, since existence has the remarkable trait of compelling an existing individual to exist whether he wills it or not. (The comical contradiction in willing to be what one is not, as when a man wills to be a bird, is not more comical than the contradiction of not willing to be what one is, as *in casu* an existing individual; just as the language finds it comical that a man forgets his name, which does not so much mean forgetting a designation, as it means forgetting the distinctive essence of one's being.) *Or* he can concentrate his entire energy upon the fact that he is an existing individual. It is from this side, in the first instance, that objection must be made to modern philosophy; not that it has a mistaken presupposition, but that it has a comical presupposition, occasioned by its having forgotten, in a sort of world-historical absent-mindedness, what it means to be a human being. Not indeed, what it means to be a human being in general; for this is the sort of thing that one might even induce a speculative philosopher to agree to; but what it means that you and I and he are human beings, each one for himself.

(b) From *The Present Age*

Throughout many changes the tendency in modern times has remained a levelling one. These changes themselves have not, however, all of them, been levelling, for they are none of them abstract enough, each having a certain concrete reality. To some extent it is true that the levelling process goes on when one great man attacks another, so that both are weakened, or when one is neutralized by the other, or when an association of people, in themselves weak, grow stronger than the eminent. Levelling can also be accomplished by one particular caste, e.g. the clergy, the bourgeois, the peasants, by the people themselves. But all that is only the first movement of an abstract power within the concreteness of individuality.

In order that everything should be reduced to the same level, it is first of all necessary to procure a phantom, its spirit, a monstrous abstraction, an all-embracing something which is nothing, a mirage – and that phantom is *the public*. It is only in an age which is without passion, yet reflective, that such a phantom can develop itself with the help of the Press which itself becomes an abstraction. In times of passion and tumult and enthusiasm, even when a people desire to realize a fruitless idea and lay waste and destroy everything: even then there is no such thing as a public. There are parties and they are concrete. The Press, in times such as those, takes on a concrete character according to the division of parties. But just as sedentary professional people are the first to take up any fantastic illusion which comes their way, so a passionless, sedentary, reflective age, in which only the Press exhibits a vague sort of life, fosters this phantom. The public is, in fact, the real Levelling-Master rather than the actual leveller, for whenever levelling is only approximately accomplished it is done by something, but the public is a monstrous nothing. The public is a concept which could not have occurred in antiquity because the people *en masse, in corpore*, took part in any situation which arose, and were responsible for the actions of the individual, and, moreover, the individual was personally present and had to submit at once to applause or disapproval for his decision. Only when the sense of association in society is no longer strong enough to give life to concrete realities is the Press able to create that abstraction 'the public', consisting of unreal individuals who never are and never can be united in an actual situation or organization – and yet are held together as a whole.

The public is a host, more numerous than all the peoples together, but it is a body which can never be reviewed, it cannot even be represented, because it is an abstraction. Nevertheless, when the age is reflective and passionless and destroys everything concrete, the public becomes everything and is supposed to include everything. And that again shows how the individual is thrown back upon himself. . . .

A public is neither a nation, nor a generation, nor a community, nor a society, nor these particular men, for all these are only what they are through the concrete; no single person who belongs to the public makes a real commitment; for some hours of the day, perhaps, he belongs to the public – at moments when he is nothing else since when he really is what he is he does not form part of the public. Made up of such individuals, of individuals at the moments when they are nothing, a public is a kind of gigantic something, an abstract and deserted void which is everything and nothing. But on this basis any one can arrogate to himself a public, and just as the Roman Church chimerically extended its frontiers by appointing bishops *in partibus infidelium*, so a public is something which every one can claim, and even a drunken sailor exhibiting a 'peep-show' has dialectically absolutely the same right to a public as the greatest man; he has just as logical a right to put all those many noughts *in front* of his single number.

A public is everything and nothing, the most dangerous of all powers and the most insignificant: one can speak to a whole nation in the name of the public, and still the public will be less than a single real man, however unimportant. The qualification 'public' is produced by the deceptive juggling of an age of reflection, which makes it appear flattering to the individual who in this way can arrogate to himself this monster, in comparison with which concrete realities seem poor. The public is the fairy story of an age of understanding, which in imagination makes the individual into something even greater than a king above his people; but the public is also a gruesome abstraction through which the individual will receive his religious formation – or sink.

The Press is an abstraction (since a paper is not a concrete part of a nation and only in an abstract sense an individual) which in conjunction with the passionless and reflective character of the age produces

ASPECTS OF THE MODERN EUROPEAN MIND

that abstract phantom: a public which in its turn is really the levelling power.

(c) From *Concluding Unscientific Postscript*, Bk 2, pt 2, ch. 2

When the question of truth is raised in an objective manner, reflection is directed objectively to the truth, as an object to which the knower is related. Reflection is not focussed upon the relationship, however, but upon the question of whether it is the truth to which the knower is related. If only the object to which he is related is the truth, the subject is accounted to be in the truth. When the question of the truth is raised subjectively, reflection is directed subjectively to the nature of the individual's relationship; if only the mode of this relationship is in the truth, the individual is in the truth even if he should happen to be thus related to what is not true. Let us take as an example the knowledge of God. Objectively, reflection is directed to the problem of whether this object is the true God; subjectively, reflection is directed to the question whether the individual is related to a something in *such a manner* that his relationship is in truth a God-relationship. On which side is the truth now to be found? Ah, may we not here resort to a mediation, and say: It is on neither side, but in the mediation of both? Excellently well said, provided we might have it explained how an existing individual manages to be in a state of mediation. For to be in a state of mediation is to be finished, while to exist is to become. Nor can an existing individual be in two places at the same time – he cannot be an identity of subject and object. When he is nearest to being in two places at the same time he is in passion; but passion is momentary, and passion is also the highest expression of subjectivity.

The existing individual who chooses to pursue the objective way enters upon the entire approximation-process by which it is proposed to bring God to light objectively. But this is in all eternity impossible, because God is a subject, and therefore exists only for subjectivity in inwardness. The existing individual who chooses the subjective way apprehends instantly the entire dialectical difficulty involved in having to use some time, perhaps a long time, in finding God objectively; and he feels this dialectical difficulty in all its painfulness, because every moment is wasted in which he does not have God. That very instant he has God, not by virtue of any objective deliberation, but by virtue of the infinite passion of inwardness. The objective inquirer, on the other hand, is not embarrassed by such dialectical difficulties as are involved in devoting an entire period of investigation to finding God – since it is possible that the inquirer may die tomorrow; and if he lives he can scarcely regard God as something to be taken along if convenient, since God is precisely that which one takes *à tout prix*, which in the understanding of passion constitutes the true inward relationship to God.

(*d*) From *The Sickness unto Death*

Is despair an advantage or a drawback? Regarded in a purely dialectical way it is both. If one were to stick to the abstract notion of despair, without thinking of any concrete despairer, one might say that it is an immense advantage. The possibility of this sickness is man's advantage over the beast, and this advantage distinguishes him far more essentially than the erect posture, for it implies the infinite erectness or loftiness of being spirit. The possibility of this sickness is man's advantage over the beast; to be sharply observant of this sickness constitutes the Christian's advantage over the natural man; to be healed of this sickness is the Christian's bliss. . . .

It is as far as possible from being true that the vulgar view is right in assuming that despair is a rarity; on the contrary, it is quite universal. It is as far as possible from being true that the vulgar view is right in assuming that everyone who does not think or feel that he is in despair is not so at all, and that only he is in despair who says that he is. On the contrary, one who without affectation says that he is in despair is after all a little bit nearer, a dialectical step nearer to being cured than all those who are not regarded and do not regard themselves as being in despair. But precisely this is the common situation (as the physician of souls will doubtless concede), that the majority of men live without being thoroughly conscious that they are spiritual beings – and to this is referable all the security, contentment with life, etc., etc., which precisely is despair. Those, on the other hand, who say that they are in despair are generally such as have a nature so much more profound that they must become conscious of themselves as spirit, or such as by the hard vicissitudes of life and its dreadful decisions have been helped to become conscious of themselves as spirit – either one or the other, for rare is the man who truly is free from despair.

Ah, so much is said about human want and misery – I seek to understand it, I have also had some acquaintance with it at close range; so much is said about wasted lives – but only that man's life is wasted who lived on, so deceived by the joys of life or by its sorrows that he never became eternally and decisively conscious of himself as spirit, as self, or (what is the same thing) never became aware and in the deepest sense received an impression of the fact that there is a God, and that he, he himself, his self, exists before this God, which gain of infinity is never attained except through despair. . . .

Sin is this: *before God, or with the conception of God, to be in despair at not willing to be oneself, or in despair at willing to be oneself.* Thus sin is potentiated weakness or potentiated defiance: sin is the potentiation of despair. The point upon which the emphasis rests is before God, or the fact that the conception of God is involved; the factor which dialectically, ethically, religiously, makes 'qualified' despair (to use a juridical term) synonymous with sin is the conception of God.

(e) From *Fear and Trembling*

The infinite resignation is the last stage prior to faith, so that one who has not made this movement has not faith; for only in the infinite resignation do I become clear to myself with respect to my eternal validity, and only then can there be any question of grasping existence by virtue of faith. . . .

Generally people are of the opinion that what faith produces is not a work of art, that it is coarse and common work, only for the more clumsy natures; but in fact this is far from the truth. The dialectic of faith is the finest and most remarkable of all; it possesses an elevation, of which indeed I can form a conception, but nothing more. I am able to make from the springboard the great leap whereby I pass into infinity, my back is like that of a tight-rope dancer, having been twisted in my childhood, hence I find this easy; with a one-two-three! I can walk about existence on my head; but the next thing I cannot do, for I cannot perform the miraculous, but can only be astonished by it. Yes, if Abraham the instant he swung his leg over the ass's back had said to himself, 'Now, since Isaac is lost, I might just as well sacrifice him here at home, rather than ride the long way to Moriah' – then I should have no need of Abraham, whereas now I bow seven times before his name and seventy times before his deed. For this indeed he did not do, as I can prove by the fact that he was glad at receiving Isaac, heartily glad, that he needed no preparation, no time to concentrate upon the finite and its joy. If this had not been the case with Abraham, then perhaps he might have loved God but not believed; for he who loves God without faith reflects upon himself, he who loves God believingly reflects upon God.

Upon this pinnacle stands Abraham. The last stage he loses sight of is the infinite resignation. He really goes further, and reaches faith; for all these caricatures of faith, the miserable lukewarm indolence which thinks, 'There surely is no instant need, it is not worth while sorrowing before the time,' the pitiful hope which says, 'One cannot know what is going to happen . . . it might possibly be after all' – these caricatures of faith are part and parcel of life's wretchedness, and the infinite resignation has already consigned them to infinite contempt.

Abraham I cannot understand, in a certain sense there is nothing I can learn from him but astonishment. If people fancy that by considering the outcome of this story they might let themselves be moved to believe, they deceive themselves and want to swindle God out of the first movement of faith, the infinite resignation. They would suck worldly wisdom out of the paradox. Perhaps one or another may succeed in that, for our age is not willing to stop with faith, with its miracle of turning water into wine, it goes further, it turns wine into water.

Would it not be better to stop with faith, and is it not revolting that everybody wants to go further? When in our age (as indeed is proclaimed in various ways) they will not stop with love, where then are they going? To earthy wisdom, to petty calculation, to paltriness and wretchedness, to everything which can make man's divine origin doubtful. Would it not be better that they should stand still at faith, and that he who stands should take heed lest he fall? For the movements of faith must constantly be made by virtue of the absurd, yet in such a way, be it observed, that one does not lose the finite but gains it every inch. For my part I can well describe the movements of faith, but I cannot make them. When one would learn to make the motions of swimming one can let oneself be hung by a swimming-belt from the ceiling and go through the motions (describe them, so to speak, as we speak of describing a circle), but one is not swimming. In that way I can describe the movements of faith, but when I am thrown into the water, I swim, it is true (for I don't belong to the beach-waders), but I make other movements, I make the movements of infinity, whereas faith does the opposite: after having made the movements of infinity, it makes those of finiteness. Hail to him who can make those movements, he performs the marvellous, and I shall never grow tired of admiring him, whether he be Abraham or a slave in Abraham's house; whether he be a professor of philosophy or a servant-girl, I look only at the movements. But at them I do look, and do not let myself be fooled, either by myself or by any other man. The knights of the infinite resignation are easily recognized: their gait is gliding and assured. Those on the other hand who carry the jewel of faith are likely to be delusive, because their outward appearance bears a striking resemblance to that which both the infinite resignation and faith profoundly despise ... to Philistinism. ...

Faith is the highest passion in a man. There are perhaps many in every generation who do not even reach it, but no one gets further. Whether there be many in our age who do not discover it, I will not decide, I dare only appeal to myself as a witness who makes no secret that the prospects for him are not the best, without for all that wanting to delude himself and to betray the great thing which is faith by reducing it to an insignificance, to an ailment of childhood which one must wish to get over as soon as possible. But for the man also who does not so much as reach faith life has tasks enough, and if one loves them sincerely, life will by no means be wasted, even though it never is comparable to the life of those who sensed and grasped the highest. But he who reached faith (it makes no difference whether he be a man of distinguished talents or a simple man) does not remain standing at faith, yea, he would be offended if anyone were to say this of him, just as the lover would be indignant if one said that he remained standing at love, for he would reply, 'I do not remain standing by any means, my whole life is in this.' Nevertheless he does not get further, does not reach anything different, for if he discovers this, he has a different explanation for it.

(f) From *The Attack on 'Christendom'*

What every religion in which there is any truth aims at, and what Christianity aims at decisively, is a total transformation in a man, to wrest from him through renunciation and self-denial all that, and precisely that, to which he immediately clings, in which he immediately has his life. This sort of religion, as 'man' understands it, is not what he wants. The upshot therefore is that from generation to generation there lives – how equivocal! – a highly respected class in the community, the priests. Their *métier* is to invert the whole situation, so that what man likes becomes religion, on the condition, however, of invoking God's name and paying something definite to the priests. The rest of the community, when one examines the case more closely, are seen to be egoistically interested in upholding the estimation in which the priests are held – for otherwise the falsification cannot succeed.

To become a Christian in the New Testament sense is such a radical change that, humanly speaking, one must say that it is the heaviest trial to a family that one of its members becomes a Christian. For in such a Christian the God-relationship becomes so predominant that he is not 'lost' in the ordinary sense of the word; no, in a far deeper sense than dying he is lost to everything that is called family. It is of this Christ constantly speaks, both with reference to himself when he says that to be his disciple is to be his mother, brother, sister, that in no other sense has he a mother, a brother, a sister; and also when he speaks continually about the collision of hating father and mother, one's own child, etc. To become a Christian in the New Testament sense is to loosen (in the sense in which the dentist speaks of loosening the tooth from the gums), to loosen the individual out of the cohesion to which he clings with the passion of immediacy, and which clings to him with the same passion.

This sort of Christianity was never – no more now, precisely no more than in the year 30 – to man's taste, but was distasteful to him in his inmost heart, mortally distasteful. Therefore the upshot is that from generation to generation there lives a highly respected class in the community whose *métier* is to transform Christianity into the exact opposite.

FURTHER READING

There are several useful essays on Kierkegaard in a number of the volumes listed under 'Existentialism' (see p. 114). See also W. Hubben, *Dostoevsky, Kierkegaard, Nietzsche and Kafka: Four Prophets of our Destiny*, New York, Collier Books, 1962. The standard life is W. Lowrie, *Kierkegaard*, 2 vols, Harper Torchbooks, 1962. The following are also worth consulting: R. Jolivet, *An Introduction to Kierkegaard*, Muller, 1950; J. Collins, *The Mind of Kierkegaard*, Chicago, Regnery, 1953; P. Rhode, *Søren Kierkegaard: an Introduction to his Life and Philosophy*, Allen & Unwin, 1963.

7 Dostoevsky

Fyodor Dostoevsky (1821–81) was born in Moscow. He was the son of a debauched and alcoholic ex-army surgeon who was murdered sixteen years later by serfs on the small country property which he had acquired in the Tula region. Dostoevsky himself graduated from the St Petersburg College of Military Engineering but decided to abandon an army career in favour of writing. This decision was confirmed by the favourable reception of 'Poor Folk' in 1846. In 1849, because of his association with a group of young socialists interested in the ideas of Fourier, he was arrested and condemned to death. The dramatic last-minute reprieve is well known and Dostoevsky's sentence was commuted to eight years penal servitude in Siberia. After four years of extreme hardship and suffering (he readily accepted this punishment) he was released on condition that he joined the army. A full pardon came only in 1859.

It was in Siberia that Dostoevsky rediscovered his faith in Christ and his hopes for the Russian Orthodox Church. It is therefore natural to see a link between his Siberian experience and the fact that so many of his characters are purified by confession and penance. One of his most influential works prior to the great novels – his 'Notes from Underground' (1864) – has as a major theme the achievement of personal salvation through suffering and degradation. The extract from 'Notes from Underground' given here (see passage (a) below) emphasizes a different, though related, point; it shows how, after Siberia, Dostoevsky lost his faith in political reform and turned to what were often mystical ideas of spiritual regeneration.

The publication of 'Crime and Punishment' (1866) marks the beginning of the great creative period of Dostoevsky's life. There followed such major novels as 'The Gambler' (1867), 'The Idiot' (1868–9), 'The Possessed' (1871) and, finally, 'The Brothers Karamazov' (1880). Passage (b) is from the famous 'Grand Inquisitor' chapter of this last novel. 'The Grand Inquisitor' is the title of a long poem which Ivan Karamazov would like to write and which he describes to Alyosha. It is set in the sixteenth century and relates to an imaginary confrontation between Christ – who has miraculously come back to earth in Spain – and the Grand Inquisitor. The latter, representing the official Church, significantly arrests and imprisons Christ. He claims that human beings seek only that food and security of mind which the Church can give them whereas the teachings of Christ impose a free and responsible faith beyond the capacity of ordinary men. An ironic counterpoint is worked out between Church religion and the Christian faith from which it sprang.

(a) From *Notes from Underground*

But these are all golden dreams. Oh, tell me, who was it first announced, who was it first proclaimed, that man only does nasty things because he does not know his own interests; and that if he were enlightened, if his eyes were opened to his real normal interests, man would at once cease to do nasty things, would at once become good and noble because, being enlightened and understanding his real advantage, he would see his own advantage in the good and nothing else, and we all know that not one man can, consciously, act against his own interests, consequently, so to say, through necessity, he would begin doing good? Oh, the babe! Oh, the pure, innocent child! ...

Why, to maintain this theory of the regeneration of mankind by means of the pursuit of his own advantage is to my mind almost the same thing as ... as to affirm, for instance, following Buckle, that through civilization mankind becomes softer, and consequently less bloodthirsty and less fitted for warfare. Logically it does seem to follow from his arguments. But man has such a predilection for systems and abstract deductions that he is ready to distort the truth intentionally, he is ready to deny the evidence of his senses only to justify his logic. I take this example because it is the most glaring instance of it. Only look about you: blood is being spilt in streams, and in the merriest way, as though it were champagne. Take the whole of the nineteenth century in which Buckle lived. Take Napoleon – the Great and also the present one. Take North America – the eternal union. Take the farce of Schleswig-Holstein. ... And what is it that civilization softens in us? The only gain of civilization for mankind is the greater capacity for variety of sensations – and absolutely nothing more. And through the development of this manysidedness man may come to finding enjoyment in bloodshed. In fact, this has already happened to him. Have you noticed that it is the most civilized gentlemen who have been the subtlest slaughterers, to whom the Attilas and Stenka Razins could not hold a candle, and if they are not so conspicuous as the Attilas and Stenka Razins it is simply because they are so often met with, are so ordinary and have become so familiar to us. In any case civilization has made mankind if not more bloodthirsty, at least more vilely, more loathsomely bloodthirsty. In the old days he saw justice in bloodshed and with his conscience at peace exterminated those he thought proper. Now we do think bloodshed abominable and yet we engage in this abomination, and with more energy than ever. Which is worse? Decide that for yourselves. They say that Cleopatra (excuse an instance from Roman history) was fond of sticking gold pins into her slave-girls' breasts and derived gratification from their screams and writhings. You will say that that was in the comparatively barbarous times; that these are barbarous times too, because also, comparatively speaking, pins are stuck in even now; that though man has now learned to see more clearly than in barbarous ages, he is still far from having learnt to act as reason and science would dictate. But yet you are fully convinced that he will be sure to learn when he gets rid of certain old bad habits, and when common sense and science have completely reeducated human nature and turned it in a normal direction. You are confident that then man will cease from *intentional* error and will, so to say, be compelled not to want to set his will against his normal interests. That is not all; then, you say, science itself will teach man (though to my mind it's a superfluous luxury) that he never has really had any caprice or will of his own, and that he himself is something of the nature of a piano-key or the stop of an organ, and that there are, besides, things called the laws of nature; so that everything he does is not done by his willing it, but is done of itself, by the laws of nature. Consequently we have only to discover these laws of nature, and man will no longer have to answer for his actions and life will become exceedingly easy for him. All human actions will then, of course, be tabulated according to these laws, mathematically, like tables of logarithms up to 108,000, and entered in an index; or, better still, there would be published certain edifying works of the nature of encyclopaedic lexicons, in which everything will be so clearly calculated and explained that there will be no more incidents or adventures in the world.

Then – this is all what you say – new economic relations will be established, all ready-made and worked out with mathematical exactitude, so that every possible question will vanish in the twinkling of an eye, simply because every possible answer to it will be provided. Then the 'Palace of Crystal' will be built. Then. ... In fact, those will be halcyon days. Of course there is no guaranteeing (this is my comment) that it will not be, for instance, frightfully dull then (for what will one have to do when everything will be calculated and tabulated), but on the other hand everything will be extraordinarily rational. Of course boredom may lead you to anything. It is boredom sets one sticking golden pins into people, but all that would not matter. What is bad (this is my comment again) is that I dare say people will be thankful for the gold pins then. Man is stupid, you know, phenomenally stupid; or rather he is not at all stupid, but he is so ungrateful that you could not find another like him in all creation. I, for instance, would not be in the least surprised if all of a sudden, *à propos* of nothing, in the midst of general prosperity a gentleman with an ignoble, or rather with a reactionary and ironical, countenance were to arise and, putting his arms akimbo, say to us all: 'I say, gentlemen, hadn't we better kick over the whole show and scatter rationalism to the winds, simply to send these logarithms to the devil, and to enable us to live once more at our own sweet foolish will!' That again would not matter, but what is annoying is that he would be sure to find followers – such is the nature of man. And all that for the most foolish reason, which, one would think, was hardly worth mentioning: that is, that man everywhere and at all times, whoever he may be, had preferred to act as he chose and not in the least as his reason and advantage dictated. And one may choose what is contrary to one's own interests, and sometimes one *positively ought* (that is my idea). One's own free unfettered choice, one's own caprice, however wild it may be, one's own fancy worked up at times to frenzy – is that very 'most advantageous advantage' which we have overlooked, which comes under no classification and against which all systems and theories are continually being shattered to atoms. And how do these wiseacres know that man wants a normal, a virtuous choice? What has made them conceive that man must want a rationally advantageous choice? What man wants is simply *independent* choice, whatever that independence may cost and wherever it may lead.

(*b*) From *The Brothers Karamazov*, Bk 5, ch. 5

'He stops on the steps of the Cathedral of Seville at the moment when a child's little, open white coffin is brought in with weeping into the church: in it lies a girl of seven, the only daughter of a prominent citizen. The dead child is covered with flowers. "He will raise up your child," people shout from the crowd to the weeping mother. The canon, who has come out to meet the coffin, looks on perplexed and knits his brows. But presently a cry of the dead child's mother is heard. She throws herself at his feet. "If it is thou," she cries, holding out her hands to him, "then raise my child from the dead!" The funeral cortège halts. The coffin is lowered on to the steps at his feet. He gazes with compassion and his lips once again utter softly the words, "Talitha cumi" – "and the damsel arose". The little girl rises in the coffin, sits up, and looks around her with surprise in her smiling, wide-open eyes. In her hands she holds the nosegay of white roses with which she lay in her coffin. There are cries, sobs, and confusion among the people, and it is at that very moment that the Cardinal himself, the Grand Inquisitor, passes by the cathedral in the square. He is an old man of nearly ninety, tall and erect, with a shrivelled face and sunken eyes, from which, though, a light like a fiery spark still gleams. Oh, he is not wearing his splendid cardinal robes in which he appeared before the people the day before, when the enemies of the Roman faith were being burnt – no, at that moment he is wearing only his old, coarse, monk's cassock. He is followed at a distance by his sombre assistants and his slaves and his "sacred" guard. He stops in front of the crowd and watches from a distance. He sees everything. He sees the coffin set down at *his* feet, he sees the young girl raised from the dead, and his face darkens. He knits his grey, beetling brows and his eyes flash with an ominous fire. He stretches forth his finger and commands the guards to seize *him*. And so great is his power and so accustomed are the people to obey him, so humble and submissive are they to his will, that the crowd immediately makes way for the guards and, amid the death-like hush that descends upon the square, they lay hands upon *him* and lead him away. The crowd, like one man, at once bows down to the ground before the old Inquisitor, who blesses them in silence and passes on. The guards take their Prisoner to the dark, narrow, vaulted prison in the old building of the Sacred Court and lock him in there. The day passes and night falls, the dark, hot and "breathless" Seville night. The air is "heavy with the scent of laurel and lemon". Amid the profound darkness, the iron door of the prison is suddenly opened and the old Grand Inquisitor himself slowly enters the prison with a light in his hand. He is alone and the door at once closes behind him. He stops in the doorway and gazes for a long time, for more than a minute, into his face. At last he approaches him slowly, puts the lamp on the table and says to him:

'"Is it you? You?"

'But, receiving no answer, he adds quickly: "Do not answer, be silent. And, indeed, what can you say? I know too well what you would say. Besides, you have no right to add anything to what you have said already in the days of old. Why, then, did you come to meddle with us? For you have come to meddle with us, and you know it. . . ."

'"The terrible and wise spirit, the spirit of self-destruction and non-existence," the old man went on, "the great spirit talked with you in the wilderness and we are told in the books that he apparently 'tempted' you. Is that so? And could anything truer have been said than what he revealed to you in his three questions and what you rejected, and what in the books are called 'temptations'? And yet if ever there has been on earth a real, prodigious miracle, it was on that day, on the day of the three temptations. Indeed, it was in the emergence of those three questions that the miracle lay. If it were possible to imagine, for the sake of argument, that those three questions of the terrible spirit had been lost without leaving a trace in the books and that we had to rediscover, restore, and invent them afresh and that to do so we had to gather together all the wise men of the earth – rulers, high priests, scholars, philosophers, poets – and set them the task of devising and inventing three questions which would not only correspond to the magnitude of the occasion, but, in addition, express in three words, in three short human sentences, the whole future history of the world and of mankind, do you think that the entire wisdom of the earth, gathered together, could have invented anything equal in depth and force to the three questions which were actually put to you at the time by the wise and mighty spirit in the wilderness? From those questions alone, from the miracle of their appearance, one can see that what one is dealing with here is not the human, transient mind, but the absolute and everlasting one. For in those three questions the whole future history of mankind is, as it were, anticipated and combined in one whole and three images are presented in which all the insoluble historical contradictions of human nature all over the world will meet. . . ."

' "Decide yourself who was right – you or he who questioned you then? Call to your mind the first question; its meaning, though not in these words, was this: 'You want to go into the world and you are going empty-handed, with some promise of freedom, which men in their simplicity and their innate lawlessness cannot even comprehend, which they fear and dread – for nothing has ever been more unendurable to man and to human society than freedom! And do you see the stones in this parched and barren desert? Turn them into loaves, and mankind will run after you like a flock of sheep, grateful and obedient, though for ever trembling with fear that you might withdraw your hand and they would no longer have your loaves.' But you did not want to deprive man of freedom and rejected the offer, for, you thought, what sort of freedom is it if obedience is bought with loaves of bread? You replied that man does not live by bread alone, but do you know that for the sake of that earthly bread the spirit of the earth will rise up against you and will join battle with you and conquer you, and all will follow him, crying 'Who is like this beast? He has given us fire from heaven!' Do you know that ages will pass and mankind will proclaim in its wisdom and science that there is no crime and, therefore, no sin, but that there are only hungry people. 'Feed them first and then demand virtue of them!' – that is what they will inscribe on their banner which they will raise against you and which will destroy your temple. A new building will rise where your temple stood, the dreadful Tower of Babel will rise up again, and though, like the first one, it will not be completed, yet you might have prevented the new tower and have shortened the sufferings of men by a thousand years – for it is to us that they will come at last, after breaking their hearts for a thousand years with their tower! Then they will look for us again under the ground, hidden in the catacombs (for we shall again be persecuted and tortured), and they will find us and cry out to us, 'Feed us, for those who have promised us fire from heaven have not given it to us!' And then we shall finish building their tower, for he who feeds them will complete it, and we alone shall feed them in your name, and we shall lie to them that it is in your name. Oh, without us they will never, never feed themselves. No science will give them bread so long as they remain free. But in the end they will lay their freedom at our feet and say to us, 'We don't mind being your slaves so long as you feed us!' They will, at last, realize themselves that there cannot be enough freedom and bread for everybody, for they will never, never be able to let everyone have his fair share! They will also be convinced that they can never be free because they are weak, vicious, worthless, and rebellious. You promised them bread from heaven, but, I repeat again, can it compare with earthly bread in the eyes of the weak, always vicious and always ignoble race of man? And if for the sake of the bread from heaven thousands and tens of thousands will follow you, what is to become of the millions and scores of thousands of millions of creatures who will not have the strength to give up the earthly bread for the bread of heaven?"'

FURTHER READING

Some of the most useful studies, from a general 'modern European mind' point of view, are: N. Berdyaev, *Dostoevsky*, New York, Meridian Books, 1957; A. Steinberg, *Dostoievsky*, Bowes & Bowes, 1966; J. Lavrin, *Dostoevsky: a Study*, Methuen, 1943. See also: W. Hubben, *Dostoevsky, Kierkegaard, Nietzsche and Kafka: four Prophets of our Destiny*, New York, Collier Books, 1962.

8 Nietzsche

Friedrich Nietzsche (1844–1900) was born at Röcken in Saxony, the son and grandson of Lutheran clergymen, and studied classical philology at the universities of Bonn and Leipzig. He was appointed to the chair of classical philology at Basel at the age of twenty-four and became, in the process, a younger colleague of Burckhardt and Franz Overbeck. He served briefly as a medical orderly in the Franco-Prussian War (1870) and returned to Basel with his health seriously affected. In 1879 he resigned from the university, continued to publish a large number of books and essays, and became insane in 1889, remaining in the care of his mother and later of his sister until his death in Weimar in 1900.

Nietzsche's first book, 'The Birth of Tragedy', was published in 1872 at a time when his classical studies were considerably influenced by the philosophy of Schopenhauer and the musical ideas of Wagner. Two features of this book are particularly important. First, his well-known distinction between the Apollonian spirit (serenity, harmony, calm) and the Dionysian (exuberance, intoxication, chaos) and his assertion – contradicting Winckelmann and most other contemporary Hellenists – that it is ultimately the Dionysian which is 'the single root of all Greek art'. Second, Nietzsche interpreted Greek tragedy as having been born from music and killed by rationalism. Hence his attack on the Socratic spirit which places reason – 'a dangerous, life-undermining force' – above instinct. Something of the way in which he preferred the Dionysian to the Apollonian, and related this preference to the ideas of Schopenhauer and Wagner, is indicated in passage (a) below. His enthusiastic call for the 'Dionysiac life' and the 'rebirth of tragedy' is set out in passage (b).

This emphasis on the Dionysian, which Nietzsche later interpreted as controlled rather than unbridled passion, underlies several of his most characteristic attitudes, more particularly his anti-rationalism, his fierce opposition to Christianity, his call for a new morality and his conception of the 'superman'. His anti-rationalism (see passage (c) from 'Twilight of the Idols' (1889)) should be related to the general scepticism which he formulated in the definition: 'Truths are illusions about which one has forgotten that this is what they are' and which is also implied by the statement: 'I mistrust all systematizers and I avoid them. The will to a system is a lack of integrity.' As regards his anti-Christian sentiments, these are repeatedly expressed in his work and reach a climax in 'The Antichrist' (written 1888, published 1895) from which passage (d) is taken. The same work contains various formulations (passage (e) is an example) of Nietzsche's anti-Christian morality, his 'transvaluation of all values', which was given historical and psychological justification in 'The Genealogy of Morals' of 1887. As a psychologist he is also a significant figure (he claimed, incidentally, that Dostoevsky was the one 'psychologist' who taught him things he did not already know) and his analysis of what he called 'the will to power' – already mentioned in passage (e) – occurs in Part II (1883) of his most famous and most enigmatic work, 'Thus Spoke Zarathustra' (see passage (f)).

Although he wrote with passion of the new morality of strength and hard-ness, and emphasized the will to power, Nietzsche's fundamental attitude was deeply pessimistic, even nihilistic, and radically opposed to social Darwin-ism. His doctrine of 'eternal recurrence' (see passages (g) and (h)) is some measure of his desperation, despite the suggestion that real strength lies in accepting 'the external hourglass of existence'. In a sense this idea of an ulti-mately meaningless, repetitive existence, to which only the superman can really measure up, is a consequence of the famous section in 'The Gay Science' (1882) on the 'death of God' (see passage (i)). For Nietzsche, our modern tragedy lies in the fact that man has proved incapable of replacing God and that we now have to live 'on the mere pittance of inherited and decaying values'.

(a) From *The Birth of Tragedy*, Sect. 16

In opposition to all who would derive the arts from a single vital prin-ciple, I wish to keep before me those two artistic deities of the Greeks, Apollo and Dionysos. They represent to me, most vividly and con-cretely, two radically dissimilar realms of art. Apollo embodies the transcendent genius of the *principium individuationis*; through him alone is it possible to achieve redemption in illusion. The mystical jubilation of Dionysos, on the other hand, breaks the spell of individuation and opens a path to the maternal womb of being. Among the great thinkers there is only one who has fully realized the immense discrepancy be-tween the plastic Apollonian art and the Dionysiac art of music. Independently of Greek religious symbols, Schopenhauer assigned to music a totally different character and origin from all the other arts, because it does not, like all the others, represent appearance, but the will directly. It is the metaphysical complement to everything that is physical in the world; the thing-in-itself where all else is appearance (*The World as Will and Idea, I*). Richard Wagner set his seal of approval on this key notion of all esthetics when he wrote in his book on Beethoven that music obeys esthetic principles quite unlike those governing the visual arts and that the category of beauty is altogether inapplicable to it – although a wrongheaded esthetic based on a mis-guided and decadent art has attempted to make music answer to criteria of beauty proper only to the plastic arts, expecting it to generate *pleasure in beautiful forms*. Once I had become aware of this antinomy I felt strongly moved to explore the nature of Greek tragedy, the pro-foundest manifestation of Hellenic genius. For the first time I seemed to possess the key enabling me to inspect the problem of tragedy in terms that were no longer derived from conventional esthetics. I was given such a strange and unfamiliar glimpse into the essence of Hellenism that it seemed to me that our classical philology, for all its air of triumphant achievement, had only dealt with phantasmagorias and externals.

We might approach this fundamental problem by posing the following question: what esthetic effect is produced when the Apollonian and Dionysiac forces of art, usually separate, are made to work alongside each other? Or, to put it more succinctly, in what relation does music stand to image and concept? . . .

In accordance with Schopenhauer's doctrine, we interpret music as the immediate language of the will, and our imaginations are stimulated to embody that immaterial world, which speaks to us with lively motion and yet remains invisible. Image and concept, on the other hand, gain a heightened significance under the influence of truly appropriate music. Dionysiac art, then, affects the Apollonian talent in a twofold manner: first, music incites us to a symbolic intuition of the Dionysiac universality; second, it endows that symbolic image with supreme significance. From these facts, perfectly plausible once we have pondered them well, we deduce that music is capable of giving birth to myth, the most significant of similitudes; and above all, to the tragic myth, which is a parable of Dionysiac knowledge. When I spoke earlier of the lyric poet I demonstrated how, through him, music strives to account for its own essence in Apollonian images. Once we grant that music raised to its highest power must similarly try to find an adequate embodiment, it stands to reason that it will also succeed in discovering a symbolic expression for its proper Dionysiac wisdom. And where should we look for that expression if not in tragedy and the tragic spirit?

(b) From *The Birth of Tragedy*, Sect. 20

No one shall wither our faith in the imminent rebirth of Greek antiquity, for here alone do we see a hope for the rejuvenation and purification of the German spirit through the fire-magic of music. What else, in the desolate waste of present-day culture, holds any promise of a sound, healthy future? In vain we look for a single powerfully branching root, a spot of earth that is fruitful: we see only dust, sand, dullness, and languor. In such hopeless isolation no better symbol comes to mind than that of 'The Knight, Death, and the Devil' of Dürer, the steely-eyed armoured knight who pursues his dreadful path, undismayed by his ghastly companions and yet without hope, alone with horse and dog. Such a knight was our Schopenhauer, devoid of hope yet persisting in the search for truth. There has been no other like him.

But what amazing change is wrought in that gloomy desert of our culture by the wand of Dionysos! All that is half-alive, rotten, broken and stunted the whirlwind wraps in a red cloud of dust and carries off like a vulture. Our distracted eyes look for all that has vanished and are confused, for what they see has risen from beneath the earth into the golden light, so full and green, so richly alive. In the midst of all this life, joy, and sorrow, tragedy sits in noble ecstasy, listening to a sad, distant song which tells of the mothers of being, whose names are Wish, Will, Woe.

Indeed, my friends, believe with me in this Dionysiac life and in the rebirth of tragedy! Socratic man has run his course; crown your heads with ivy, seize the thyrsus, and do not be surprised if tiger and panther lie down and caress your feet! Dare to lead the life of tragic man, and you will be redeemed. It has fallen to your lot to lead the Dionysiac procession out of India into Greece. Gird yourselves for a severe conflict, but have faith in the thaumaturgy of your god!

(c) From *Twilight of the Idols*

'Reason' is the cause of our falsification of the testimony of the senses. Insofar as the senses show becoming, passing away, and change, they do not lie. But Heraclitus will remain eternally right with his assertion that being is an empty fiction. The 'apparent' world is the only one: the 'true' world is merely added by a lie.

And what magnificent instruments of observation we possess in our senses! This nose, for example, of which no philosopher has yet spoken with reverence and gratitude, is actually the most delicate instrument so far at our disposal: it is able to detect minimal differences of motion which even a spectroscope cannot detect. Today we possess science precisely to the extent to which we have decided to *accept* the testimony of the senses – to the extent to which we sharpen them further, arm them, and have learned to think them through. The rest is miscarriage and not-yet-science – in other words, metaphysics, theology, psychology, epistemology – or formal science, a doctrine of signs, such as logic and that applied logic which is called mathematics. In them reality is not encountered at all, not even as a problem – no more than the question of the value of such a sign-convention as logic.

(d) From *The Antichrist*

The religious man, as the church wants him, is a typical decadent; the moment when a religious crisis overcomes a people is invariably marked by epidemics of the nerves; the 'inner world' of the religious man looks exactly like the 'inner world' of the overexcited and the exhausted; the 'highest' states that Christianity has hung over mankind as the value of all values are epileptoid forms – only madmen or great impostors have been pronounced holy by the church *in maiorem dei honorem*. I once permitted myself to designate the whole Christian repentance and redemption training (which today is best studied in England) as a methodically produced *folie circulaire*, as is proper, on soil prepared for it, that is to say, thoroughly morbid soil. Nobody is free to become a Christian: one is not 'converted' to Christianity – one has to be sick enough for it.

We others who have the *courage* to be healthy and also to despise – how may we despise a religion which taught men to misunderstand the body! which does not want to get rid of superstitious belief in souls! which turns insufficient nourishment into something 'meritorious'! which fights health as a kind of enemy, devil, temptation! which fancies that one can carry around a 'perfect soul' in a cadaver of a body, and which therefore found it necessary to concoct a new conception of 'perfection' – a pale, sickly, idiotic-enthusiastic character, so-called 'holiness'. Holiness – merely a series of symptoms of an impoverished, unnerved, incurably corrupted body.

The Christian movement, as a European movement, has been from the start a collective movement of the dross and refuse elements of every kind (these want to get power through Christianity). It does *not* express the decline of a race, it is an aggregate of forms of decadence flocking together and seeking each other out from everywhere. It is *not*, as is supposed, the corruption of antiquity itself, of *noble* antiquity, that made Christianity possible. The scholarly idiocy which upholds such ideas even today cannot be contradicted harshly enough. At the very time when the sick, corrupt chandala strata in the whole *imperium* adopted Christianity, the *opposite type*, nobility, was present in its most beautiful and most mature form. The great number became master; the democratism of the Christian instincts *triumphed*. Christianity was not 'national', not a function of a race – it turned to every kind of man who was disinherited by life, it had allies everywhere. At the bottom of Christianity is the rancour of the sick, instinct directed *against* the healthy, *against* health itself. Everything that has turned out well, everything that is proud and prankish, beauty above all, hurts its ears and eyes. Once more I recall the inestimable words of Paul: 'The *weak* things of the world, the *foolish* things of the world, the *base* and *despised* things of the world hath God chosen.' This was the formula; *in hoc signo* decadence triumphed.

God on the cross – are the horrible secret thoughts behind this symbol not understood yet? All that suffers, all that is nailed to the cross, is *divine*. All of us are nailed to the cross, *we* are divine. We alone are divine. Christianity was a victory, a nobler outlook perished of it – Christianity has been the greatest misfortune of mankind so far.

Christianity also stands opposed to every *spirit* that has turned out well; it can use only sick reason as Christian reason, it sides with everything idiotic, it utters a curse against the spirit, against the *superbia* of the healthy spirit. Because sickness is of the essence of Christianity, the typical Christian state, 'faith', must also be a form of sickness, and all straight, honest, scientific paths to knowledge must be rejected by the church as forbidden paths. Even doubt is a sin.

(e) From *The Antichrist*

What is good? Everything that heightens the feeling of power in man, the will to power, power itself.

What is bad? Everything that is born of weakness.

What is happiness? The feeling that power is *growing*, that resistance is overcome.

Not contentedness but more power; not peace but war; not virtue but fitness (Renaissance virtue, *virtù*, virtue that is moraline-free).

The weak and the failures shall perish: first principles of *our* love of man. And they shall even be given every possible assistance.

What is more harmful than any vice? Active pity for all the failures and all the weak: Christianity.

(f) From *Thus Spoke Zarathustra*, Pt 2

Hear, then, my word, you who are wisest. Test in all seriousness whether I have crawled into the very heart of life and into the very roots of its heart.

Where I found the living, there I found will to power; and even in the will of those who serve I found the will to be master.

That the weaker should serve the stronger, to that it is persuaded by its own will, which would be master over what is weaker still: this is the one pleasure it does not want to renounce. And as the smaller yields to the greater that it may have pleasure and power over the smallest, thus even the greatest still yields, and for the sake of power risks life. That is the yielding of the greatest: it is hazard and danger and casting dice for death.

And where men make sacrifices and serve and cast amorous glances, there too is the will to be master. Along stealthy paths the weaker steals into the castle and into the very heart of the more powerful – and there steals power.

And life itself confided this secret to me: 'Behold,' it said, 'I am *that which must always overcome itself*. Indeed, you call it a will to procreate or a drive to an end, to something higher, farther, more manifold: but all this is one, and one secret.

'Rather would I perish than forswear this; and verily, where there is perishing and a falling of leaves, behold, there life sacrifices itself – for power. That I must be struggle and a becoming and an end and an opposition to ends – alas, whoever guesses what is my will should also guess on what *crooked* paths it must proceed.

'Whatever I create and however much I love it – soon I must oppose it and my love; thus my will wills it. And you too, lover of knowledge, are only a path and footprint of my will; verily, my will to power walks also on the heels of your will to truth.

'Indeed, the truth was not hit by him who shot at it with the word of the "will to existence": that will does not exist. For, what does not exist cannot will; but what is in existence, how could that still want existence? Only where there is life is there also will: not will to life but – thus I teach you – will to power.

'There is much that life esteems more highly than life itself; but out of the esteeming itself speaks the will to power.'

Thus life once taught me; and with this I shall yet solve the riddle of your heart, you who are wisest.

(*g*) From *The Gay Science*

The greatest stress. How, if some day or night a demon were to sneak after you into your loneliest loneliness and say to you, 'This life as you now live it and have lived it, you will have to live once more and in-numerable times more; and there will be nothing new in it, but every pain and every joy and every thought and sign and everything im-measurably small or great in your life must return to you – all in the same succession and sequence – even this spider and this moonlight between the trees, and even this moment and I myself. The eternal hourglass of existence is turned over and over, and you with it, a dust grain of dust.' Would you not throw yourself down and gnash your teeth and curse the demon who spoke thus? Or did you once experience a tremendous moment when you would have answered him, 'You are a god, and never have I heard anything more godly.' If this thought were to gain possession of you, it would change you, as you are, or perhaps crush you. The question in each and every thing, 'Do you want this once more and innumerable times more?' would weigh upon your actions as the greatest stress. Or how well disposed would you have to become to yourself and to life to *crave nothing more fervently* than this ultimate eternal confirmation and seal?

(*h*) From *Thus Spoke Zarathustra*, Pt 3

'O Zarathustra,' the animals said, 'to those who think as we do, all things themselves are dancing: they come and offer their hands and laugh and flee – and come back. Everything goes, everything comes back; eternally rolls the wheel of being. Everything dies, everything blossoms again; eternally runs the year of being. Everything breaks, everything is joined anew; eternally the same house of being is built. Everything parts, everything greets every other thing again; eternally the ring of being remains faithful to itself. In every Now, being begins; round every Here rolls the sphere There. The centre is everywhere. Bent is the path of eternity.'

(*i*) From *The Gay Science*

The Madman. Have you not heard of that madman who lit a lantern in the bright morning hours, ran to the market place, and cried incessantly, 'I seek God! I seek God!' As many of those who do not believe in God were standing around just then, he provoked much laughter. Why, did he get lost? said one. Did he lose his way like a child? said another. Or is he hiding? Is he afraid of us? Has he gone on a voyage? or emigrated? Thus they yelled and laughed. The madman jumped into their midst and pierced them with his glances.

'Whither is God?' he cried. 'I shall tell you. *We have killed him* – you and I. All of us are his murderers. But how have we done this? How were we able to drink up the sea? Who gave us the sponge to wipe away the entire horizon? What did we do when we unchained this earth from its sun? Whither is it moving now? Whither are we moving

now? Away from all suns? Are we not plunging continually? Back-
ward, sideward, forward, in all directions? Is there any up or down
left? Are we not straying as through an infinite nothing? Do we not
feel the breath of empty space? Has it not become colder? Is not night
and more night coming on all the while? Must not lanterns be lit in the
morning? Do we not hear anything yet of the noise of the gravediggers
who are burying God? Do we not smell anything yet of God's de-
composition? Gods too decompose. God is dead. God remains dead.
And we have killed him. How shall we, the murderers of all murderers,
comfort ourselves? What was holiest and most powerful of all that the
world has yet owned has bled to death under our knives. Who will
wipe this blood off us? What water is there for us to clean ourselves?
What festivals of atonement, what sacred games shall we have to
invent? Is not the greatness of this deed too great for us? Must not we
ourselves become gods simply to seem worthy of it? There has never
been a greater deed; and whoever will be born after us – for the sake
of this deed he will be part of a higher history than all history
hitherto.'

Here the madman fell silent and looked again at his listeners; and they
too were silent and stared at him in astonishment. At last he threw his
lantern on the ground, and it broke and went out. 'I come too early,'
he said then; 'my time has not come yet. This tremendous event is still
on its way, still wandering – it has not yet reached the ears of man.
Lightning and thunder require time, the light of the stars requires time,
deeds require time even after they are done, before they can be seen
and heard. This deed is still more distant from them than the most
distant stars – *and yet they have done it themselves.*'

It has been related further that on that same day the madman entered
divers churches and there sang his *requiem aeternam deo.* Led out and
called to account, he is said to have replied each time, 'What are these
churches now if they are not the tombs and sepulchres of God?'

FURTHER READING·

There are important essays on Nietzsche in some of the volumes listed
under 'Existentialism' (see p. 114) and in E. Heller, *The Disinherited
Mind*, Bowes, 1952; Penguin, 1961. Other useful studies of his thought
include: W. Kaufmann, *Nietzsche: Philosopher. Psychologist. Antichrist,*
New York, Meridian Books, 1956; F. A. Lea, *The Tragic Philosopher:
a Study of Friedrich Nietzsche*, Methuen, 1957; C. Brinton, *Nietzsche,*
Harper Torchbooks, 1965. Mention should also be made of the

interesting ideas contained in K. Jaspers, *Nietzsche and Christianity*, Chicago, Regnery, 1961.

9 Frazer

James George Frazer (1854–1941) was born in Glasgow, became a life fellow of Trinity College, Cambridge, and was knighted in 1914. Beginning his academic career as a classical scholar, he was soon led by the nature of his studies into the wider 'anthropological' fields of magic, mythology, comparative religion and primitive customs. He was strongly influenced by a reading of Edward Tylor's 'Primitive Culture' (1871) and by his friendship with William Robertson Smith who, as editor of the 'Encyclopaedia Britannica', invited him in 1885 to contribute the articles on 'Totem' and 'Taboo'. Frazer's outstanding reputation as an anthropologist was established in 1890 with the publication of 'The Golden Bough: a Study in Magic and Religion' (the original two volumes were extended to twelve between 1907 and 1915; a one-volume abridgement was first published in 1922). Among those who acknowledged his influence we find such varied names as Herbert Spencer, Freud, Durkheim, Malinowski, T. S. Eliot and Ezra Pound.

Frazer has been called a 'classical evolutionist' in the sense that he elaborated an approximate mental equivalent to the physical evolution propounded by Darwin. 'The Golden Bough' develops a universal scheme of gradually succeeding modes of thought from magic, through religion, to science (reminiscent of Comte's earlier theological/metaphysical/scientific or positivist schema). This is now rejected by anthropologists who have shown the frequent coexistence of magical, religious and scientific ways of understanding the world. Nevertheless, Frazer's distinction between magic and religion (see passage (a) below) is still valuable and, in general, 'The Golden Bough' remains a remarkable source-book of primitive customs and beliefs.

It is now commonplace to criticize Frazer not only as an over-simplifying 'evolutionist' but also as an 'armchair anthropologist'. He himself travelled relatively little, obtained much of his data from correspondence with missionaries, administrators, etc., and then proceeded to 'think himself into the minds' of the primitive peoples about whom he wrote. This led him on occasion into false psychology and false deduction. However, it is only right to point out that he contributed a great deal to the modern readiness to study the 'primitive mind' seriously. Hence the choice of passages (b) and (c), taken from less well-known works among his voluminous list of publications.

(a) From *The Golden Bough*, ch. 4

Wherever sympathetic magic occurs in its unadulterated form, it assumes that in nature one event follows another necessarily and invariably without the intervention of any spiritual or personal agency. Thus its fundamental conception is identical with that of modern science; underlying the whole system is a faith, implicit but real and firm, in the order and uniformity of nature. The magician does not doubt that the same causes will always produce the same effects, that the performance of the proper ceremony, accompanied by the appropriate spell, will inevitably be attended by the desired result, unless, indeed, his incantations should chance to be thwarted and foiled by the more potent charms of another sorcerer. He supplicates no higher power: he sues the favour of no fickle and wayward being: he abases himself before no awful deity. Yet his power, great as he believes it to be, is by no means arbitrary and unlimited. He can wield it only so long as he strictly conforms to the rules of his art, or to what may be called the laws of nature as conceived by him. To neglect these rules, to break these laws in the smallest particular, is to incur failure, and may even expose the unskilful practitioner himself to the utmost peril. If he claims a sovereignty over nature, it is a constitutional sovereignty rigorously limited in its scope and exercised in exact conformity with ancient usage. Thus the analogy between the magical and the scientific conceptions of the world is close . . . .

If magic is thus next of kin to science, we have still to enquire how it stands related to religion. But the view we take of that relation will necessarily be coloured by the idea which we have formed of the nature of religion itself; hence a writer may reasonably be expected to define his conception of religion before he proceeds to investigate its relation to magic. There is probably no subject in the world about which opinions differ so much as the nature of religion, and to frame a definition of it which would satisfy every one must obviously be impossible. All that a writer can do is, first, to say clearly what he means by religion, and afterwards to employ the word consistently in that sense throughout his work. By religion, then, I understand a propitiation or conciliation of powers superior to man which are believed to direct and control the course of nature and of human life. Thus defined, religion consists of two elements, a theoretical and a practical, namely, a belief in powers higher than man and an attempt to propitiate or please them. Of the two, belief clearly comes first, since we must believe in the existence of a divine being before we can attempt to please him . . . .

But if religion involves, first, a belief in superhuman beings who rule the world, and, second, an attempt to win their favour, it clearly assumes that the course of nature is to some extent elastic or variable, and that we can persuade or induce the mighty beings who control it to deflect, for our benefit, the current of events from the channel in which they would otherwise flow. Now this implied elasticity or variability of nature is directly opposed to the principles of magic as well as of science, both of which assume that the processes of nature are rigid and invariable in their operation, and that they can as little be turned from their course by persuasion and entreaty as by threats and intimidation. The distinction between the two conflicting views of the universe turns on their answer to the crucial question, Are the forces which govern the world conscious and personal, or unconscious and impersonal? Religion, as a conciliation of the superhuman powers, assumes the former member of the alternative. For all conciliation implies that the being conciliated is a conscious or personal agent, that his conduct is in some measure uncertain, and that he can be prevailed upon to vary it in the desired direction by a judicious appeal to his interests, his appetites, or his emotions. Conciliation is never employed towards things which are regarded as inanimate, nor towards persons whose behaviour in the particular circumstances is known to be determined with absolute certainty. Thus in so far as religion assumes the world to be directed by conscious agents who may be turned from their purpose by persuasion, it stands in fundamental antagonism to magic as well as to science, both of which take for granted that the course of nature is determined, not by the passions or caprice of personal beings, but by the operation of immutable laws acting mechanically.
(*From the abridged version*)

(*b*) From 'The Scope and Method of Mental Anthropology' in *Garnered Sheaves*

Not the least important branch of what we may call the new anatomy was the science of embryology, which by a comparison of the human and animal embryos was able to demonstrate their close resemblance for a considerable period of their development, and thus to supply a powerful argument in favour of the conclusion that man and what he calls the lower animals have had a common origin, and that for an incalculable time they probably pursued nearly parallel lines of evolution. In fact, embryology shows that the very process of evolution, which we postulate for the past history of our race, is summarily reproduced in the life-history of every man and woman who is born into the world.

Turning now from the physical to the mental side of man's nature, we may say that the evolution theory has in like manner opened up a new province of inquiry which has been left unoccupied by the older philosophy. Whenever in former days a philosopher set himself to inquire into the principles of the human mind, it was his own particular mind, or at most the minds of his civilized contemporaries, that he proceeded to investigate. When Descartes turned his eyes inwards and reflected on the operations of his own mind, he believed himself to be probing to the very deepest foundations accessible to human intelligence. It never occurred to him, I imagine, to apply for information to the mind of a Zulu or a Hottentot, still less of a baboon or a chimpanzee. Yet the doctrine of evolution has rendered it highly probable that the mind of the philosopher is indissolubly linked to the minds of these barbarous peoples and strange animals, and that, if we would fully understand it, we must not disdain to investigate the intelligence of these our humble relations.

(c) From 'The Scope of Social Anthropology' in *Psyche's Task*

If we examine the superstitious beliefs which are tacitly but firmly held by many of our fellow-countrymen, we shall find, perhaps to our surprise, that it is precisely the oldest and crudest superstitions which are most tenacious of life, while views which, though also erroneous, are more modern and refined, soon fade from the popular memory. For example, the high gods of Egypt and Babylon, of Greece and Rome, have for ages been totally forgotten by the people and survive only in the books of the learned; yet the peasants, who never even heard of Isis and Osiris, of Apollo and Artemis, of Jupiter and Juno, retain to this day a firm belief in witches and fairies, in ghosts and hobgoblins, those lesser creatures of mythical fancy in which their fathers believed long before the great deities of the ancient world were ever thought of, and in which, to all appearance, their descendants will continue to believe long after the great deities of the present day shall have gone the way of all their predecessors. The reason why the higher forms of superstition or religion (for the religion of one generation is apt to become the superstition of the next) are less permanent than the lower is simply that the higher beliefs, being a creation of superior intelligence, have

85

little hold on the minds of the vulgar, who nominally profess them for a time in conformity with the will of their betters, but readily shed and forget them as soon as these beliefs have gone out of fashion with the educated classes. But while they dismiss without a pang or an effort articles of faith which were only superficially imprinted on their minds by the weight of cultured opinion, the ignorant and foolish multitude cling with a sullen determination to far grosser beliefs which really answer to the coarser texture of their undeveloped intellect. Thus while the avowed creed of the enlightened minority is constantly changing under the influence of reflection and enquiry, the real, though unavowed, creed of the mass of mankind appears to be almost stationary, and the reason why it alters so little is that in the majority of men, whether they are savages or outwardly civilized beings, intellectual progress is so slow as to be hardly perceptible. The surface of society, like that of the sea, is in perpetual motion; its depths, like those of the ocean, remain almost unmoved. . . .

The savage is not a different sort of being from his civilized brother: he has the same capacities, mental and moral, but they are less fully developed: his evolution has been arrested, or rather retarded, at a lower level. And as savage races are not all on the same plane, but have stopped or tarried at different points of the upward path, we can to a certain extent, by comparing them with each other, construct a scale of social progression and mark out roughly some of the stages on the long road that leads from savagery to civilization. In the kingdom of mind such a scale of mental evolution answers to the scale of morphological evolution in the animal kingdom.

FURTHER READING

S. E. Hyman, *The Tangled Bank: Darwin, Marx, Frazer and Freud as Imaginative Writers*, New York, Atheneum, 1962, *passim*.

10 Jung

In the development of modern psychological theory a unique place is occupied by Carl Gustav Jung (1875–1961). After a conventional medical training at the University of Basel (Jung was the son of a Swiss Protestant pastor and, apart from travel, lived in Switzerland throughout his life) he entered on a career in psychiatry at Zürich in 1900. In 1902 he worked for a time under Janet at the

Salpêtrière in Paris. Eventually, he branched out into studies of history, literature, philosophy, mythology and alchemy. He emphasized the need for a broad geographical and historical approach – Eastern mysticism as well as medieval alchemy – to the psychological understanding of man. He further declared, speaking as an analytical psychologist, that 'we moderns are faced with the necessity of rediscovering the life of the spirit'. Something of his general attitude, at once comprehensive and undogmatic, is suggested by passage (a) below. Jung's work is universalist in intention and possesses a mystical element that contrasts sharply with the late nineteenth-century empirico-rationalism of Freud.

Freud and Jung first met shortly after the publication of Jung's 'The Psychology of Dementia Praecox' (German original, 1907; English trans. 1909). They collaborated closely but were by no means in continual agreement. The break between them occurred some time after the publication of Jung's 'The Psychology of the Unconscious' (German original, 1912; English trans. 1917). The animosity between Freudians and Jungians (not to mention the less influential Adlerians) has been a feature of psychoanalytic theory ever since as, for example, in E. Glover's presentation of Jung as 'a psycho-analytical schismatic' in 'Freud or Jung' (Allen and Unwin, 1950). Jung criticized Freud's ideas on various grounds. He considered that Freudian theory offers 'an over-emphasized sexuality piled up behind a dam'. Furthermore, 'it shrinks at once to normal proportions as soon as the way to development is opened'. Therefore, he asked, in an image that might itself seem particularly significant to the Freudian: 'what is the use of paddling about in this flooded country?' On related though more general grounds Jung asserted that 'Freud's is not a psychology of the healthy mind' and also suggested, as a major weakness in Freud's writings, 'his inability to understand religious experience, as is clearly shown in his book: "The Future of an Illusion".'

Perhaps the two major contributions of Jung to analytical psychology are his classification of psychological types and his account of the 'collective unconscious'. His psychological classification, set out in most detail in 'Psychological Types' (German original, 1921; English trans. 1923), distinguished two main classes of people: introverts and extraverts. Within each of these classes Jung drew up four further categories of 'temperamental function': thinking, feeling, sensation and intuition – any one of which will predominate in a particular individual. Part of Jung's own brief sketch of his typology, included in 'Modern Man in Search of a Soul' (1933), is given in passage (b).

Passages (c) and (d) are chiefly concerned with the nature and contents of the collective unconscious. They also contain a hint of the way in which his studies led Jung into the spheres of magic, symbolism and mythology. Like Freud,

Jung posited an unconscious area of the mind – the personal unconscious – consisting for the most part of complexes (or emotionally toned groups of ideas) formed by repressed memories, wishes, emotions, etc. But Jung differed from Freud in positing an important non-personal part of the unconscious mind – the collective *unconscious – made up of archetypes (a kind of deposit inherited from our early ancestors and forming the basis of certain patterns of instinctual behaviour). These ideas are worked out most fully in 'The Archetypes and the Collective Unconscious' which forms vol. IX of the English translation of Jung's collected works. This latter venture, which is still in progress (under the auspices of the Bollingen Foundation), has regrouped a large number of Jung's essays and lectures and includes important works not mentioned above such as 'Psychology and Religion: West and East', 'Psychology and Alchemy' and 'The Spirit in Man, Art and Literature'.*

(a) From *Modern Man in Search of a Soul*

The spirit of the age cannot be compassed by the processes of human reason. It is an inclination, an emotional tendency that works upon weaker minds, through the unconscious, with an overwhelming force of suggestion that carries them along with it. To think otherwise than our contemporaries think is somehow illegitimate and disturbing; it is even indecent, morbid or blasphemous, and therefore socially dangerous for the individual. He is stupidly swimming against the social current. Just as formerly the assumption was unquestionable that everything that exists takes its rise from the creative will of a God who is spirit, so the nineteenth century discovered the equally unquestionable truth that everything arises from material causes. Today the psyche does not build itself a body, but on the contrary, matter, by chemical action, produces the psyche. This reversal of outlook would be ludicrous if it were not one of the outstanding features of the spirit of the age. It is the popular way of thinking, and therefore it is decent, reasonable, scientific and normal. Mind must be thought to be an epiphenomenon of matter. The same conclusion is reached even if we say not 'mind' but 'psyche', and in place of matter speak of brain, hormones, instincts or drives. To grant the substantiality of the soul or psyche is repugnant to the spirit of the age, for to do so would be heresy.

We have now discovered that it was intellectually unjustified presumption on our forefathers' part to assume that man has a soul; that that soul has substance, is of divine nature and therefore immortal; that there is a power inherent in it which builds up the body, supports its life, heals its ills and enables the soul to live independently of the body; that there are incorporeal spirits with which the soul associates; and that beyond our empirical present there is a spiritual world from which the soul receives knowledge of spiritual things whose origins cannot be discovered in this visible world. But people who are not above the general level of consciousness have not yet discovered that it is just as presumptuous and fantastic for us to assume that matter produces spirit; that apes give rise to human beings; that from the harmonious interplay of the drives of hunger, love, and power Kant's *Critique of Pure Reason* should have arisen; that the brain-cells manufacture thoughts, and that all this could not possibly be other than it is.

(b) From *Modern Man in Search of a Soul*

... there is a whole class of men who at the moment of reaction to a given situation at first draw back a little as if with an unvoiced 'No', and only after that are able to react; and there is another class who, in the same situation, come forward with an immediate reaction, apparently confident that their behaviour is obviously right. The former class would therefore be characterized by a certain negative relation to the object, and the latter by a positive one.

As we know, the former class corresponds to the introverted and the second to the extraverted attitude. But with these two terms in themselves as little is gained as when Molière's *bourgeois gentilhomme* discovered that he ordinarily spoke in prose. These distinctions attain meaning and value only when we realize all the other characteristics that go with the type ....

What struck me now was the undeniable fact that while people may be classed as introverts or extraverts, these distinctions do not cover all the dissimilarities between the individuals in either class. So great, indeed, are these differences that I was forced to doubt whether I had observed correctly in the first place. It took nearly ten years of observation and comparison to clear up this doubt.

The question as to the great variation observable among the members of each class entangled me in unforeseen difficulties which for a long time I could not master. To observe and recognize the differences gave me comparatively little trouble, the root of my difficulties being now, as before, the problem of criteria. How was I to find the right terms for the characteristic differences? Here I realized for the first time and to the full extent how young psychology really is. It is still little more than a chaos of arbitrary opinions, the better part of which seems to have been produced in the study and consulting-room by spontaneous generation from the isolated and therefore Jovian brains of learned scholars . . . .

Since I must restrict myself here to a mere sketch of the basic ideas of a psychological theory of types, I must unfortunately forego a detailed description of individual traits and actions in the light of this theory. The total result of my work in this field up to the present is the presentation of two general types covering the attitudes which I call extraversion and introversion. Besides these, I have worked out a four-fold classification corresponding to the functions of thinking, feeling, sensation and intuition. Each of these functions varies according to the general attitude, and thus eight variants are produced. I have been asked almost reproachfully why I speak of four functions and not of more or fewer. That there are exactly four is a matter of empirical fact. But as the following consideration will show, a certain completeness is attained by these four. Sensation establishes what is actually given, thinking enables us to recognize its meaning, feeling tells us its value, and finally intuition points to the possibilities of the whence and whither that lie within the immediate facts. In this way, we can orientate ourselves with respect to the immediate world as completely as when we locate a place geographically by latitude and longitude. The four functions are somewhat like the four points of the compass; they are just as arbitrary and just as indispensable. Nothing prevents our shifting the cardinal points as many degrees as we like in one direction or the other, nor are we precluded from giving them different names. It is merely a question of convention and comprehensibility.

But one thing I must confess: I would not for anything dispense with this compass on my psychological journeys of discovery. This is not merely for the obvious, all-too-human reason that everyone is in love with his own ideas. I value the type-theory for the objective reason that it offers a system of comparison and orientation which makes possible something that has long been lacking, a critical psychology.

(c) From *Modern Man in Search of a Soul*

Modern investigation of animal instinct, as for example in insects, has brought together a rich fund of empirical findings which show that if man acted as certain insects do he would possess a higher intelligence than at present. It cannot, of course, be proved that insects possess conscious knowledge, but common-sense cannot doubt that their unconscious action-patterns are psychic functions. Man's unconscious likewise contains all the patterns of life and behaviour inherited from his ancestors, so that every human child, prior to consciousness, is possessed of a potential system of adapted psychic functioning. In the conscious life of the adult, as well, this unconscious, instinctive functioning is always present and active. In this activity all the functions of the conscious psyche are prepared for. The unconscious perceives, has purposes and intuitions, feels and thinks as does the conscious mind. We find sufficient evidence for this in the field of psycho-pathology and the investigation of dream-processes. Only in one respect is there an essential difference between the conscious and the unconscious functioning of the psyche. While consciousness is intensive and concentrated, it is transient and is directed upon the immediate present and the immediate field of attention; moreover, it has access only to material that represents one individual's experience stretching over a few decades. A wider range of 'memory' is artificially acquired and consists mostly of printed paper. But matters stand very differently with the unconscious. It is not concentrated and intensive, but shades off into obscurity; it is highly extensive and can juxtapose the most heterogeneous elements in the most paradoxical way. More than this, it contains, besides an indeterminable number of subliminal perceptions, an immense fund of accumulated inheritance-factors left by one genera-tion of men after another, whose mere existence marks a step in the differentiation of the species. If it were permissible to personify the unconscious, we might call it a collective human being combining the characteristics of both sexes, transcending youth and age, birth and death, and, from having at his command a human experience of one or two million years, almost immortal. If such a being existed, he would be exalted above all temporal change; the present would mean neither more nor less to him than any year in the one hundredth century before Christ; he would be a dreamer of age-old dreams and, owing to his immeasurable experience, he would be an incomparable prognosticator. He would have lived countless times over the life of the individual, of the family, tribe and people, and he would possess the living sense of the rhythm of growth, flowering and decay.

Unfortunately – or rather let us say, fortunately – this being dreams. At least it seems to us as if the collective unconscious, which appears to us in dreams, had no consciousness of its own contents – though of course we cannot be sure of this, any more than we are in the case of insects. The collective unconscious, moreover, seems not to be a person, but something like an unceasing stream or perhaps an ocean of images and figures which drift into consciousness in our dreams or in abnormal states of mind.

It would be positively grotesque for us to call this immense system of experience of the unconscious psyche an illusion, for our visible and tangible body itself is just such a system. It still carries within it the discernible traces of primeval evolution, and it is certainly a whole that functions purposively – for otherwise we could not live. It would never occur to anyone to look upon comparative anatomy or physiology as nonsense. And so we cannot dismiss the collective unconscious as illusion, or refuse to recognize and study it as a valuable source of knowledge.

(d) From *The Archetypes and the Collective Unconscious*

The hypothesis of a collective unconscious belongs to the class of ideas that people at first find strange but soon come to possess and use as familiar conceptions. This has been the case with the concept of the unconscious in general. After the philosophical idea of the unconscious, in the form presented chiefly by Carus and von Hartmann, had gone down under the overwhelming wave of materialism and empiricism, leaving hardly a ripple behind it, it gradually reappeared in the scientific domain of medical psychology.

At first the concept of the unconscious was limited to denoting the state of repressed or forgotten contents. Even with Freud, who makes the unconscious – at least metaphorically – take the stage as the acting subject, it is really nothing but the gathering place of forgotten and repressed contents, and has a functional significance thanks only to these. For Freud, accordingly, the unconscious is of an exclusively personal nature, although he was aware of its archaic and mythological thought-forms.

A more or less superficial layer of the unconscious is undoubtedly personal. I call it the *personal unconscious*. But this personal unconscious rests upon a deeper layer, which does not derive from personal experience and is not a personal acquisition but is inborn. This deeper layer I call the *collective unconscious*. I have chosen the term 'collective' because this part of the unconscious is not individual but universal; in contrast to the personal psyche, it has contents and modes of behaviour that are more or less the same everywhere and in all individuals. It is, in other words, identical in all men and thus constitutes a common psychic substrate of a suprapersonal nature which is present in every one of us.

Psychic existence can be recognized only by the presence of contents that are *capable of consciousness*. We can therefore speak of an unconscious only in so far as we are able to demonstrate its contents. The contents of the personal unconscious are chiefly the *feeling-toned complexes*, as they are called; they constitute the personal and private side of psychic life. The contents of the collective unconscious, on the other hand, are known as *archetypes* . . . .

'Archetype' is an explanatory paraphrase of the Platonic εἶδος. For our purposes this term is apposite and helpful, because it tells us that so far as the collective unconscious contents are concerned we are dealing with archaic or – I would say – primordial types, that is, with universal images that have existed since the remotest times. The term 'représentations collectives', used by Lévy-Bruhl to denote the symbolic figures in the primitive view of the world, could easily be applied to unconscious contents as well, since it means practically the same thing. Primitive tribal lore is concerned with archetypes that have been modified in a special way. They are changed into conscious formulae taught according to tradition, generally in the form of esoteric teaching. This last is a typical means of expression for the transmission of collective contents originally derived from the unconscious.

Another well-known expression of the archetypes is myth and fairytale. But here too we are dealing with forms that have received a specific stamp and have been handed down through long periods of time. The term 'archetype' thus applies only indirectly to the 'représentations collectives', since it designates only those psychic contents which have not yet been submitted to conscious elaboration and are therefore an immediate datum of psychic experience.

FURTHER READING

The following general studies of Jung's thought are particularly useful: F. Fordham, *An Introduction to Jung's Psychology*, Penguin, 1953; E. A. Bennet, *C. G. Jung*, Barrie & Rockliff, 1961; E. A. Bennet, *What Jung really said*, Macdonald, 1966.

11 Spengler

Oswald Spengler (1880–1936) was born at Blankenburg am Harz and died in Munich. He studied mathematics and natural science and in 1904 completed his thesis on Heraclitus – a significant subject in view of his own later

writings on historical cycles. In 1911, when he was working as a school-
master, a small inheritance enabled him to retire and devote himself to the
writing of his major work, 'The Decline of the West'. The draft was finished
by 1914 and the two volumes were published in 1918 and 1922. A revised
version of Vol. I appeared in 1923 and an English translation of the two
volumes was completed in 1926 and 1928.

'The Decline of the West' is Spengler's one really important work. How-
ever, because of its enormous length and scope, only a very general impression
of some of its basic ideas can be conveyed by the passages below. Passage (a)
sets out the fundamental concept of historical morphology on which the whole
work is based – something like the application to history of the biologist's
conception of living forms. As Spengler himself puts it: 'Cultures are
organisms, and world-history is their collective biography.' *This morpho-*
logical approach enables him to discern a four-fold cycle through which, he
claims, all civilizations pass: 'pre-Culture', 'Culture', 'Civilization' and
'Decline'. Spengler is using the terms 'Culture' and 'Civilization' here in a
second and special sense. They represent, respectively, a period of creativity and
a succeeding stage of conscious intellectuality and material comfort. It is in this
sense that 'Civilization' is the destiny *of a 'Culture' (see passage (b) below)*
and beyond this stage there can only be decay.

This view of inevitable decline (with its overtones of Nietzsche and its anti-
Darwinian emphasis) means, among other things, that Spengler regarded post-
Industrial Revolution art as a marked falling away from the high standards
and achievements of the 'Cultural' stage (see passage (c)). More generally, he
denied the capacity of modern Western man for political and moral progress and
his ability to control his actions by reason. He regarded political democracy as
a sham and considered a return of extreme violence to be inevitable (see
passages (d) and (e)).

Spengler's prophecy of the inevitable doom of European civilization, when
it first appeared just after the First World War, gave comfort to a number of
his German compatriots who argued that the downfall of their victors would
not be long delayed. 'The Decline of the West' was widely read in the nihilistic
atmosphere of the 1920's (100,000 copies were sold in eight years) and even
more widely discussed and criticized. Spengler's pessimism may not be generally
acceptable today – and many of his historical 'facts' and interpretations are now
rejected – but his attempt to construct a philosophy of history and to disclose
the close relationships existing within a given cultural pattern continue to have
considerable influence. It could be argued, for instance, that André Malraux's
'Voices of Silence' (1951) is basically an attempt to refute Spengler.

(a) From *The Decline of the West*, Vol. I, Introduction

Thus our theme ... expands into the conception of a *morphology of world history*, of the world-as-history in contrast to the morphology of the world-as-nature that hitherto has been almost the only theme of philosophy. And it reviews once again the forms and movements of the world in their depths and final significance, but this time according to an entirely different ordering which groups them, not in an ensemble picture inclusive of everything known, but in a picture of *life*, and presents them not as things-become, but as things-becoming.

The *world-as-history*, conceived, viewed and given form from out of its opposite the *world-as-nature* – here is a new aspect of human existence on this earth. As yet, in spite of its immense significance, both practical and theoretical, this aspect has not been realized, still less presented. Some obscure inkling of it there may have been, a distant momentary glimpse there has often been, but no one has deliberately faced it and taken it in with all its implications. We have before us two possible ways in which man may inwardly possess and experience the world around him. With all rigour I distinguish (as to form, not substance) the organic from the mechanical world-impression, the content of images from that of laws, the picture and symbol from the formula and the system, the instantly actual from the constantly possible, the intents and purposes of imagination ordering according to plan from the intents and purposes of experience dissecting according to scheme; and – to mention even thus early an opposition that has never yet been noted, in spite of its significance – the domain of *chronological* from that of *mathematical number* ....

Present-day historians think they are doing a work of supererogation in bringing in religions and social, or still more art-history, details to 'illustrate' the political sense of an epoch. But the decisive factor – decisive, that is, in so far as visible history is the expression, sign and embodiment of soul – they forget. I have not hitherto found one who has carefully considered the *morphological relationship* that inwardly binds together the expression-forms of *all* branches of a Culture, who has gone beyond politics to grasp the ultimate and fundamental ideas of Greeks, Arabians, Indians and Westerners in mathematics, the meaning of their early ornamentation, the basic forms of their architecture, philosophies, dramas and lyrics, their choice and development of great arts, the detail of their craftsmanship and choice of materials – let alone appreciated the decisive importance of these matters for the form-problems of history. Who amongst them realizes that between the Differential Calculus and the dynastic principle of politics in the age of Louis XIV, between the Classical city-state and the Euclidean geometry, between the space-perspective of Western oil-painting and the conquest of space by railroad, telephone and long-range weapon, between contrapuntal music and credit economics, there are deep uniformities? Yet, viewed from this morphological standpoint, even the humdrum facts of politics assume a symbolic and even a metaphysical character, and – what has perhaps been impossible hitherto – things such as the Egyptian administrative system, the Classical coinage, analytical geometry, the cheque, the Suez Canal, the book-printing of the Chinese, the Prussian Army, and the Roman road-engineering can, as symbols, be made *uniformly* understandable and appreciable.

(*b*) From *The Decline of the West*, Vol. I, Introduction

What is Civilization, understood as the organic-logical sequel, fulfilment and finale of a culture?

For every Culture has *its own* Civilization. In this work, for the first time the two words, hitherto used to express an indefinite, more or less ethical, distinction are used in a *periodic* sense, to express a strict and necessary *organic succession*. The Civilization is the inevitable *destiny* of the Culture, and in this principle we obtain the viewpoint from which the deepest and gravest problems of historical morphology become capable of solution. Civilizations are the most external and artificial states of which a species of developed humanity is capable. They are a conclusion, the thing-become succeeding the thing-becoming, death following life, rigidity following expansion, intellectual age and the stone-built, petrifying world-city following mother-earth and the spiritual childhood of Doric and Gothic. They are an end, irrevocable, yet by inward necessity reached again and again.

So, for the first time, we are enabled to understand the Romans as the *successors* of the Greeks, and light is projected into the deepest secrets of the late-Classical period. What, but this, can be the meaning of the fact – which can only be disputed by vain phrases – that the Romans were barbarians who did not *precede* but *closed* a great development? Unspiritual, unphilosophical, devoid of art, clannish to the point of brutality, aiming relentlessly at tangible successes, they stand between the Hellenic Culture and nothingness. An imagination directed purely to practical objects – they had religious laws governing godward relations as they had other laws governing human relations, but there was no specifically Roman saga of gods – was something which is not found at all in Athens. In a word, Greek *soul* – Roman *intellect*; and this antithesis is the differentia between Culture and Civilization . . . .

The transition from Culture to Civilization was accomplished for the Classical world in the 4th, for the Western in the 19th Century. From these periods onward the great intellectual decisions take place, not as in the days of the Orpheus-movement or the Reformation in the 'whole world' where not a hamlet is too small to be unimportant, but in three or four world-cities that have absorbed into themselves the whole content of History, while the old wide landscape of the Culture, become merely provincial, serves only to feed the cities with what remains of its higher mankind . . . .

To the world-city belongs not a folk but a mass. Its uncomprehending hostility to all the traditions representative of the Culture (nobility, church, privileges, dynasties, convention in art and limits of knowledge in science), the keen and cold intelligence that confounds the wisdom of the peasant, the new-fashioned naturalism that in relation to all matters of sex and society goes back far beyond Rousseau and Socrates to quite primitive instincts and conditions, the reappearance of the *panem et circenses* in the form of wage-disputes and football-grounds – all these things betoken the definite closing-down of the Culture and the opening of a quite new phase of human existence – anti-provincial, late, futureless, but quite inevitable.

(c) From *The Decline of the West*, Vol. I, ch. 8

I have said that oil-painting faded out at the end of the 17th Century, when one after another all its great masters died, and the question will naturally, therefore, be asked – is Impressionism (in the current narrow sense) a creation of the 19th Century? Has painting lived, after all, two centuries more? Is it still existing? But we must not be deceived by appearances. Not only was there a dead space between Rembrandt and Delacroix or Constable – for when we think of the living art of high symbolism that was Rembrandt's the purely decorative artists of the 18th Century do not count – but, further, that which began with Delacroix and Constable was, notwithstanding all technical continuity, something quite different from that which had ended with Rembrandt. The new episode of painting that in the 19th Century (i.e. beyond the 1800 frontier and in 'Civilization') has succeeded in awakening some illusion of a great culture of painting, has itself chosen the word *Plein-air* (*Freilicht*) to designate its special characteristic. The very designation suffices to show the significance of the fleeting phenomenon that it is. It implies the conscious, intellectual, cold-blooded rejection of that for which a sudden wit invented the name 'brown sauce', but which the great masters had, as we know, regarded as the only truly metaphysical colour. On it had been built the painting-culture of the schools, and especially the Dutch school, that had vanished irretrievably in the Rococo. This brown, the symbol of a spatial infinity, which had for Faustian mankind created a spiritual something out of a mere canvas, now came to be regarded, quite suddenly, as an offence to Nature. What had happened? Was it not simply this, that the *soul* for which this supernal colour was something religious, the sign of wistfulness, the whole meaning of 'Living Nature', had quietly slipped away? The materialism of a Western cosmopolis blew into the ashes and rekindled this curious brief flicker – a brief flicker of two generations, for with the generation of Manet all was ended again. I have (as the reader will recall) characterized the noble green of Grünewald and Claude and Giorgione as the Catholic space-colour and the transcendent brown of Rembrandt as the colour of the Protestant worldfeeling. On the other hand, *Plein-air* and its new colour scale stand for irreligion. From the spheres of Beethoven and the stellar expanses of Kant, Impressionism has come down again to the crust of the earth. Its space is cognized, not experienced, seen, not contemplated; there is tunedness in it, but not Destiny. It is the mechanical object of physics and not the felt world of the pastorale that Courbet and Manet give us in their landscapes. . . . Rembrandt's mighty landscapes lie essentially in the universe, Manet's near a railway station.

(*d*) From *The Decline of the West*, Vol. II, ch. 10

The bourgeoisie has definite limits; it belongs to the Culture; it embraces, in the best sense, all who adhere to it, and under the name of people, *populus, demos,* rallies nobility and priesthood, money and mind, craftsman and wage-earner, as constituents of itself.

This is the idea that Civilization finds prevailing when it comes on the scene, and this is what it destroys by its notion of the Fourth Estate, *the Mass,* which rejects the Culture and its matured forms, lock, stock, and barrel. It is the absolute of formlessness, persecuting with its hate every sort of form, every distinction of rank, the orderliness of property, the orderliness of knowledge. It is the new nomadism of the Cosmopolis, for which slaves and barbarians in the Classical world, Sudras in the Indian, and in general anything and everything that is merely human, provide an undifferentiated floating something that falls apart the moment it is born, that recognizes no past and possesses no future. Thus the Fourth Estate becomes the expression of the passing of a history over into the historyless. The mass is the end, the radical nullity.

(e) From *The Decline of the West*, Vol. II, ch. 14

A power can be overthrown only by another power, not by a principle, and no power that can confront money is left but this one. Money is overthrown and abolished only by blood. *Life* is alpha and omega, the cosmic onflow in microcosmic form. It is *the* fact of facts within the world-as-history. Before the irresistible rhythm of the generation-sequence, everything built up by the waking-consciousness in its intellectual world vanishes at the last. Ever in History it is life and life only – race-quality, the triumph of the will-to-power – and not the victory of truths, discoveries, or money that signifies. *World-history is the world court,* and it has ever decided in favour of the stronger, fuller, and more self-assured life – decreed to it, namely, the right to exist, regardless of whether its right would hold before a tribunal of waking-consciousness. Always it has sacrificed truth and justice to might and race, and passed doom of death upon men and peoples in whom truth was more than deeds, and justice than power. And so the drama of a high Culture – that wondrous world of deities, arts, thoughts, battles, cities – closes with the return of the pristine facts of the blood eternal that is one and the same as the ever-circling cosmic flow. The bright imaginative Waking-Being submerges itself into the silent service of Being, as the Chinese and Roman empires tell us. Time triumphs over Space, and it is Time whose inexorable movement embeds the ephemeral incident of the Culture, on this planet, in the incident of Man – a form wherein the incident life flows on for a time, while behind it all the streaming horizons of geological and stellar histories pile up in the light-world of our eyes.

FURTHER READING

The best general book on Spengler is S. Hughes, *Oswald Spengler: A Critical Estimate*, Scribner, 1962 (first publ. 1952). There is also a suggestive chapter entitled 'Oswald Spengler and the predicament of the historical imagination' in E. Heller, *The Disinherited Mind*, Bowes, 1952; Penguin, 1961.

III

Ideologies

In 1960 Sartre published the first volume of his *Critique de la raison dialectique*. The opening section of the work is a long essay separately entitled 'Question de méthode' and translated into English, in book form, as *The Problem of Method* (Methuen, 1963). In the opening pages of *The Problem of Method* Sartre makes a distinction between a 'philosophy' and an 'ideology', a distinction which lies behind the descriptive title of this section. In Sartre's sense of the term, a properly creative 'philosophy' offers a clear methodology, is governed by a genuinely original idea or set of ideas, totalizes knowledge and reflects the increasing self-awareness of a 'rising' social class. On this basis he identifies three 'moments' of authentic philosophical creation since the seventeenth century: those of Descartes and Locke, of Kant and Hegel, and of Marx. None of these philosophies could be refuted until men had advanced beyond the particular historical moment of which each is a reflection. And indeed, in the case of Marxism, Sartre argues that the historical reality it mirrors is still with us so that it is the one current, authentic 'philosophy' and cannot be philosophically controverted. Attempts so far made to 'go beyond' Marxism either misunderstand its doctrines or simply revive pre-Marxist ideas as distinct from creating post-Marxist ones.

Having cleared the ground in this way Sartre continues:

Those intellectuals who come after the great flowering and who undertake to set the systems in order or to use the new methods to conquer territory not yet fully explored, those who provide practical applications for the theory and employ it as a tool to destroy and to construct – they should not be called philosophers. They cultivate the domain, they take an inventory, they erect certain structures there, they may even bring about certain internal changes; but they still get their nourishment from the living thought of the great dead. They are borne along by the crowd on the march, and it is the crowd which constitutes their cultural milieu and their future, which determines the field of their investigations, and even of their 'creation'. These *relative* men I propose to call '*ideologists*'.

In the sense suggested here we clearly live in an age of 'ideologies'. Our intellectual life is typified by ultimately derivative, yet widely influential doctrines, lacking the distinctive status of an authentically original and creative philosophy. Among such doctrines, and in their very different ways, Fascism, Nazism, phenomenology and existentialism have all had important consequences, both direct and indirect, for the mind of modern Europe.

FASCISM AND NAZISM

Contempt for European liberalism, together with the belief that the Western civilization nurtured by that liberalism was suffering a steady decline, were widely held viewpoints immediately before and just after the First World War (cf. Spengler, pp. 93–99). An atmosphere existed in which the twin ideologies of Fascism and Nazism were able to develop as radical, non-Marxist solutions promising to cure the ills of Europe.

Fascism began in Italy in 1919 when the former radical socialist, Benito Mussolini (1883–1945), organized the Fascio di Combattimento in Milan. The movement came to power with his 'March on Rome' on 28 October 1922. The term 'Fascism' was derived from the Latin *fasces* – the bunch of rods, with an axe, representing authority in ancient Rome – and the authoritarian aspects of the doctrine emerge in passage (12) below from Mussolini's *La Dottrina del Fascismo* (1932). This statement of his ideas by Mussolini was originally a long article in the official *Enciclopedia Italiana*. The arguments put forward were almost certainly influenced by the 'philosopher of Fascism', Giovanni Gentile (1875–1944).

Nazism is in several ways the German version of Fascism, though the Nazis emphasized more strongly than the Italian Fascists the ideal of racial 'purity'. Adolf Hitler (1889–1945) regarded what he called 'the race war' as an inflexible law of both nature and history and this can be seen (passage 13 below) in a brief but typical extract from his book *Mein Kampf* (vol. 1, 1925; vol. 2, 1927).

Both Fascism and Nazism were anti-bourgeois and anti-communist movements in which the inevitability of violence and war, in the pursuit of social and political ends, were regarded as axiomatic (cf. Mussolini: 'War is to the man what maternity is to the woman').

12 Mussolini

From *La Dottrina del Fascismo*

Being anti-individualistic, the Fascist system of life stresses the importance of the State and recognizes the individual only in so far as his interests coincide with those of the State, which stands for the consciousness and the universality of man as an historic entity. It is opposed to classic Liberalism which arose as a reaction to absolutism and exhausted its historical function when the State became the expression of the consciousness and the will of the people. Liberalism denied the State in the name of the individual; Fascism reasserts the rights of the State as expressing the real essence of the individual. And if liberty is to be the attribute of living men and not that of abstract dummies invented by individualistic Liberalism, then Fascism stands for liberty and for the only liberty worth having, the liberty of the State and of the individual within the State. The Fascist conception of the State is all-embracing; outside of it no human or spiritual values may exist, much less have any value. Thus understood, Fascism is totalitarian and the Fascist State, as a synthesis and a unit which includes all values, interprets, develops and lends additional power to the whole life of people.

A nation, as expressed in the State, is a living, ethical entity only in so far as it is progressive. Inactivity means death. Therefore the State does not only stand for Authority which governs and confers legal form and spiritual value on individual wills, but it is also Power which makes its will felt and respected beyond its own boundaries, thus affording practical evidence of the universal character of the decisions necessary to ensure its development. This implies organization and expansion, potential if not actual. . . .

Fascism, in short, is not only a lawgiver and a founder of institutions, but an educator and a promoter of spiritual life. It does not merely aim at remoulding the forms of life, but also their content, man, his character and his faith. To achieve this purpose it enforces discipline and makes use of authority, entering into the mind and ruling with undisputed sway. Therefore it has chosen as its emblem the Lictor's rods, the symbol of unity, strength and justice. . . .

Fascism is definitely and absolutely opposed to the doctrines of Liberalism, both in the political and in the economic sphere. The importance of Liberalism in the nineteenth century must not be exaggerated for present-day controversial purposes, nor should we make of one of the many theories which flourished in that century a religion for mankind for the present and for all time to come. It is symptomatic that throughout the nineteenth century the religion of Liberalism was totally unknown to so highly civilized a people as the Germans, except for a single case, which has been described as the 'ridiculous Parliament of Frankfurt' which lasted just one season. Germany attained her national unity outside Liberalism and in opposition to Liberalism, a doctrine which seems to be foreign to the German temperament, an essentially Monarchist one, whereas Liberalism is the historic and logical prelude to anarchy. The three stages of the achievement of German unity were the three wars of 1864, 1866 and 1870, directed by such 'Liberals' as Moltke and Bismarck. And Liberalism played a very minor part in building up Italian unity, if we compare it to the contribution made by Mazzini and Garibaldi who were not Liberals. But for the intervention of the illiberal Napoleon III we would not have had Lombardy, and without that of the illiberal Bismarck at Sadowa and Sedan very probably we would not have had Venetia in 1866, nor would we have entered Rome in 1870. . . .

The Fascist negation of Socialism, Democracy, Liberalism should not, however, be interpreted as implying a desire to drive the world backwards to positions occupied prior to 1789. Monarchist absolutism is of the past, and so is Church rule. Dead and done for are feudal privileges and the division of society into closed, secluded castes. Neither has the Fascist conception of authority anything in common with that of the police-ridden State.

The State educates its members to citizenship, makes them aware of their mission, urges them to unity; its justice harmonizes their divergent interests; it hands down to future generations the conquests of the mind in the fields of science, art, law, human solidarity; it leads them up from primitive tribal life to imperial rule, the highest expression of human power. The State hands down to future generations the memory of those who laid down their lives to ensure its safety or to obey its laws; it sets up as examples and records for future ages the names of captains who enlarged its territory and of the men of genius who have made it famous. Whenever respect for the State declines and the disintegrating and centrifugal tendencies of individuals and groups prevail, nations are heading for decay. . . .

If Liberalism spells individualism, Fascism spells collectivism.

13 Hitler

From *Mein Kampf*, I, ch. 11

Just as little as Nature desires a mating between weaker individuals and stronger ones, far less she desires the mixing of a higher race with a lower one, as in this case her entire work of higher breeding, which has perhaps taken hundreds of thousands of years, would tumble at one blow.

Historical experience offers countless proofs of this. It shows with terrible clarity that with any mixing of the blood of the Aryan with lower races the result was the end of the culture-bearer. North America, the population of which consists for the greatest part of Germanic elements – which mix only very little with the lower, coloured races – displays a humanity and a culture different from those of Central and South America, where chiefly the Romanic immigrants have sometimes mixed with the aborigines on a large scale. By this example alone one may clearly and distinctly recognize the influence of the race mixture. The Germanic of the North American continent, who has remained pure and less intermixed, has become the master of that continent; he will remain so until he, too, falls victim to the shame of blood-mixing.

The result of any crossing, in brief, is always the following:

(*a*) Lowering of the standard of the higher race.
(*b*) Physical and mental regression, and, with it, the beginning of a slowly but steadily progressive lingering illness.

To bring about such a development means nothing less than sinning against the will of the Eternal Creator.

This action, then, is also rewarded as a sin.

Man, by trying to resist this iron logic of Nature, becomes entangled in a fight against the principles to which alone he, too, owes his existence as a human being. Thus his attack is bound to lead to his own doom.

Of course, now comes the typically Jewish, impudent, but just as stupid, objection by the modern pacifist: 'Man conquers Nature!' . . .

Everything that today we admire on this earth – science and art, technique and inventions – is only the creative product of a few peoples and perhaps originally of *one* race. On them now depends also the existence of this entire culture. If they perish, then the beauty of this earth sinks into the grave with them. . . .

If one were to divide mankind into three groups: culture-founders, culture-bearers, and culture-destroyers, then, as representative of the first kind, only the Aryan would come in question. . . .

Therefore, it is no accident that the first cultures originated in those places where the Aryan, by meeting lower peoples, subdued them and made them subject to his will. They, then, were the first technical instrument in the service of a growing culture.

With this the way that the Aryan had to go was clearly lined out. As a conqueror he subjected the lower peoples and then he regulated their practical ability according to his command and his will and for his aims. But while he thus led them towards a useful, though hard activity, he not only spared the lives of the subjected, but perhaps he even gave them a fate which was better than that of their so-called 'freedom'. As long as he kept up ruthlessly the master's standpoint, he not only really remained 'master' but also the preserver and propagator of the culture. For the latter was based exclusively on his abilities, and, with it, on his preservation in purity. But as soon as the subjected peoples themselves began to rise (probably) and approached the conqueror linguistically, the sharp separating wall between master and slave fell. The Aryan gave up the purity of his blood and therefore he also lost his place in the Paradise which he had created for himself. . . .

The blood-mixing, with the lowering of the racial level caused by it, is the sole cause of the dying-off of old cultures; for the people do not perish by lost wars, but by the loss of that force of resistence which is contained only in the pure blood.

All that is not race in this world is trash. . . .

All really important symptoms of decay of the pre-War time ultimately go back to racial causes.

PHENOMENOLOGY

The foundations of twentieth-century phenomenology were largely laid by Edmund Husserl (1859–1938) and extended in various directions by such thinkers as Heidegger (metaphysics), Scheler (ethics) and Pfänder (aesthetics). After some years as a student of mathematics, Husserl came under the influence of Franz Brentano in the University of Vienna and decided to make philosophy, rather than mathematics, his career. This double interest and training is indicated by the title of his first book, *Philosophie der Arithmetik* (1891), and goes a long way to explaining Husserl's cartesian ambition in which he sought to make of phenomenology a 'science of essence' (*Wesenswissenschaft*) on the lines of pure mathematics.

During a long academic career Husserl taught philosophy at Halle, Göttingen and Freiburg (where he spent the last twenty-two years of his life). His first widely influential work was the two-volume *Logische Untersuchungen* (1900–1). His phenomenological theories were developed further in the book which English readers know best: *Ideen zu einer reinen Phänomenologie* (1913) (translated into English as *Ideas: General Introduction to Pure Phenomenology*). Later works include *Formale und Transzendentale Logik* (1929) and the *Cartesianische Meditationen* (1931) which were translated into English in 1960.

Like Heidegger's existentialism, Husserl's phenomenology is difficult to understand, let alone to sum up in a couple of paragraphs. As the name implies, it has links with earlier forms of philosophical realism but Husserl's emphasis on intuition and insight led him to an idealist position (cf. his statement: 'We shall never know if there is a world') rejected by some of his best-known intellectual beneficiaries, including Heidegger and Sartre.

Husserl's thought was much concerned with various types of 'reduction' or the setting on one side of things that get in the way of necessary knowledge in the philosophical sense. Thus at an early stage he argued against the view (of Mill, among others) that the laws of logic are fundamentally laws of psychology. He also opposed the claim that genuine knowledge can only come to us via the natural sciences, or that a philosophical system, to achieve objective validity, must synthesize scientific theories. In a word, he mapped out a clear and autonomous area for philosophy by separating it from psychology and science.

The phenomenological system itself similarly proceeds by a series of methodological reductions. Husserl prefigured existentialist thought by introducing the experiencing self, from the outset, into the world of phenomena (physical and psychical). Now the self's experience is always directed towards an object, it is experience *of something*, and this characteristic Husserl calls 'intentionality'. But by the same token this experience is contingent and affected by what he terms 'the natural viewpoint'. In order, therefore, to achieve necessary rather than contingent knowledge, we must suspend belief in the world of phenomena and investigate further the 'experiences'. This 'phenomenological reduction' of the world is what Husserl also calls 'bracketing' (*epoché*).

But the 'experiences' on which we now concentrate have a structure or essence (*eidos*) which must be analysed further. In the course of this analysis or 'eidetic reduction' we isolate a 'pure ego' to which the psychical selves involved in the experiences analysed are objectively present. It is study of this 'pure ego' which takes us through what Husserl calls 'the entrance gate of phenomenology'; the closing sentence of the *Cartesian Meditations* sums up his position: 'I must lose the world by epoché, in order to regain it by a universal self-examination.'

The two passages below give some general idea of the nature of Husserl's thought. The first sets out some aspects of phenomenological reduction; the second contains a brief indication of what eidetic reduction means.

14 Husserl

From *Ideas: General Introduction to Pure Phenomenology*, II, ch. 1.

§ 30. THE GENERAL THESIS OF THE NATURAL STANDPOINT. That which we have submitted towards the characterization of what is given to us from the natural standpoint, and thereby of the natural standpoint itself, was a piece of pure description *prior to all 'theory'*. In these studies we stand bodily aloof from all theories, and by 'theories' we here mean anticipatory ideas of every kind. Only as facts of our environment, not as agencies for uniting facts validly together, do theories concern us at all. But we do not set ourselves the task of continuing the pure description and raising it to a systematically inclusive and exhaustive characterization of the data, in their full length and breadth, discoverable from the natural standpoint (or from any standpoint, we might add, that can be knit up with the same in a common consent). A task such as this can and must – as scientific – be undertaken, and it is one of extraordinary importance, although so far scarcely noticed. Here it is not ours to attempt. For us who are striving towards the entrance-gate of phenomenology all the necessary work in this direction has already been carried out; the few features pertaining to the natural standpoint which we need are of a quite general character, and have already figured in our descriptions, and been sufficiently *and fully clarified*. We even made a special point of securing this full measure of clearness.

We emphasize a most important point once again in the sentences that follow: I find continually present and standing over against me the one spatio-temporal fact-world to which I myself belong, as do all other men found in it and related in the same way to it. This 'fact-world', as the word already tells us, I find to *be out there*, and also *take it just as it gives itself to me as something that exists out there.* All doubting and rejecting of the data of the natural world leaves standing the *general thesis of the natural standpoint.* 'The' world is as fact-world always there; at the most it is at odd points 'other' than I supposed, this or that under such names as 'illusion', 'hallucination', and the like, must be struck *out of it*, so to speak; but the 'it' remains ever, in the sense of the general thesis, a world that has its being out there. To know it more comprehensively, more trustworthily, more perfectly than the naïve lore of experience is able to do, and to solve all the problems of scientific knowledge which offer themselves upon its ground, that is the goal of the *sciences* of *the natural standpoint.*

§ 31. RADICAL ALTERATION OF THE NATURAL THESIS: 'DIS-CONNEXION', 'BRACKETING'. *Instead now of remaining at this standpoint, we propose to alter it radically.* Our aim must be to convince ourselves of the possibility of this alteration on grounds of principle.

The General Thesis according to which the real world about me is at all times known not merely in a general way as something apprehended, but as a fact-world *that has its being out there*, does *not* consist of course *in an act proper*, in an articulated judgment *about* existence. It is and remains something all the time the standpoint is adopted, that is, it endures persistently during the whole course of our life of natural endeavour. What has been at any time perceived clearly, or obscurely made present, in short everything out of the world of nature known through experience and prior to any thinking, bears in its totality and in all its articulated sections the character 'present' 'out there', a character which can function essentially as the ground of support for an explicit (predicative) existential judgment which is in agreement with the character it is grounded upon. If we express that same judgment, we know quite well that in so doing we have simply put into the form of a statement and grasped as a prediction what already lay somehow in the original experience, or lay there as the character of something 'present to one's hand'.

We can treat the potential and unexpressed thesis exactly as we do the thesis of the explicit judgment. A procedure of this sort, *possible at any time*, is, for instance, *the attempt to doubt everything* which *Descartes*, with an entirely different end in view, with the purpose of setting up an absolutely indubitable sphere of Being, undertook to carry through. We link on here, but add directly and emphatically that this attempt to doubt everything should serve us *only as a device of method*, helping us to stress certain points which by its means, as though secluded in its essence, must be brought clearly to light.

The attempt to doubt everything has its place in the realm of our *perfect freedom*. We can *attempt to doubt* anything and everything, however convinced we may be concerning what we doubt, even though the evidence which seals our assurance is completely adequate.

Let us consider what is essentially involved in an act of this kind. He who attempts to doubt is attempting to doubt 'Being' of some form or other, or it may be Being expanded into such predicative forms as 'It is', 'It is this or thus', and the like. The attempt does not affect the form of Being itself. He who doubts, for instance, whether an object, whose Being he does not doubt, is constituted in such and such a way, doubts *the way it is constituted*. We can obviously transfer this way of speaking from the doubting to the *attempt* at doubting. It is clear that we cannot doubt the Being of anything, and in the same act of consciousness (under the unifying form of simultaneity) bring what is substantive to this Being under the terms of the Natural Thesis, and so confer upon it the character of 'being actually there' (*vorhanden*). Or to put the same in another way: we cannot at once doubt and hold for certain one and the same quality of Being. It is likewise clear that the *attempt* to doubt any object of awareness in respect of its *being actually there necessarily conditions a certain suspension* (*Aufhebung*) *of the thesis*; and it is precisely this that interests us. It is not a transformation of the thesis into antithesis, of positive into negative; it is also not a transformation into presumption, suggestion, indecision, doubt (in one or another sense of the word); such shifting indeed is not at our free pleasure. *Rather is it something quite unique. We do not abandon the thesis we have adopted, we make no change in our conviction*, which remains in itself what it is so long as we do not introduce new motives of judgment, which we precisely refrain from doing. And yet the thesis undergoes a modification – whilst remaining in itself what it is, *we set it as it were 'out of action', we 'disconnect it', 'bracket it'*. It still remains there like the bracketed in the bracket, like the disconnected outside the connexional system. We can also say: The thesis is experience as lived (*Erlebnis*), *but we make 'no use' of it*, and by that, of course, we do not indicate privation (as when we say of the ignorant that he makes no use of a certain thesis); in this case rather, as with all parallel expressions, we are dealing with indicators

that point to a definite but *unique form of consciousness*, which clamps on
to the original simple thesis (whether it actually or even predicatively
posits existence or not), and transvalues it in a quite peculiar way. *This
transvaluing is a concern of our full freedom, and is opposed to all cognitive
attitudes* that would set themselves up as co-ordinate with *the thesis*, and
yet within the unity of 'simultaneity' remain incompatible with it, as
indeed it is in general with all attitudes whatsoever in the strict sense of
the word.

In *the attempt to doubt* applied to a thesis which, as we presuppose,
is certain and tenaciously held, the 'disconnexion' takes place in and with
a modification of the antithesis, namely, with the *'supposition'* (*Anset-
zung*) *of Non-Being*, which is thus the partial basis of the attempt to
doubt. With Descartes this is so markedly the case that one can say
that his universal attempt at doubt is just an attempt at universal denial.
We disregard this possibility here, we are not interested in every
analytic component of the attempt to doubt, nor therefore in its exact
and completely sufficing analysis. *We extract only the phenomenon of*
'bracketing' or 'disconnecting', which is obviously not limited to that of
the attempt to doubt, although it can be detached from it with special
ease, but can appear *in other contexts also*, and with no less ease *independently*. In relation to *every* thesis and wholly uncoerced we can use
this peculiar ἐποχή (epoché), *a certain refraining from judgment which is*
*compatible with the unshaken and unshakable because self-evidencing convic-
tion of Truth*. The thesis is 'put out of action', bracketed, it passes off into
the modified status of a 'bracketed thesis', and the judgment *simpliciter*
into *'bracketed judgment'*.

Naturally one should not simply identify this consciousness with that
of 'mere supposal', that nymphs, for instance, are dancing in a ring;
for thereby *no disconnecting* of a living conviction that goes on living
takes place, although from another side the close relation of the two
forms of consciousness lies clear. Again, we are not concerned here with
supposal in the sense of *'assuming'* or *taking for granted*, which in the
equivocal speech of current usage may also be expressed in the words:
'I suppose (I make the assumption) that it is so and so.'

Let us add further that nothing hinders us *from speaking of bracketing
correlatively* also, in respect of *an objectivity to be posited*, whatever be
the region or category to which it belongs. What is meant in this case
is that *every thesis related to this objectivity* must be *disconnected* and
changed into its bracketed counterpart. On closer view, moreover, the
'bracketing' image is from the outset better suited to the sphere of the

object, just as the expression 'to put out of action' better suits the sphere of the Act or of Consciousness.

From *Ideas: . . .*, III, ch. 2

§ 80. THE RELATION OF EXPERIENCES TO THE PURE EGO. Among the essential peculiarities of a general kind, distinctive of the transcendentally purified field of experience, the first place should be kept for the relation of that experience to the 'pure' Ego. Every *'cogito'*, every act in a specially marked sense, is characterized as act of the Ego, 'proceeding from the Ego', 'actually living' in it. We have already spoken on this point, and recall in a few sentences what we previously worked out.

When observing, *I* perceive something; similarly in recollection I am often 'busied' with something; again, observing in a sense, *I* follow in imaginative fancy what goes on in the world of fancy. Or I meditate, draw inferences; I revoke a judgment, 'refrain' if need be from judging at all. I approve or disapprove, I am glad or grieved, I wish, or I will and do; or again, I 'refrain' from being glad, from wishing, willing, and action. In all such acts I am present, *actually* present. In reflexion I apprehend myself herein as the human being that I am.

But if I perform the phenomenological ἐποχή, the whole world of the natural setting is suspended, and with it, 'I, the man'. The pure experience as act with its own proper essence then remains as residue. But I also see that the apprehension of the same as human experience, quite apart from the question of existence, introduces various features which do not need to be there, and that on the other side no disconnecting can remove the form of the *cogito* and cancel the 'pure' subject of the act. The 'being directed towards', 'the being busied with', 'adopting an attitude', 'undergoing or suffering from', has this *of necessity* wrapped in its very essence, that it is just something 'from the Ego', or in the reverse direction 'to the Ego'; and this Ego is the *pure* Ego, and no reduction can get any grip on it.

We have hitherto spoken of experiences of the special 'cogito' type. The remaining experiences which supply the general *milieu* for the actuality of the Ego certainly lack the marked relation to the Ego, of which we have just been speaking. And yet they too have their part in the pure Ego, and the latter in them. They 'belong' to it as 'its own', they are *its* background of consciousness, *its* field of freedom.

Yet notwithstanding these peculiar complications with all 'its' experiences, the experiencing Ego is still nothing that might be taken *for itself* and made into an object of inquiry on its *own* account. Apart from its 'ways of being related' or 'ways of behaving', it is completely empty of essential components, it has no content that could be unravelled, it is in and for itself indescribable: pure Ego and nothing further.

There is therefore occasion for a variety of important descriptions, bearing on the special forms or modes of experience of the experiencing Ego, *as* actually enjoyed. In this connexion we continue to distinguish – despite the necessary interrelationship – the *experience itself* from the *pure Ego* of the experiencing process; and again: the *pure subjective phase of the way of experiencing* from the remaining, *Ego-diverted content of the experience*, so to speak. Thus there is a certain, extraordinarily important two-sidedness in the essential nature of the sphere of experience, concerning which we can also say that in experiences we must distinguish between a *subjectively and an objectively oriented* aspect.

FURTHER READING

The most authoritative work on Husserl's thought is undoubtedly M. Farber, *The Foundation of Phenomenology*, New York, Paine-Whitman, 1962.

Shorter accounts of Husserl, with comments on Heidegger and the general philosophic movement in Germany in the twentieth century, will be found in I. M. Bocheński, *Contemporary European Philosophy*, University of California Press, 1965, and G. L. Kline, ed., *European Philosophy Today*, Chicago, Quadrangle Books, 1965. There is an essay on Husserl in J. Passmore, *A Hundred Years of Philosophy*, Duckworth, 1957, pp. 187–97.

EXISTENTIALISM

The 'existentialist' label has been widely applied since the Second World War and has given rise to a large number of expository books and articles. The term has been used to describe the philosophical ideas of both Christian and atheist thinkers – Berdyaev, Maritain, Buber and Marcel as well as Heidegger, Sartre and Merleau-Ponty (not to mention the non-Christian theist, Jaspers). Such nineteenth-century writers as Kierkegaard, Dostoevsky and Nietzsche are often classed as existentialists and the tradition of thought they represent has been traced back through Pascal to Augustine.

For our immediate purposes here, and in very general terms, two main attitudes which these various thinkers have in common need to be stated. All of them, in different ways, have emphasized existence as the starting point of philosophy. They have adopted an 'existentialist' rather than an abstract, 'essentialist' position. Secondly, it follows that they have underlined the role of the human subject in all knowing and have had much to say about the situation and the potentialities of man, his 'human condition' and his capacity for freedom. They have argued ingeniously in defence of a position variously described by their critics as 'subjective', 'romantic' and 'self-punishingly gloomy'.

Almost all existentialists, whether Christian or atheist, owe a special debt to Kierkegaard (see pp. 55–65). Since Kierkegaard was a Christian thinker who is already well represented earlier in this book, I have chosen to illustrate, in the passages which follow, the rather different emphases of two influential atheist existentialists: Heidegger and Sartre.

Although he has rejected the term 'existentialist', Martin Heidegger has been a major figure in the movement. He was born at Messkirch in the Black Forest in 1889, had an early training with strong Thomist elements, and wrote his thesis on the doctrine of categories and concepts in the work of Duns Scotus. He published his major work (never actually completed), *Sein und Zeit* (translated into English as *Being and Time*) in 1927 and within two years had succeeded Husserl at Freiburg on the latter's retirement. His relations with Nazism were cordial, at least in the early stages, and his inaugural address as Rector of Freiburg University in 1933 endorsed Nazi ideology.

The difficulty of reading and understanding Heidegger is increased by the fact that he has largely created a special philosophical vocabulary. Hence the proliferation, in English translations, of such words as 'thrownness', 'care', 'facticity', 'falling', etc. In order to understand being (*Sein*) Heidegger approaches it through human existence (*Dasein*) which is 'being there'. Man is 'thrown' into existence not so much in the sense of being created by some blind force as in the sense that he can only and always find himself *already there*. 'I am' can only be grasped by man as 'I have already been'. Man is a being always in advance of himself, as it were, and subject to being–towards–death. Hence the experience of 'care', 'anxiety', etc., inseparable from 'authenticity'. 'Authenticity' recognizes these conditions of *Dasein* whereas 'inauthentic' existence ignores them by dint of absorption in day-to-day matters. Some idea of Heidegger's analysis of 'anxiety' and of 'being–towards–death' is contained in passages 15 (*a*) and (*b*) below. Other works by Heidegger available in English include *Existence and Being* (1949), *An Introduction to Metaphysics* (1959) and *Essays in Metaphysics: Identity and Difference* (1960).

Jean-Paul Sartre was born in Paris in 1905. His novels, plays and essays brought him a worldwide reputation and have helped to popularize and dramatize both his own brand of existentialism and some of the more general consequences which he draws from it. His original training, however, was a strictly philosophical one and he taught philosophy in various French *lycées* between 1928 and 1944, apart from a year's study of modern German philosophy at the Institut Français in Berlin (1933–4) and a period in the army and as a prisoner of war (1939–41). His main philosophical works are: *The Transcendence of the Ego* ('La Transcendance de l'égo', 1936), *Imagination: a Psychological Critique* (*L'Imagination: étude critique*, 1936), *Sketch for a Theory of the Emotions* (*Esquisse d'une théorie des émotions*, 1939), *The Psychology of the Imagination* (*L'Imaginaire: psychologie phénoménologique de l'imagination*, 1940), *Being and Nothingness* (*L'Etre et le néant: essai d'ontologie phénoménologique*, 1943), *Existentialism and Humanism* (*L'Existentialisme est un humanisme*, 1946) and *Critique de la raison dialectique* (1960) of which the first section has been translated into English as *The Problem of Method*. The two extracts 16 (*a*) and (*b*), show something of Sartre's thinking on one of his most central themes: the fact of human freedom and responsibility.

FURTHER READING

The general literature on existentialism is formidable in volume. Apart from a useful introduction and selection of texts by W. Kaufmann, *Existentialism from Dostoevsky to Sartre*, New York, Meridian Books, 1956, the following critical works are all worth reading: E. Mounier, *Existentialist Philosophies*, Rockliff, 1948; H. J. Blackman, *Six Existentialist Thinkers*, Routledge & Kegan Paul, 1952; F. H. Heinemann, *Existentialism and the Modern Predicament*, A. and C. Black, 1958; K. F. Reinhardt, *The Existentialist Revolt*, New York, Ungar Publishing Co., 1960; R. G. Olson, *An Introduction to Existentialism*, New York, Dover Books, 1962; W. Barrett, *Irrational Man: a Study in Existentialism*, Heinemann (Mercury Books), 1964; P. Roubiczek, *Existentialism: For and Against*, Cambridge University Press, 1964.

15 Heidegger

(a) From *Being and Time*, § 40

Anxiety is not only anxiety in the face of something, but, as a state-of-mind, it is also *anxiety about* something. That which anxiety is profoundly anxious [*sich abängstet*] about is not a *definite* kind of Being for Dasein or a *definite* possibility for it. Indeed the threat itself is indefinite, and therefore cannot penetrate threateningly to this or that factically concrete potentiality-for-Being. That which anxiety is anxious about is Being-in-the world itself. In anxiety what is environmentally ready-to-hand sinks away, and so, in general, do entities within-the-world. The 'world' can offer nothing more, and neither can the Dasein-with of Others. Anxiety thus takes away from Dasein the possibility of understanding itself, as it falls, in terms of the 'world' and the way things have been publicly interpreted. Anxiety throws Dasein back upon that which it is anxious about – its authentic potentiality-for-Being-in-the-world. Anxiety individualizes Dasein for its ownmost Being-in-the-world, which as something that understands, projects itself essentially upon possibilities. Therefore, with that which it is anxious about, anxiety discloses Dasein *as Being-possible*, and indeed as the only kind of thing which it can be of its own accord as something individualized in individualization [*vereinzeltes in der Vereinzelung*].

Anxiety makes manifest in Dasein its *Being towards* its ownmost potentiality-for-Being – that is, its *Being-free for* the freedom of choosing itself and taking hold of itself. Anxiety brings Dasein face to face with its *Being-free for* (*propensio in* . . .) the authenticity of its Being, and for this authenticity as a possibility which it always is. But at the same time, this is the Being to which Dasein as Being-in-the-world has been delivered over.

That *about which* anxiety is anxious reveals itself as that *in the face of which* it is anxious – namely, Being-in-the-world. The selfsameness of that in the face of which and that about which one has anxiety, extends even to anxiousness [*Sichängsten*] itself. For, as a state-of-mind, anxiousness is a basic kind of Being-in-the-world. *Here the disclosure and the disclosed are existentially selfsame in such a way that in the latter the world has been disclosed as world, and Being-in has been disclosed as a potentiality-for-Being which is individualized, pure, and thrown; this makes it plain that with the phenomenon of anxiety a distinctive state-of mind has become a theme for Interpretation.* Anxiety individualizes Dasein and thus discloses it as *'solus ipse'*. But this existential 'solipsism' is so far from the displacement of putting an isolated subject-Thing into the innocuous emptiness of a worldless occurring, that in an extreme sense what it does is precisely to bring Dasein face to face with its world as world, and thus bring it face to face with itself as Being-in-the-world.

(*b*) From *Being and Time*, § 51

The analysis of the phrase 'one dies' reveals unambiguously the kind of Being which belongs to everyday Being-towards-death. In such a way of talking, death is understood as an indefinite something which, above all, must duly arrive from somewhere or other, but which is proximally not *yet present-at-hand* for oneself, and is therefore no threat. The expression 'one dies' spreads abroad the opinion that what gets reached, as it were, by death, is the 'they'. In Dasein's public way of interpreting, it is said that 'one dies', because everyone else and oneself can talk himself into saying that 'in no case is it I myself', for this 'one' is the *'nobody'*. 'Dying' is levelled off to an occurrence which reaches Dasein, to be sure, but belongs to nobody in particular. If idle talk is always ambiguous, so is this manner of talking about death. Dying, which is essentially mine in such a way that no one can be my representative, is perverted into an event of public occurrence which the 'they' encounters. In the way of talking which we have characterized, death is spoken of as a 'case' which is constantly occurring. Death gets passed off as always something 'actual'; its character as a possibility gets concealed, and so are the other two items that belong to it – the fact that it is non-relational and that it is not to be outstripped. By such ambiguity, Dasein puts itself in the position of losing itself in the 'they' as regards a distinctive potentiality-for-Being which belongs to Dasein's ownmost Self. The 'they' gives its approval, and aggravates the *temptation* to cover up from oneself one's ownmost Being-towards-death. This evasive concealment in the face of death dominates everydayness so stubbornly that, in Being with one another, the 'neighbours' often still keep talking the 'dying person' into the belief that he will escape death and soon return to the tranquillized everydayness of the world of his concern. Such 'solicitude' is meant to 'console' him. It insists upon bringing him back into Dasein, while in addition it helps him to keep his ownmost non-relational possibility-of-Being completely concealed. In this manner the 'they' provides [*besorgt*] a *constant tranquillization about death*. At bottom, however, this is a tranquillization not only for him who is 'dying' but just as much for those who 'console' him. And even in the case of a demise, the public is still not to have its own tranquillity upset by such an event, or be disturbed in the carefreeness with which it concerns itself. Indeed the dying of Others is seen often enough as a social inconvenience, if not even a downright tactlessness, against which the public is to be guarded.

But along with this tranquillization, which forces Dasein away from its death, the 'they' at the same time puts itself in the right and makes itself respectable by tacitly regulating the way in which *one* has to comport oneself towards death. It is already a matter of public acceptance that 'thinking about death' is a cowardly fear, a sign of insecurity on the part of Dasein, and a sombre way of fleeing from the world. *The 'they' does not permit us the courage for anxiety in the face of death.* The dominance of the manner in which things have been publicly interpreted by the 'they', has already decided what state-of-mind is to determine our attitude towards death. In anxiety in the face of death, Dasein is brought face to face with itself as delivered over to that possibility which is not to be outstripped. The 'they' concerns itself with transforming this anxiety which has been made ambiguous as fear, is passed off as a weakness with which no self-assured Dasein may have any acquaintance. What is 'fitting' [*Was sich* ... *'gehört'*] according to the unuttered decree of the 'they', is indifferent tranquillity as to the 'fact' that one dies. The cultivation of such a 'superior' indifference *alienates* Dasein from its ownmost non-relational potentiality-for-Being.

But temptation, tranquillization, and alienation are distinguishing marks of the kind of Being called '*falling*'. As falling, everyday Being-towards-death is a constant *fleeing in the face of death*. Being-*towards*-the-end has the mode of *evasion in the face of it* – giving new explanations for it, understanding it inauthentically, and concealing it. Factically one's own Dasein is always dying already; that is to say, it is in a Being-towards-its-end. And it hides this Fact from itself by recoining 'death' as just a 'case of death' in Others – an everyday occurrence which, if need be, gives us the assurance still more plainly that 'oneself' is still 'living'. But in thus falling and fleeing *in the face of* death, Dasein's everydayness attests that the very 'they' itself already has the definite character of *Being-towards-death*, even when it is not explicitly engaged in 'thinking about death'.

FURTHER READING

The following books on Heidegger are all helpful in their different ways: M. Grene, *Martin Heidegger*, Bowes & Bowes, 1957; T. Langan, *The Meaning of Heidegger*, Routledge & Kegan Paul, 1959; M. King, *Heidegger's Philosophy*, Blackwell, 1964.

16 Sartre

(a) From *Existentialism and Humanism*

When we speak of 'abandonment' – a favourite word of Heidegger – we only mean to say that God does not exist, and that it is necessary to draw the consequences of his absence right to the end. The existentialist is strongly opposed to a certain type of secular moralism which seeks to suppress God at the least possible expense. Towards 1880, when the French professors endeavoured to formulate a secular morality, a society and a law-abiding world, it is essential that certain values should be taken seriously; they must have an *a priori* existence ascribed to them. It must be considered obligatory *a priori* to be honest, not to lie, not to beat one's wife, to bring up children and so forth; so we are going to do a little work on this subject, which will enable us to show that these values exist all the same, inscribed in an intelligible heaven although, of course, there is no God. In other words – and this is, I believe, the purport of all that we in France call radicalism – nothing will be changed if God does not exist; we shall re-discover the same norms of honesty, progress and humanity, and we shall have disposed of God as an out-of-date hypothesis which will die away quietly of itself. The existentialist, on the contrary, finds it extremely embarrassing that God does not exist, for there disappears with Him all possibility of finding values in an intelligible heaven. There can no longer be any good *a priori*, since there is no infinite and perfect consciousness to think it. It is nowhere written that 'the good' exists, that one must be honest or must not lie, since we are now upon the plane where there are only men. Dostoievsky once wrote 'If God did not exist, everything would be permitted'; and that, for existentialism, is the starting point. Everything is indeed permitted if God does not exist, and man is in consequence forlorn, for he cannot find anything to depend upon either within or outside himself. He discovers forthwith, that he is without excuse. For if indeed existence precedes essence, one will never be able to explain one's action by reference to a given and specific human nature; in other words, there is no determinism – man is free, man is freedom. Nor, on the other hand, if God does not exist, are we provided with any values or commands that could legitimise our behaviour. Thus we have neither behind us, nor before us in a luminous realm of values, any means of justification or excuse. We are left alone, without excuse. That is what I mean when I say that man is condemned to be free. Condemned, because he did not create himself, yet is nevertheless at liberty, and from the moment that he is thrown into this world he is responsible for everything he does.

(b) From *Being and Nothingness*, Pt IV, ch. 1

The essential consequence of our earlier remarks is that man being condemned to be free carries the weight of the whole world on his shoulders; he is responsible for the world and for himself as a way of being. We are taking the word 'responsibility' in its ordinary sense as 'consciousness [of] being the incontestable author of an event or of an object'. In this sense the responsibility of the for-itself is overwhelming since he is the one by whom it happens that *there* is a world; since he is also the one who makes himself be, then whatever may be the situation in which he finds himself, the for-itself must wholly assume this situation with its peculiar coefficient of adversity, even though it be insupportable. He must assume the situation with the proud consciousness of being the author of it, for the very worst disadvantages or the worst threats which can endanger my person have meaning only in and through my project; and it is on the ground of the engagement which I am that they appear. It is therefore senseless to think of complaining since nothing foreign has decided what we feel, what we live, or what we are.

Furthermore this absolute responsibility is not resignation; it is simply the logical requirement of the consequences of our freedom. What happens to me happens through me, and I can neither affect myself with it nor revolt against it nor resign myself to it. Moreover everything which happens to me is *mine*. By this we must understand first of all that I am always equal to what happens to me *qua* man, for what happens to a man through other men and through himself can be only human. The human state of things; there is no non-human situation. It is only through fear, flight, and recourse to magical types of conduct that I shall decide on the non-human, but this decision is human, and I shall carry the entire responsibility for it. But in addition the situation is *mine* because it is the image of my free choice of myself, and everything which it presents to me is *mine* in that this represents me and symbolizes me. Is it not I who decide the coefficient of adversity in things and even their unpredictability by deciding myself?

Thus there are no *accidents* in a life; a community event which suddenly bursts forth and involves me in it does not come from the outside. If I am mobilized in a war, this war is *my* war; it is in my image and I deserve it. I deserve it first because I could always get out of it by suicide or by desertion; these ultimate possibles are those which must always be present for us when there is a question of envisaging a situation. For lack of getting out of it, I have *chosen* it. This can be due to inertia, to cowardice in the face of public opinion, or because I prefer certain other values to the value of the refusal to join in the war (the good opinion of my relatives, the honour of my family, etc.). Any way you look at it, it is a matter of a choice. This choice will be repeated later on again and again without a break until the end of the war. Therefore we must agree with the statement by J. Romains, 'In war there are no innocent victims.' If therefore I have preferred war to death or to dishonour, everything takes place as if I bore the entire responsibility for this war. Of course others have declared it, and one might be tempted perhaps to consider me as a simple accomplice. But this notion of complicity has only a juridical sense, and it does not hold here. For it depended on me that for me and by me this war should not exist, and I have decided that it does exist. There was no compulsion here, for the compulsion could have got no hold on a freedom. I did not have any excuse; for as we have said repeatedly in this book, the peculiar character of human reality is that it is without excuse. . . .

Yet this responsibility is of a very particular type. Someone will say, 'I did not ask to be born.' This is a naïve way of throwing greater emphasis on our facticity. I am responsible for everything, in fact, except for my very responsibility, for I am not the foundation of my being. Therefore everything takes place as if I were compelled to be responsible. I am *abandoned* in the world, not in the sense that I might remain abandoned and passive in a hostile universe like a board floating on the water, but rather in the sense that I find myself suddenly alone and without help, engaged in a world for which I bear the whole responsibility without being able, whatever I do, to tear myself away from this responsibility for an instant. For I am responsible for my very desire of fleeing responsibilities. To make myself passive in the world, to refuse to act upon things and upon Others is still to choose myself, and suicide is one mode among others of being-in-the-world.

FURTHER READING

There are a good many general books on Sartre. Those that deal more particularly with his philosophical ideas include I. Murdoch, *Sartre: Romantic Rationalist*, Collins, 1953; Fontana, 1967; A. Stern, *Sartre: his Philosophy and Psycho-analysis*, New York, Liberal Arts Press, 1953; A. Manser, *Sartre: a Philosophic Study*, Athlone Press, 1966; in French, F. Jeanson, *Le Problème moral et la pensée de Sartre*, Paris, Edition du Myrte, 1947.

IV
The Study of Society

Preoccupation with the nature of society as a whole is characteristic of the modern mind. The assumption is widespread that our society can be analysed, shaped and improved by making the right deductions from social investigations and experiments. There has been a steady growth in the importance of the social sciences and an emphasis on the possibility of generalized answers to collective problems. Central to this activity is the discipline of sociology which is concerned with a systematic study of the whole life of man in society.

The term 'sociology' was coined by the French positivist thinker, Auguste Comte, in his *Cours de philosophie positive* (1830–42). Nevertheless his use of the word, by which he meant something like the synthesis of all knowledge about human life and activity, is much too comprehensive to define presentday sociology. Indeed, one of the first tasks of the founding fathers of sociology, such as Durkheim, was to define the legitimate concerns of this new 'science' and to outline an appropriate methodology. It is significant, however, that sociology as we now know it first developed during a period of widespread belief in scientific positivism and inevitable human progress. It concerned itself with the identification and discussion of social and economic 'laws' on analogy with the physical 'laws' revealed by natural scientists.

This emphasis on laws and system-building gradually led to a rejection of the earlier view of man in society as a self-aware and highly rational being making free and consciously considered choices. There emerged a new emphasis, in keeping with the determinist implications of Darwinism and Freudian psychology, on the limited nature of the individual's freedom in social action. One is struck too by the extent to which sociologists such as Pareto and Weber found that, as far as laws exist, they must often be related to the emotional and non-rational behaviour of human beings rather than to their consciously rational actions.

Apart from the role of positivism, many other tendencies contributed in varying degrees to the growth of sociology in the late nineteenth century and early 1900s. On the model of Darwinism, it was widely held that society should be properly conceived of as an evolving organism. In psychology the study of groups increased. Marx was another major influence, and the accelerating pace of industrialization and urbanization throughout the nineteenth century focused attention on the nature and function of classes within society and on the relationship of economic and political problems to the wider social structure.

It is against this rapidly expanding intellectual background that the foundations of modern sociology were laid. In the selections which follow representative passages have been chosen from three of the main pioneers: Durkheim, Pareto and Max Weber.

FURTHER READING

Two essential books which trace the late nineteenth-century development of social thought and emphasize the roles of Durkheim, Pareto and Weber are: Talcott Parsons, *The Structure of Social Action*, New York, Free Press of Glencoe, 1949, and S. Hughes, *Consciousness and Society*, New York, Vintage Books, 1958.

17 Durkheim

Emile Durkheim (1858–1917) was born in Alsace and studied philosophy at the Ecole Normale Supérieure in Paris. In 1887 a lectureship in sociology was created for him in the University of Bordeaux where he later occupied a chair of sociology (the first in France) before moving back to Paris and the Sorbonne. One significant reason for his change from philosophy to sociology was his conviction that philosophy was too abstract an intellectual study. He had been much influenced by the 'scientific' positivism of Comte and set out to apply 'the principle of causality' to social phenomena in the belief that social relationships can and must be scrutinized by objective, scientific methods (hence his use of organized statistical methods – however unsophisticated these may be by current standards). One consequence of this positivist inheritance is seen, in passage (a) below, in his insistence that social facts must be regarded as 'things', though this is a position that he had – at least unconsciously – abandoned towards the end of his life. It was this same positivist emphasis which led him, like Pareto, to deny the scientific validity of much of Marx's theory.

Durkheim's well-known concept of 'collective consciousness' ('la conscience collective'), by which he meant groups of ideas or symbols that are widely accepted and effective in a given society, suggests that his sociology was often more scientific or mechanistic in intention than in fact. Indeed, he emphasized the role of moral values in society, as in his idea of anomy (anomie). *This is the phenomenon of social disequilibrium resulting from the overthrow of a previously accepted hierarchy of values which Durkheim discusses in passage* (b) *below. Where, for example, individual suicide is brought about by anomy it may be prompted by a sudden change in marital or economic status (e.g. sudden prosperity or sudden poverty may equally well lead to suicide). The wider application of the idea of anomy obviously has a great deal of relevance to the rapidly changing social patterns which we witness today.*

The main publications of Durkheim are a book on method, 'The Rules of Sociological Method' (first published in French, 'Les Règles de la méthode sociologique', 1895) and three books on particular problems: moral aspects of the division of labour in 'The Division of Labour in Society' ('De la division du travail social', 1893); the question of suicide in 'Suicide: a Study in Sociology' ('Le Suicide: étude de sociologie', 1897); the social significance of religion in 'The Elementary Forms of the Religious Life' ('Les Formes élémentaires de la vie religieuse', 1912).

(a) From *The Rules of Sociological Method*, ch. 2

Ethical theory is limited merely to a few discussions on the idea of duty, the good and right. And even these abstract speculations do not constitute a science, strictly speaking, since their object is the determination not of that which is, in fact, the supreme rule of morality but of what it ought to be. Similarly, economists are today principally occupied with the problem of whether society *ought to* be organized on an individualistic or socialistic basis, whether it is *better* that the state should intervene in industrial and commercial relations, or whether it is *better* to abandon them to private initiative; whether one ought to use a single monetary standard, or a bimetallic system, etc. It contains few laws in the proper sense of the word; even what are commonly called 'laws' are generally unworthy of this designation since they are merely maxims for action, or practical precepts in disguise. The famous law of supply and demand, for example, has never been inductively established, as should be the case with a law referring to economic reality. No experiment or systematic comparison has ever been undertaken for the purpose of establishing that, *in fact*, economic relations *do* conform to this law. All that these economists could do, and actually did do, was to demonstrate by dialectics that, in order properly to promote their interests, individuals ought to proceed according to this law, and that every other line of action would be harmful to those who engage in it and would imply a serious error of judgement. It is fair and logical that the most productive industries should be the most attractive and that the holders of the products most in demand and most scarce should sell them at the highest prices. But this quite logical necessity resembles in no way the necessity that the true laws of nature present. The latter express the regulations according to which facts are really inter-connected, not the way in which it is good that they should be inter-connected.

What we say of this law may be repeated for all those that orthodox economics designates as 'natural' and which, moreover, are scarcely more than particular cases of it. They are natural, if one likes, in the sense that they enunciate the means which it is really or seemingly natural to employ in order to attain a certain hypothetical end, but they do not deserve this designation if natural law means an inductively determined way of behaviour in nature. In brief, they are merely maxims of practical wisdom; and they have been more or less plausibly presented as the very expression of reality only because it was supposed, rightly or wrongly, that these counsels were indeed followed by the average man in the average case.

In spite of all these doctrines, social phenomena are things and ought to be treated as things. To demonstrate this proposition, it is un-necessary to philosophize on their nature and to discuss the analogies they present with the phenomena of lower realms of existence. It is sufficient to note that they are the unique data of the sociologist. All that is given, all that is subject to observation, has thereby the character of a thing. To treat phenomena as things is to treat them as data, and these constitute the point of departure of science. Now, social pheno-mena present this character incontestably. What is given is not the idea that men form of value, for that is inaccessible, but only the values established in the course of economic relations; not conceptions of the moral ideal, but the totality of rules which actually determine conduct; not the idea of utility or wealth, but all the details of economic organiza-tion. Even assuming the possibility that social life is merely the develop-ment of certain ideas, these ideas are nevertheless not immediately given. They cannot be perceived or known directly, but only through the phenomenal reality expressing them. We do not know *a priori* whether ideas form the basis of the diverse currents of social life, nor what they are. Only after having traced these currents back to their sources shall we know whence they issue.

We must, therefore, consider social phenomena in themselves as distinct from the consciously formed representations of them in the mind; we must study them objectively as external things, for it is this character that they present to us. If this exteriority should prove to be only apparent, the advance of science will bring the disillusionment and we shall see our conception of social phenomena change, as it were, from the objective to the subjective. But in any case, the solution cannot be anticipated; and even if we finally arrive at the result that social phenomena do not possess all the intrinsic characteristics of the thing, we ought at first to treat them as if they had. This rule is applicable, then, to all social reality without exception. Even phenomena which give the strongest impression of being arbitrary arrangements ought to be thus considered. *The voluntary character of a practice or an institution should never be assumed beforehand.* Moreover, if we may introduce our personal observation, it has always been our experience that, when this procedure is followed, facts most arbitrary in appearance will come to present, after more attentive observation, qualities of consistency and regularity that are symptomatic of their objectivity.

(*b*) From *Suicide: a Study in Sociology*, Bk II, ch. 5

It would be of little use for everyone to recognize the justice of the hierarchy of functions established by public opinion, if he did not also consider the distribution of these functions just. The workman is not in harmony with his social position if he is not convinced that he has his deserts. If he feels justified in occupying another, what he has would not satisfy him. So it is not enough for the average level of needs for each social condition to be regulated by public opinion, but another, more precise rule, must fix the way in which these conditions are open to individuals. There is no society in which such regulation does not exist. It varies with times and places. Once it regarded birth as the almost exclusive principle of social classification; today it recognizes no other inherent inequality than hereditary fortune and merit. But in all these various forms its object is unchanged. It is also only possible, everywhere, as a restriction upon individuals imposed by superior authority, that is, by collective authority. For it can be established only by requiring of one or another group of men, usually of all, sacrifices and concessions in the name of the public interest.

Some, to be sure, have thought that this moral pressure would become unnecessary if men's economic circumstances were only no longer determined by heredity. If inheritance were abolished, the argument runs, if everyone began life with equal resources and if the competitive struggle were fought out on a basis of perfect equality, no one could think its results unjust. Each would instinctively feel that things are as they should be.

Truly, the nearer this ideal equality were approached, the less social restraint will be necessary. But it is only a matter of degree. One sort of heredity will always exist, that of natural talent. Intelligence, taste, scientific, artistic, literary or industrial ability, courage and manual dexterity are gifts received by each of us at birth, as the heir to wealth receives his capital or as the nobleman formerly received his title and function. A moral discipline will therefore still be required to make those less favoured by nature accept the lesser advantages which they owe to the chance of birth. Shall it be demanded that all have an equal share and that no advantage be given those more useful and deserving? But then there would have to be a discipline far stronger to make these accept a treatment merely equal to that of the mediocre and incapable.

But like the one first mentioned, this discipline can be useful only if considered just by the peoples subject to it. When it is maintained only by custom and force, peace and harmony are illusory; the spirit of unrest and discontent are latent; appetites superficially restrained are ready to revolt. This happened in Rome and Greece when the faiths underlying the old organization of the patricians and plebians were shaken, and in our modern societies when aristocratic prejudices began to lose their old ascendancy. But this state of upheaval is exceptional; it occurs only when society is passing through some abnormal crisis. In normal conditions the collective order is regarded as just by the great majority of persons. Therefore, when we say that an authority is necessary to impose this order on individuals, we certainly do not mean that violence is the only means of establishing it. Since this regulation is meant to restrain individual passions, it must come from a power which dominates individuals; but this power must also be obeyed through respect, not fear.

It is not true, then, that human activity can be released from all restraint. Nothing in the world can enjoy such a privilege. All existence being a part of the universe is relative to the remainder; its nature and method of manifestation accordingly depend not only on itself but on other beings, who consequently restrain and regulate it. Here there are only differences of degree and form between the mineral realm and the thinking person. Man's characteristic privilege is that the bond he accepts is not physical but moral; that is, social. He is governed not by a material environment brutally imposed on him, but by a conscience superior to his own, the superiority of which he feels. Because the greater, better part of his existence transcends the body, he escapes the body's yoke, but is subject to that of society.

But when society is disturbed by some painful crisis or by beneficent but abrupt transitions, it is momentarily incapable of exercising this influence; thence come the sudden rises in the curve of suicides which we have pointed out above.

In the case of economic disasters, indeed, something like a declassification occurs which suddenly casts certain individuals into a lower state than their previous one. Then they must reduce their requirements, restrain their needs, learn greater self-control. All the advantages of social influence are lost so far as they are concerned; their moral education has to be recommenced. But society cannot adjust them instantaneously to this new life and teach them to practise the increased self-repression to which they are unaccustomed. So they are not adjusted to the condition forced on them, and its very prospect is intolerable; hence the suffering which detaches them from a reduced existence even before they have made trial of it.

It is the same if the source of the crisis is an abrupt growth of power and wealth. Then, truly, as the conditions of life are changed, the standard according to which needs were regulated can no longer remain the same; for it varies with social resources, since it largely determines the share of each class of producers. The scale is upset; but a new scale cannot be immediately improvised. Time is required for the public conscience to reclassify men and things. So long as the social forces thus freed have not regained equilibrium, their respective values are unknown and so all regulation is lacking for a time. The limits are unknown between the possible and the impossible, what is just and what is unjust, legitimate claims and hopes and those which are immoderate. Consequently, there is no restraint upon aspirations. If the disturbance is profound, it affects even the principles controlling the distribution of men among various occupations. Since the relations between various parts of society are necessarily modified, the ideas expressing these relations must change. Some particular class especially favoured by the crisis is no longer resigned to its former lot, and, on the other hand, the example of its greater good fortune arouses all sorts of jealousy below and about it. Appetites, not being controlled by a public opinion become disoriented, no longer recognize the limits proper to them. Besides, they are at the same time seized by a sort of natural erethism simply by

the greater intensity of public life. With increased prosperity desires
increase. At the very moment when traditional rules have lost their
authority, the richer prize offered these appetites stimulates them and
makes them more exigent and impatient of control. The state of de-
regulation or anomy is thus further heightened by passions being less
disciplined, precisely when they need more disciplining.

FURTHER READING

Useful books in English on Durkheim include: C. E. Gehlke, *Emile
Durkheim's Contributions to Sociological Theory*, Columbia University
Press, 1915; H. Alpert, *Emile Durkheim and his Sociology*, New York,
Russell & Russell, 1961; R. A. Nisbet, *Emile Durkheim*, Prentice-Hall
(Spectrum Books), 1965.

18 Pareto

*In contrast to both Durkheim and Max Weber, Vilfredo Pareto (1848–1923)
has been called 'the great rationalizer of authoritarian conservatism in our
time'. He was born in Paris, where his father was living in exile, but the
family returned to their native Italy in the mid-1850s. As a young man
Pareto studied mathematics and physics, becoming a railway engineer and,
subsequently, a businessman. He took up the study of classics, philosophy and
politics, and his learning was impressively wide-ranging when he succeeded
Walras as Professor of Political Economy at Lausanne in 1893. His encyclopaedic knowledge was put to particularly effective use when, relatively late in
life, he began publishing work on sociology.*

*As an economic theorist in Lausanne Pareto achieved distinction, if not
genuine originality, by his application of mathematics to political economy
(e.g. in his 'Cours d'économie politique' of 1896). He was a political radical at
this time and became a keen dreyfusard during the Affair in France. And yet,
within a few years, he had moved to a sophisticated anti-left-wing position.
His two-volume 'Les Systèmes socialistes' (1902) is a major attack on Marxist
economics and sociology. While a number of its arguments are not now
generally accepted, Pareto's emphasis on the subjective element underlying
ostensibly 'logical' social doctrines – and his general theory of the social utility
of myths – remain important (see passage (a) below). Later, for example in the
'Manuale di economia politica' (1906), he made further refinements in the
distinction between logical (i.e. rational) and non-logical (i.e. non-rational,*

but not illogical) action, underlining the deep-seated human tendency to make non-logical behaviour appear logical.

In his major work, the 'Tratto di sociologia generale' (1916) which is usually referred to in English as the 'Treatise' and has been translated under the title 'The Mind and Society', Pareto continued to develop these ideas and analysed various residues – *non-logical human impulses and attitudes* – *and what he called* derivations – *the pseudo-logical form given to these residues. These analyses, together with the sceptical spirit which they presuppose, represent one of his chief contributions to social analysis. The same sceptical spirit is never far removed from his cyclical theory of social change and his study of what he termed 'the circulation of élites' (see passage (b) below). Among his later works 'Fatti e Theorie' (1920) and 'Transformazione della Democrazia' (1921) are important.*

(a) From *Les Systèmes Socialistes*, I

Given the conditions in which an individual lives, certain opinions can be expected of him; nevertheless he may not be aware of this relationship between his opinions and his circumstances, and will seek to justify the former on quite different grounds. Many people who are socialists are not socialists because they have been persuaded by a particular line of reasoning; quite the reverse: they acquiesce in this line of reasoning because they are socialists.

The sources of men's illusions about the motives determining their behaviour are manifold. A main one lies in the fact that a very large number of human actions are not the outcome of reasoning. They are purely instinctive actions, although the man performing them experiences a feeling of pleasure in giving them, quite arbitrarily, logical causes. He is, generally speaking, not very exacting as to the soundness of this logic, and is very easily satisfied by a semblance of rationality. Nevertheless, he would feel very uncomfortable if there were lacking a smattering of logic. . . .

The diffusion of a doctrine depends hardly at all on its logical value. Quite the contrary; and any one trying to assess the social effects of a doctrine according to its logical value would expose himself to enormous errors.

It is not thus that the phenomenon is reflected in the awareness of men. When they feel drawn by certain religious, moral or humanitarian movements, human beings believe – and almost all of them entirely in good faith – that their convictions have been formed by a series of strict syllogisms deriving from real and incontestable facts. We shall guard against falling prey to this illusion, and shall make every effort to reveal its origins. This enquiry will frequently impress on us the fact that economic factors modify social institutions and doctrines, and as such are reflected in the awareness of men, as is claimed by the materialist theory of history. But frequently we shall also find that there are other factors which are not reducible, at least in the present state of our knowledge, to purely economic categories.

The materialist theory of history, indeed, has its point of departure in a principle which is true; but it errs in trying to claim too much: a claim taking it beyond the conclusions which are legitimately derivable from experience. This tendency to claim too much is, it seems, natural to the human mind, for a similar defect is to be found in the theory of Malthus, in Ricardo's theory of rent, and in many other theories. It is only by successive rectifications and by pruning away propositions which are found to be false that the truth is reached.

Human beings habitually make all their actions dependent on a small number of rules of conduct in which they have a religious faith. It is inevitable that this should be so, for the great mass of men possess neither the character nor the intelligence necessary for them to be capable of relating these actions to their real causes. Indeed, even the most intelligent men are obliged to condense their rules of conduct into a few axioms for, when one has to act, there really is not time for indulging in long and theoretical deliberations.

Yet the causes of social phenomena are enormously greater in number and variety than the small number of religious or other axioms which are posited. The desire – indeed it is an obligation – to relate all one's behaviour to these axioms necessarily leads to assigning fictive causes for one's conduct; hence, among other consequences, the need for a casuistry. Social life makes it impossible to accept all the logical consequences of the principles one seeks to respect. A way therefore must be found for interpreting these principles in such a way that their consequences do not conflict with the circumstances of real life. A certain principle X, in which individuals have a religious faith, has – let us say – as its logical consequences the actions M, N, etc., which are useful to society; and also other actions, P, Q etc., which would clash too strongly with the conditions of social life. To deny X in order to avoid P, Q, etc. is generally a bad way out, for X would inevitably be replaced by Z, and this might have logical consequences worse than P, Q, etc. The dilemma is usually resolved by giving a few gentle twists to logic in such a way as to exclude P, Q, etc., from the consequences of X.

This is the task of casuists and exegetists. If judged from the viewpoint of logic, it has no value at all; but judged from the viewpoint of practical life, it is indispensable, and in fact is seen to have been operative at all times. At a certain stage in the evolution of Graeco-Roman polytheism, the attempt was made, by elaborate feats of interpretation, to reconcile a purified morality with the legendary crimes of the gods. When Christianity experienced an enormous increase of proselytes in the Roman world, it had to make considerable efforts to reconcile precepts, which were obviously relevant solely to people in very humble stations of life, with the conditions of life in a society embracing the rich and the powerful. Socialism in its turn is now beginning to enter this phase.

(b) From *Manuale di economia politica*, ch. 2

Human society is not homogeneous; it is made up of elements which differ to a greater or lesser degree, not only in respect to very obvious characteristics – like sex, age, physical strength, health, etc. – but also in respect to less obvious but no less important characteristics – like intellectual and moral qualities, energy, courage, etc. The assertion that men are objectively equal is so patently absurd that it is not worth refuting. On the other hand, the subjective idea of human equality is a fact of great importance and one which has a powerful influence in determining the changes which occur in society.

Just as one can distinguish the rich and the poor in a society, even though incomes may show an almost imperceptible increase as one traces them upwards from the very lowest to the very highest, so one can distinguish the élite in a society – the aristocratic groups (in the etymological sense of the word, i.e., 'best') – and the commonalty. But it must always be remembered that these groups imperceptibly merge into one another.

The notion of an élite is governed by the qualities which are looked for in it. There can be an aristocracy of saints or an aristocracy of brigands, an aristocracy of the learned, an aristocracy of the criminal and so on. The totality of qualities promoting the well-being and domination of a class in society constitutes something which we will call simply *the élite*.

This élite exists in all societies and governs them even in cases where the regime in appearance is highly democratic. In conformity with a law which is of great importance and is the principal explanation of many social and historical factors, these aristocracies do not last but are continually renewed. This phenomenon may be called *the circulation of élites*. . . .

Let us suppose there is a society in which a dominant section, A, and a subject section, B, are hostile to one another. Both could appear as they really are. But more often than not it will be the case that the dominant group will want to appear to be acting for the common good, hoping thus to reduce the opposition of the subject group. This latter, on the other hand, will frankly stake its claim to the advantages it is seeking.

The situation is similar when the two sections are of different nationalities; for example, English and Irish, Russians and Poles. The phenomenon becomes more complex in a society which has a national homogeneity or – which amounts to the same thing – is considered to have such homogeneity by its members.

In such a society, there emerges between the two hostile sections, A and B, a third section, C, which has links with both and may be found sometimes on one side and sometimes on the other. Eventually section A splits into two groups: one group – which we will call A^1 – has still enough strength to defend its portion of authority; the other group – A^2 – consists of degenerate individuals, weak in intelligence and will: in our day they are called humanitarians. Similarly section B splits in two. One group – B^1 – constitutes the new nascent aristocracy; it receives elements from A who, out of greed and ambition, betray their own class and put themselves at the head of its adversaries. The other group of B – B^2 – comprises the common mass which forms the largest section in human society . . . .

The degenerate element in the élite, the A^2, is the real victim of the deception, and it is made to go where it would not. The mass of the people, the B^2, often end up by gaining something, either during the conflict or when it has a change of masters. The élite of the old aristocracy, the A^1, is not deceived: it succumbs to force. The new aristocracy is victorious.

The work of the humanitarians in eighteenth-century France paved the way for the slaughter of the Terror. The work of liberals in the first half of the nineteenth century paved the way for that era of demagogic oppression which is now dawning. Those who demanded the equality of all citizens before the law certainly did not envisage the privileges the masses now enjoy. The old special jurisdictions have been suppressed, but the same thing in a new form is being instituted: a system of arbitration which operates always in favour of the workers. Those who demanded the freedom to strike did not imagine that this freedom, for the strikers, would consist of beating up workers who want to continue working, and of burning down factories with impunity. Those who sought equal taxation to help the poor did not imagine that it would lead to progressive taxation at the expense of the rich, and to a system in which taxes are voted by those who do not pay them – a system of such a kind as to encourage people to advance unblushingly the following style of argument: 'Such-and-such tax only hits rich people, and it will go to meet expenditure of benefit only to the less fortunate; it will be sure to find favour with the majority of the electors.'

The ingenuous people who, in some countries, have disorganised the army in their obsession with high-sounding phrases about justice and equality, become astounded and indignant at the growth of anti-militarism, and yet they are the begetters of it. They have not the wit to realise that as a man sows so shall he reap.

The great error of the present age is of believing that men can be governed by pure reasoning, without resort to force. Yet force is the foundation of all social organisation. It is interesting to note that the antipathy of the contemporary bourgeoisie to force results in giving a free hand to violence. Criminals and rioters, their impunity assured, do more or less as they like. The most peaceable people form combinations and have recourse to threats and violence, compelled thereto by governments which leave open to them no other way of defending their interests.

The humanitarian religion will very probably disappear when its work of social dissolution is accomplished and when a new élite has arisen from the ruins of the old. This religion, which has nothing more to it than the naïve imperception of a bourgeoisie in decadence, will be of no further use from the day when the enemies of the bourgeoisie become strong enough not to need to hide their hand any more. The best among them have already reached this stage. Syndicalism is here and now giving us an insight into what is likely to be the strength and dignity of the new élite. One of the most remarkable works of our epoch is Georges Sorel's *Réflexions sur la violence*. In its utter rejection of the meaningless declamations of humanitarianism and its entry into the realm of scientific reality, it anticipates the future.

FURTHER READING

An early study is: G. C. Homans and C. P. Curtis, *An Introduction to Pareto*, Knopf, 1934. There is an excellent expository essay on Pareto's thought in *Pareto: Sociological Writings selected and introduced by S. E. Finer*, Pall Mall Press, 1966.

19 Weber

It is usual to regard Max Weber (1864–1920) as the co-founder, with Durkheim, of modern sociology. However, whereas Durkheim grew up in the French positivist tradition, Weber was a product of German idealism with its emphasis on spiritual values and its distrust of the material world. Weber was born at Erfurt and studied legal and economic history (he maintained throughout his writings a strong historical sense which Durkheim largely lacked). He taught economics in the universities of Berlin, Freiburg and Heidelberg. It was only towards the end of his life, first in Vienna and later in Munich (where he died), that he taught sociology.

In his 'Methodology of the Social Sciences' (first published in German, 1922) Weber emphasized the differences between scientific and humane studies. He placed sociology in the latter category, insisted that 'moral indifference' is not to be confused with 'scientific objectivity', and gave an important role to sympathetic understanding and evaluative procedures in the study of social phenomena. Indeed, knowledge of the meaning of an activity is a prerequisite to any causal correlation of facts. In view of his general attitude to the analysis of society it is not surprising that some of Weber's most important work was done in the sphere of religion. He wrote generally on the sociology of religion and produced separate works on the religions of India and China. Probably his best-known book – the first of this series of studies of religion – is 'The Protestant Ethic and the Spirit of Capitalism' (first published in German, 1904–5) in which, as against the exclusiveness of Marxist economic determinism, he showed the importance of religious and ethical ideas in any study of historical causation. He explained the identification of spiritual salvation with business success in order to point to the creative contribution (not a direct causal connection) of the consequences of the Reformation to the capitalist spirit.

Weber also wrote on the sociology of the city, but his other single major work is the posthumously edited 'Wirtschaft und Gesellschaft' in two volumes of which the first has been translated as 'The Theory of Social and Economic Organization'. Among the many subjects discussed are bureaucratic government (see (a) below) and the nature of charismatic authority (see (b) below) – two topics on which Weber's views have become particularly well known.

(*a*) From *Wirtschaft und Gesellschaft*, II, ch. 9, § 2

The decisive reason for the advance of bureaucratic organization has always been its purely technical superiority over any other form of organization. The fully developed bureaucratic mechanism compares with other organizations exactly as does the machine with the non-mechanical modes of production.

Precision, speed, unambiguity, knowledge of the files, continuity, discretion, unity, strict subordination, reduction of friction and of material and personal costs – these are raised to the optimum point in the strictly bureaucratic administration, and especially in its monocratic form. As compared with all collegiate, honorific, and avocational forms of administration, trained bureaucracy is superior on all these points. And as far as complicated tasks are concerned, paid bureaucratic work is not only more precise but, in the last analysis, it is often cheaper than even formally unremunerated honorific service.

Honorific arrangements make administrative work an avocation and, for this reason alone, honorific service normally functions more slowly; being less bound to schemata and being more formless. Hence it is less precise and less unified than bureaucratic work because it is less dependent upon superiors and because the establishment and exploitation of the apparatus of subordinate officials and filing services are almost unavoidably less economical. Honorific service is less continuous than bureaucratic and frequently quite expensive. This is especially the case if one thinks not only of the money costs to the public treasury – costs which bureaucratic administration, in comparison with administration by notables, usually substantially increases – but also of the frequent economic losses of the governed caused by delays and lack of precision. The possibility of administration by notables normally and permanently exists only where official management can be satisfactorily discharged as an avocation. With the qualitative increase of tasks the administration has to face, administration by notables reaches its limits – today, even in England. Work organized by collegiate bodies causes friction and delay and requires compromises between colliding interests and views. The administration, therefore, runs less precisely and is more independent of superiors; hence, it is less unified and slower. All advances of the Prussian administrative organization have been and will in the future be advances of the bureaucratic, and especially of the monocratic, principle.

Today, it is primarily the capitalist market economy which demands

THE STUDY OF SOCIETY

that the official business of the administration be discharged precisely, unambiguously, continuously, and with as much speed as possible. Normally, the very large, modern capitalist enterprises are themselves unequalled models of strict bureaucratic organization. Business management throughout rests on increasing precision, steadiness, and, above all, the speed of operations. This, in turn, is determined by the peculiar nature of the modern means of communication, including, among other things, the news service of the press. The extraordinary increase in the speed by which public announcements, as well as economic and political facts, are transmitted exerts a steady and sharp pressure in the direction of speeding up the tempo of administrative reaction towards various situations. The optimum of such reaction time is normally attained only by a strictly bureaucratic organization.

Bureaucratization offers above all the optimum possibility for carrying through the principle of specializing administrative functions according to purely objective considerations. Individual performances are allocated to functionaries who have specialized training and who by constant practice learn more and more. The 'objective' discharge of business primarily means a discharge of business according to *calculable rules* and 'without regard for persons'.

'Without regard for persons' is also the watchword of the 'market' and, in general, of all pursuits of naked economic interests. A consistent execution of bureaucratic domination means the levelling of status 'honour'. Hence, if the principle of the free-market is not at the same time restricted, it means the universal domination of the 'class situation'. That this consequence of bureaucratic domination has not set in everywhere, parallel to the extent of bureaucratization, is due to the differences among possible principles by which polities may meet their demands.

The second element mentioned, 'calculable rules', also is of paramount importance for modern bureaucracy. The peculiarity of modern culture, and specifically of its technical and economic basis, demands this very 'calculability' of results. When fully developed, bureaucracy also stands, in a specific sense, under the principle of *sine ira ac studio*. Its specific nature, which is welcomed by capitalism, develops the more perfectly the more the bureaucracy is 'dehumanized', the more completely it succeeds in eliminating from official business love, hatred, and all purely personal, irrational, and emotional elements which escape calculation. This is the specific nature of bureaucracy and it is appraised as its special virtue.

137

The more complicated and specialized modern culture becomes, the more its external supporting apparatus demands the personally detached and strictly 'objective' *expert*, in lieu of the master of older social structures, who was moved by personal sympathy and favour, by grace and gratitude. Bureaucracy offers the attitudes demanded by the external apparatus of modern culture in the most favourable combination. As a rule, only bureaucracy has established the foundation for the administration of a rational law conceptually systematized on the basis of such enactments as the latter Roman imperial period first created with a high degree of technical perfection. During the Middle Ages, this law was received along with the bureaucratization of legal administration, that is to say, with the displacement of the old trial procedure which was bound to tradition or to irrational presuppositions, by the rationally trained and specialized expert.

(b) From *Wirtschaft und Gesellschaft*, II, ch. 9 § 5

Bureaucratic and patriarchal structures are antagonistic in many ways, yet they have in common a most important peculiarity: permanence. In this respect they are both institutions of daily routine. Patriarchal power especially is rooted in the provisioning of recurrent and normal needs of the workaday life. Patriarchal authority thus has its original locus in the economy, that is, in those branches of the economy that can be satisfied by means of normal routine. The patriarch is the 'natural leader' of the daily routine. And in this respect, the bureaucratic structure is only the counter-image of patriarchalism transposed into rationality. As a permanent structure with a system of rational rules, bureaucracy is fashioned to meet calculable and recurrent needs by means of a normal routine.

The provisioning of all demands that go beyond those of everyday routine has had, in principle, an entirely heterogeneous, namely, a *charismatic*, foundation; the further back we look in history, the more we find this to be the case. This means that the 'natural' leaders – in times of psychic, physical, economic, ethical, religious, political distress – have been neither officeholders nor incumbents of an 'occupation' in the present sense of the word, that is, men who have acquired expert knowledge and who serve for remuneration. The natural leaders in distress have been holders of specific gifts of the body and spirit; and these gifts have been believed to be supernatural, not accessible to everybody. The concept of 'charisma' is here used in a completely 'value-neutral' sense . . . .

The charismatic leader gains and maintains authority solely by proving his strength in life. If he wants to be a prophet, he must perform miracles; if he wants to be a war lord, he must perform heroic deeds. Above all, however, his divine mission must 'prove' itself in that those who faithfully surrender to him must fare well. If they do not fare well, he is obviously not the master sent by the gods.

This very serious meaning of genuine charisma evidently stands in radical contrast to the convenient pretensions of present rulers to a 'divine right of kings', with its reference to the 'inscrutable' will of the Lord, 'to whom alone the monarch is responsible'. The genuinely charismatic ruler is responsible precisely to those whom he rules. He is responsible for but one thing, that he personally and actually be the God-willed master.

During these last decades we have witnessed how the Chinese monarch impeaches himself before all the people because of his sins and insufficiencies if his administration does not succeed in warding off some distress from the governed, whether it is inundations or unsuccessful wars. Thus does a ruler whose power, even in vestiges and theoretically, is genuinely charismatic deport himself. And if even this penitence does not reconcile the deities, the charismatic emperor faces dispossession and death, which often enough is consummated as a propitiatory sacrifice.

Meng-tse's (Mencius') thesis that the people's voice is 'God's voice' (according to him the *only* way in which God speaks!) has a very specific meaning: if the people cease to recognize the ruler, it is expressly stated that he simply becomes a private citizen; and if he then wishes to be more, he becomes a usurper deserving of punishment. The state of affairs that corresponds to these phrases, which sound highly revolutionary, recurs under primitive conditions without any such pathos. The charismatic character adheres to almost all primitive authorities with the exception of domestic power in the narrowest sense, and the chieftain is often enough simply deserted if success does not remain faithful to him.

The subjects may extend a more active or passive 'recognition' to the personal mission of the charismatic master. His power rests upon this purely factual recognition and springs from faithful devotion. It is devotion to the extraordinary and unheard-of, to what is strange to all rule and tradition and which therefore is viewed as divine. It is a devotion born of distress and enthusiasm.

Genuine charismatic domination therefore knows of no abstract legal

139

codes and statutes and of no 'formal' way of adjudication. Its 'objective' law emanates concretely from the highly personal experience of heavenly grace and from the god-like strength of the hero. Charismatic domination means a rejection of all ties to any external order in favour of the exclusive glorification of the genuine mentality of the prophet and hero. Hence, its attitude is revolutionary and transvalues everything; it makes a sovereign break with all traditional or rational norms: 'It is written, but I say unto you.'

The specifically charismatic form of settling disputes is by way of the prophet's revelation, by way of the oracle, or by way of 'Solomonic' arbitration by a charismatically qualified sage. This arbitration is determined by means of strictly concrete and individual evaluations, which, however, claim absolute validity. Here lies the proper locus of 'Kadi-justice' in the proverbial – not the historical – sense of the phrase. In its actual historical appearance the jurisdiction of the Islamic Kadi is, of course, bound to sacred tradition and is often a highly formalistic interpretation.

Only where these intellectual tools fail does jurisdiction rise to an unfettered individual act valuing the particular case; but then it does indeed. Genuinely charismatic justice always acts in this manner. In its pure form it is the polar opposite of formal and traditional bonds, and it is just as free in the face of the sanctity of tradition as it is in the face of any rationalist deductions from abstract concepts.

FURTHER READING

Two illuminating recent books are: R. Bendix, *Max Weber: an Intellectual Portrait*, Methuen, 1966, and K. Loewenstein, *Max Weber's Political Ideas in the Perspective of our Time*, Univ. of Massachusetts Press, 1966.

V

Religious Thought and the Post-Christian World

Theologians and other religious scholars must necessarily take account of changes and developments in the intellectual life of their times. This has never been more true than in the last hundred years, and as a result of the scientific, philosophical, psychological and social ideas expressed in the preceding four sections of this book. But there are two quite different ways in which the religious thinker may react. He may use the resources of certain contemporary disciplines – archaeology, anthropology, philology, comparative religion, etc. – in order to obtain new insights into the text of the Bible and the whole Judaeo-Christian tradition which it sums up. Such activity has been widespread and continuous since the nineteenth century. In the second place, the theologian (while possibly remaining a biblical scholar) may consider it his chief duty not so much to use modern knowledge for his own ends as to look afresh at his beliefs in the light of this knowledge. He may ask such questions as: what is the meaning of religion in our own age? or, in what way can belief in God remain tenable for twentieth-century man?

It is with this second activity, a questioning of what meaning religious belief can have for themselves and their contemporaries, that the religious thinkers quoted in the following pages have been mainly concerned. Naturally, they have adopted very different approaches and come, with varying emphases, to different conclusions. Thus Teilhard de Chardin, both a Jesuit priest and an authority on evolution, is best known for his discussion of Christianity from the standpoint of 'natural religion' and his attempt to reconcile scientific knowledge with religious values. At what is almost the opposite end of the scale, Karl Barth starts from the standpoint of revelation and his theology proclaims a 'faith by which men live'. Buber, Bultmann and Bonhoeffer all, though again in different ways, write from the standpoint of philosophical enquiry rather than from that of revealed truth. They show something of the influence of Kierkegaard, perhaps even of Pascal, by approaching religious ideas from an existential basis, emphasizing the study of man's situation in the world, underlining the nature of individual experience of the world and discussing ideas of Christian commitment and social concern.

The range of religious thought represented here, beginning with the personalist emphasis of Buber and ending with the 'religionless Christianity' meditated on by Bonhoeffer in a Nazi prison, impresses one by its humanity and its flexibility. Yet apart from Teilhard de Chardin, whose interests and training are rather different, perhaps the most striking and significant feature of these writers is the extent to which they challenge the assumptions of the professing Christian. They have done much to encourage the modesty of the dialogue, rather than the condescension of the sermon, between the theologian and his intellectual contemporary.

FURTHER READING

Good selections of recent theological writing are readily available in W. Herberg (ed), *Four Existentialist Theologians*, New York, Doubleday Anchor, 1958 and J. Bowden and J. Richmond (eds), *A Reader in Contemporary Theology*, SCM Press (SCM Paperbacks), 1967.

Among the many expository works on recent religious thought I would pick out: H. R. Mackintosh, *Types of Modern Theology*, Collins (Fontana Library), 1964 (first published 1937 and stops at Barth); J. Macquarrie, *Twentieth Century Religious Thought*, SCM Press, 1963; J. Macquarrie, *Studies in Christian Existentialism*, SCM Press, 1966; D. Jenkins, *Beyond Religion*, SCM Press, 1962. Two interesting studies of the status of religious belief in the twentieth century are: F. C. Happold, *Religious Faith and Twentieth Century Man*, Penguin Books, 1966 and A. Isaacs, *The Survival of God in the Scientific Age*, Penguin Books, 1966 (a detached presentation of the pros and cons).

20 Buber

The most influential Jewish religious thinker of this century is undoubtedly Martin Buber (1878–1965). Born in Vienna, Buber had a traditionally

Jewish upbringing and education before going on to study philosophy and art history at the universities of Vienna and Berlin. From his student days he was associated with Zionism, in its cultural and spiritual rather than its political forms, and his ideas were expressed in the periodical, 'Der Jude', which he founded and edited from 1916 to 1924. In 1923 he became professor of Jewish religion and ethics at the University of Frankfurt, and in 1938 left Germany to become professor of social philosophy in the Hebrew University of Jerusalem until his retirement in 1951.

Apart from the influence of Hasidism and such early German mystics as Meister Eckhart and Jakob Boehme, Buber acknowledged a particular intellectual debt to Kierkegaard, Dostoevsky and Nietzsche. Among his contemporaries he showed considerable interest in the existentialism of Heidegger and Sartre and the psychological ideas of Jung. At the same time, his own thought is distinctive and unique, finding its first major expression in 'I and Thou' (1923). Here, in what is often a mystical and hermetic manner, Buber distinguishes between the I – Thou (dialogic) and the I – It (instrumental) relationship with others. Authentic being is personalist and the depersonalization of life is evil. Passage (a) below shows Buber's insistence that 'all real living is meeting' and his claim that a real relationship with God grows out of an authentic relationship with other men. What he means by 'being lived in dialogue' is set out in the more discursive terms of 'Between Man and Man' (1947) in passage (b), while passage (c), from the same collection of writings dated between 1929 and 1939, shows him arguing against both individualism and collectivism and in favour of community.

(a) From *I and Thou*

The *Thou* meets me through grace – it is not found by seeking. But my speaking of the primary word to it is an act of my being, is indeed *the* act of my being.

The *Thou* meets me. But I step into direct relation with it. Hence the relation means being chosen and choosing, suffering and action in one; just as any action of the whole being, which means the suspension of all partial actions and consequently of all sensations of actions grounded only in their particular limitation, is bound to resemble suffering.

The primary word *I – Thou* can be spoken only with the whole being. Concentration and fusion into the whole being can never take place through my agency, nor can it ever take place without me. I become through my relation to the *Thou*; as I become *I*, I say *Thou*.

All real living is meeting . . . .

The extended lines of relations meet in the eternal *Thou*.

Every particular *Thou* is a glimpse through to the eternal *Thou*; by means of every particular *Thou* the primary word addresses the eternal *Thou*. Through this mediation of the *Thou* of all beings fulfilment, and non-fulfilment, of relations comes to them: the inborn *Thou* is realised in each relation and consummated in none. It is consummated only in the direct relation with the *Thou* that by its nature cannot become *It*.

Men have addressed their eternal *Thou* with many names. In singing of Him who was thus named they always had the *Thou* in mind: the first myths were hymns of praise. Then the names took refuge in the language of *It*; men were more and more strongly moved to think of and to address their eternal *Thou* as an *It*. But all God's names are hallowed, for in them He is not merely spoken about, but also spoken to.

Many men wish to reject the word God as a legitimate usage, because it is so misused. It is indeed the most heavily laden of all the words used by men. For that very reason it is the most imperishable and most indispensable. What does all mistaken talk about God's being and works (though there has been, and can be, no other talk about these) matter in comparison with the one truth that all men who have addressed God had God Himself in mind? For he who speaks the word God and really has *Thou* in mind (whatever the illusion by which he is held), addresses the true *Thou* of his life, which cannot be limited by another *Thou*, and to which he stands in a relation that gathers up and includes all others.

But when he, too, who abhors the name, and believes himself to be godless, gives his whole being to addressing the *Thou* of his life, as a *Thou* that cannot be limited by another, he addresses God.

(b) From 'Dialogue' in *Between Man and Man*

Responsibility which does not respond to a word is a metaphor of morality. Factually, responsibility only exists when the court is there to which I am responsible, and 'self-responsibility' has reality only when the 'self' to which I am responsible becomes transparent into the absolute. But he who practices real responsibility in the life of dialogue does not need to name the speaker of the word to which he is responding – he knows him in the word's substance which presses on and in, assuming the cadence of an inwardness, and stirs him in his heart of hearts. A man can ward off with all his strength the belief that 'God' is there, and he tastes him in the strict sacrament of dialogue.

Yet let it not be supposed that I make morality questionable in order to glorify religion. Religion, certainly, has this advantage over morality, that it is a phenomenon and not a postulate, and further that it is able to include composure as well as determination. The reality of morality, the demand of the demander, has a place in religion, but the reality of religion, the unconditioned being of the demander, has no place in morality. Nevertheless, when religion does itself justice and asserts itself, it is much more dubious than morality, just because it is more actual and inclusive. Religion as risk, which is ready to give itself up, is the nourishing stream of the arteries; as system, possessing, assured and assuring, religion which believes in religion is the veins' blood, which ceases to circulate. And if there is nothing that can so hide the face of our fellow-man as morality can, religion can hide from us as nothing else can the face of God. Principle there, dogma here, I appreciate the 'objective' compactness of dogma, but behind both there lies in wait the – profane or holy – war against the situation's power of dialogue, there lies in wait the 'once-for-all' which resists the unforeseeable moment. Dogma, even when its claim of origin remains uncontested, has become the most exalted form of invulnerability against revelation. Revelation will tolerate no perfect tense, but man with the arts of his craze for security props it up to perfectedness. . . .

Being, lived in dialogue, receives even in extreme dereliction a harsh and strengthening sense of reciprocity; being, lived in monologue, will not, even in the tenderest intimacy, grope out over the outlines of the self.

This must not be confused with the contrast between 'egoism' and 'altruism' conceived by some moralists. I know people who are absorbed in 'social activity' and have never spoken from being to being with a fellow-man. I know others who have no personal relation except to their enemies, but stand in such a relation to them that it is the enemies' fault if the relation does not flourish into one of dialogue.

Nor is dialogic to be identified with love. I know no one in any time who has succeeded in loving every man he met. Even Jesus obviously loved of 'sinners' only the loose, lovable sinners, sinners against the Law; not those who were settled and loyal to their inheritance and sinned against him and his message. Yet to the latter as to the former he stood in a direct relation. Dialogic is not to be identified with love. But love without dialogic, without real outgoing to the other, reaching to the other, and companying with the other, the love remaining with itself – this is called Lucifer.

Certainly in order to be able to go out to the other you must have the starting place, you must have been, you must be, with yourself. Dialogue between mere individuals is only a sketch, only in dialogue between persons is the sketch filled in. But by what could a man from being an individual so really become a person as by the strict and sweet experiences of dialogue which teach him the boundless contents of the boundary?

What is said here is the real contrary of the cry, heard at times in twilight ages, for universal unreserve. He who can be unreserved with each passer-by has no substance to lose; but he who cannot stand in a direct relation to each one who meets him has a fullness which is futile.

(c) From 'What is Man' in *Between Man and Man*

Criticism of the individualistic method starts usually from the standpoint of the collectivist tendency. But if individualism understands only a part of man, collectivism understands man only as a part: neither advances to the wholeness of man, to man as a whole. Individualism sees man only in relation to himself, but collectivism does not see *man* at all, it sees only 'society'. With the former man's face is distorted, with the latter it is masked. . . .

The second reaction, collectivism, essentially follows upon the foundering of the first. Here the human being tries to escape his destiny of solitude by becoming completely embedded in one of the massive modern group formations. The more massive, unbroken and powerful in its achievements this is, the more the man is able to feel that he is saved from both forms of homelessness, the social and the cosmic. There is obviously no further reason for dread of life, since one needs only to fit oneself into the 'general will' and let one's own responsibility for an existence which has become all too complicated be absorbed in collective responsibility, which proves itself able to meet all complications. Likewise, there is obviously no further reason for dread of the universe, since technicized nature – with which society as such manages well, or seems to – takes the place of the universe which has become uncanny and with which, so to speak, no further agreement can be reached. The collective pledges itself to provide total security. There is nothing imaginary here, a dense reality rules, and the 'general' itself appears to have become real; but modern collectivism is essentially illusory. The person is joined to the reliably functioning 'whole', which embraces the masses of men; but it is not a joining of man to man. Man in a collective is not man with man. Here the person is not freed from his isolation, by communing with living beings, which thenceforth live with him; the 'whole', with its claim on the wholeness of every man, aims logically and successfully at reducing, neutralizing, devaluating, and desecrating every bond with living beings. That tender surface of personal life which longs for contact with other life is progressively deadened or desensitized. Man's isolation is not overcome here, but overpowered and numbed. Knowledge of it is suppressed, but the actual condition of solitude has its insuperable effect in the depths, and rises secretly to a cruelty which will become manifest with the scattering of the illusion. Modern collectivism is the last barrier raised by man against a meeting with himself.

When imaginings and illusions are over, the possible and inevitable meeting of man with himself is able to take place only as the meeting of the individual with his fellow-man – and this is how it must take place. Only when the individual knows the other in all his otherness as himself, as man, and from there breaks through to the other, has he broken through his solitude in a strict and transforming meeting. . . .

The fundamental fact of human existence is neither the individual as such nor the aggregate as such. Each, considered by itself, is a mighty abstraction. The individual is a fact of existence in so far as he steps into a living relation with other individuals. The aggregate is a fact of existence in so far as it is built up of living units of relation. The fundamental fact of human existence is man with man. What is peculiarly characteristic of the human world is above all that something takes place between one being and another the like of which can be found nowhere in nature. Language is only a sign and a means for it, all achievement of the spirit has been incited by it. Man is made man by it; but on its way it does not merely unfold, it also decays and withers away. It is rooted in one being turning to another as another, as this particular other being, in order to communicate with it in a sphere which is common to them but which reaches out beyond the special sphere of each. I call this sphere, which is established with the existence of man as man but which is conceptually still uncomprehended, the sphere of 'between'. Though being realized in very different degrees, it is a primal category of human reality. This is where the genuine third alternative must begin. . . .

This reality provides the starting-point for the philosophical science of man; and from this point an advance may be made on the one hand to a transformed understanding of the person and on the other to a transformed understanding of community. The central subject of this science is neither the individual nor the collective but man with man. That essence of man which is special to him can be directly known only in a living relation. The gorilla, too, is an individual, a termitary, too is a collective, but *I* and *Thou* exist only in our world, because man exists, and the *I*, moreover, exists only through the relation to the *Thou*. The philosophical science of man, which includes anthropology and sociology, must take as its starting-point the consideration of this subject, 'man with man'. If you consider the individual by himself, then you see of man just as much as you see of the moon; only man with man provides a full image. If you consider the aggregate by itself, then you see of man just as much as we see of the Milky Way; only man with man is a completely outlined form. Consider man with man, and you see human life, dynamic, twofold, the giver and the receiver, he who does and he who endures, the attacking force and the defending force, the nature which investigates and the nature which supplies information, the request begged and granted – and always both together, completing one another in mutual contribution, together showing forth man. Now you can turn to the individual and you recognize him as man according to the possibility of relation which he shows; you can turn to the aggregate and you recognize it as man according to the fullness of relation which he shows. We may come nearer the answer to the question what man is when we come to see him as the eternal meeting of the One with the Other.

21 Teilhard de Chardin

Pierre Teilhard de Chardin (1881–1955), being at once priest, scientist and mystic, has been attacked from many quarters both on grounds of religious heresy and scientific incompetence. Yet he also has his fervent admirers, and his basic enterprise – the reconciliation of the facts of religious experience with the most recent findings of natural science – is important above all as an attempt to reinterpret the cosmic dimension of Christian belief.

Born in the Puy-de-Dôme area of France, Teilhard de Chardin was trained as a palaeontologist and biologist. He travelled widely in various areas including Burma, Java and the Gobi desert, but his main work was done in China, where he played a major role in the discovery of Peking Man in 1929. During the Second World War he was a virtual prisoner in Peking, returned to France for a period after 1946, and moved on to the U.S.A., where he died.

Teilhard de Chardin's thought begins from the naturalistic standpoint of the scientist. He sees the natural world in terms of evolutionary process activated by energy and possessing pattern and direction. He rejects a dualistic outlook, interpreting the physical and the mental as two aspects of a single complex of energy systems. Inevitably, he found it necessary to create certain neologisms to convey his ideas, and four of these may be briefly mentioned. 'Hominization' is that stage in the evolutionary process in which, with man, self-awareness and responsibility develop. By the 'biosphere' he means the network of life which, as it were, clothes the purely physical world, while the 'noosphere' is a kind of mental envelope containing both human beings and the products of the human intellect. Finally, extrapolating from the evolutionary process he posits an eventual 'omega-point' towards which consciousness will further evolve and which he appears to identify with God. As one writer puts it, 'God, on this view, would seem to be the final rather than the efficient cause of the universe, gathering all things into a perfect unity in himself.' All these ideas are set out in Teilhard de Chardin's book, 'The Phenomenon of Man', which was first published in France in 1955. The passage given below comes from an essay of 1949 included in a posthumously published work, 'The Future of Man', which first appeared in France in 1959.

From 'The Heart of the Problem' in *The Future of Man*

Any effort to understand what is now taking place in the human conscience must of necessity proceed from the fundamental change of view which since the sixteenth century has been steadily exploding and rendering fluid what had seemed to be the ultimate stability – our concept of the world itself. To our clearer vision the universe is no longer a State but a Process. The cosmos has become a Cosmogenesis. And it may be said without exaggeration that, directly or indirectly, all the intellectual crises through which civilisation has passed in the last four centuries arise out of the successive stages whereby a static *Weltanschauung* has been and is being transformed, in our minds and hearts, into a *Weltanschauung* of movement.

In the early stage, that of Galileo, it may have seemed that the stars alone were affected. But the Darwinian stage showed that the cosmic process extends from sidereal space to life on earth; with the result that, in the present phase, Man finds himself overtaken and borne on the whirlwind which his own science has discovered and, as it were, unloosed. From the time of the Renaissance, in other words, the cosmos has looked increasingly like a cosmogenesis; and now we find that Man in his turn is identified with an anthropogenesis. This is a major event which must lead, as we shall see, to the profound modification of the whole structure not only of our Thought but of our Beliefs.

Many biologists, and not the least eminent among them (all being convinced that Man, like everything else, emerged by evolutionary means, i.e. was *born* in Nature) undoubtedly still believe that the human species, having attained the level of *Homo sapiens*, has reached an upper organic limit beyond which it cannot develop, so that anthropogenesis is only of retrospective interest. But I am convinced that, in opposition to this wholly illogical and arbitrary idea of arrested hominisation, a new concept is arising, out of the growing accumulation of analogies and facts, which must eventually replace it. This is that, under the combined influence of two irresistible forces of planetary dimensions (the geographical curve of the Earth, by which we are physically compressed, and the psychic curve of Thought, which draws us closer together), the power of reflection of the human mass, which means its degree of *humanisation*, far from having come to a stop, is entering a critical period of intensification and renewed growth.

What we see taking place in the world today is not merely the multiplication of *men* but the continued shaping of *Man*. Man, that is to say, is not yet zoologically mature. Psychologically he has not spoken his last word. In one form or another something ultra-human is being born which, through the direct or indirect effect of socialisation, cannot fail to make its appearance in the near future: a future that is not simply the unfolding of Time, but which is being constructed in advance of us. ... Here is a vision which Man, we may be sure, having first glimpsed it in our day, will never lose sight of.

This being postulated, do those in high places realise the revolutionary power of so novel a concept (it would be better to use the word 'doctrine') in its effect on religious Faith? For the spiritually minded, whether in the East or the West, one point has hitherto not been in doubt: that Man could only attain to a fuller life by rising 'vertically' above the material zones of the world. Now we see the possibility of an entirely different line of progress. The Higher Life, the Union, the long dreamed-of-consummation that has hitherto been sought *Above*, in the direction of some kind of transcendency: should we not rather look for it *Ahead*, in the prolongation of the inherent forces of evolution?

Above or ahead – or both? ....

This is the question that must be forced upon every human conscience by our increasing awareness of the tide of anthropogenesis on which we are borne. It is, I am convinced, the vital question, and the fact that we have thus far left it unconfronted is the root cause of all our religious troubles: whereas an answer to it, which is perfectly possible, would mark a decisive advance on the part of Mankind towards God. That is the heart of the problem. . . .

On the one hand, neo-human faith in the World, to the extent that it is truly a Faith (that is to say, entailing sacrifice and the final abandonment of self for something greater) necessarily implies an element of worship, the acceptance of something 'divine'. Every conversation I have ever had with communist intellectuals has left me with a decided impression that Marxist atheism is not absolute, but that it simply rejects an 'extrinsical' God, a *deus ex machina* whose existence can only undermine the dignity of the Universe and weaken the springs of human endeavour – a 'pseudo-God', in short, whom no one in these days any longer wants, least of all the Christians.

And on the other hand, Christian faith (I stress the word Christian, as opposed to those 'oriental' faiths for which spiritual ascension often expressly signifies the negation or condemnation of the phenomenal world), by the very fact that it is rooted in the idea of Incarnation, has always based a large part of its tenets on the tangible values of the World and of Matter. A too humble and subordinate part, it may seem to us now (but was not this inevitable in the days when Man, not having become aware of the genesis of the Universe in progress, could not apprehend the spiritual possibilities still buried in the entrails of the Earth?) yet still a part so intimately linked with the essence of Christian dogma that, like a living bud, it needed only a sign, a ray of light, to cause it to break into flower. To clarify our ideas let us consider a single case, one which sums up everything. We continue from force of habit to think of the Parousia,[1] whereby the Kingdom of God is to be consummated on Earth, as an event of a purely catastrophic nature – that is to say, liable to come about at any moment in history, irrespective of any definite state of Mankind. But why should we not assume, in accordance with the latest scientific view of Mankind in a state of anthropogenesis, that the parousiac spark can, of physical and organic necessity, only be kindled between Heaven and a Mankind which has biologically reached a certain critical evolutionary point of collective maturity?

For my own part I can see no reason at all, theological or traditional, why this 'revised' approach should give rise to any serious difficulty.

[1] i.e. the Second Coming of Christ. J. C.

And it seems to me certain, on the other hand, that by the very fact of making this simple readjustment in our 'eschatological' vision we shall have performed an operation having incalculable consequences. For if truly, in order that the Kingdom of God may come (in order that the Pleroma[1] may close in upon its fullness), it is necessary, as an essential physical condition, that the human Earth should already have attained the natural completion of its evolutionary growth, then it must mean that the ultra-human perfection which neo-humanism envisages for Evolution will coincide in concrete terms with the crowning of the Incarnation awaited by all Christians. The two vectors, or components as they are better called, veer and draw together until they give a possible resultant. The super-naturalising Christian Upward is incorporated (not immersed) in the human Forward! And at the same time Faith in God, in the very degree in which it assimilates and sublimates within its own spirit the spirit of Faith in the World, regains all its power to attract and convert!

I said at the beginning of this paper that the human world of today has not grown cold, but that it is ardently searching for a God proportionate to the newly discovered immensities of a Universe whose aspect exceeds the present compass of our power of worship. And it is because the total Unity of which we dream still seems to beckon in two different directions, towards the zenith and towards the horizon, that we see the dramatic growth of a whole race of 'spiritual expatriates' – human beings torn between a Marxism whose depersonalising effect revolts them and a Christianity so lukewarm in human terms that it sickens them.

But let there be revealed to us the possibility of believing *at the same time and wholly* in God *and* the World, the one through the other; let this belief burst forth, as it is ineluctably in process of doing under the pressure of these seemingly opposed forces, and then, we may be sure of it, a great flame will illumine all things: for a Faith will have been born (or re-born) containing and embracing all others – and, inevitably, it is the strongest Faith which sooner or later must possess the Earth.

[1] i.e. the fullness or plenitude of the spiritual world. A term used by the Gnostics – the heretical early Christian sect claiming superior knowledge of spiritual things. J. C.

22 Barth

Karl Barth was born at Basel in 1886 and after study in the universities of Berne, Berlin, Tübingen and Marburg he spent a dozen years as a Reformed Church pastor in Switzerland. This pastoral experience, together with the study of such writers as Kierkegaard and Dostoevsky, had a profound effect on his thinking. As a result he broke away completely from the nineteenth-century man-centred type of theology in his teaching at the universities of Göttingen, Münster and Bonn. Having been dismissed from Bonn in 1935 by the Nazi government he took up a post in his native Basel.

Although he no longer wishes it to be regarded as an authoritative source of his theology, Barth's revolutionary position first became clear with the publication of his commentary on the Epistle to the Romans in 1918. The most detailed statement of his ideas is to be found in the various volumes of his 'Church Dogmatics' which have appeared from 1932 onwards. Perhaps his position can be most nearly summed up by saying that he insists on seeing the Christian faith as produced solely by God's action on man, not by man's various attempts to find God. This position leads to the distinction between 'revelation' and 'religion' set out in the passage quoted below. The idea that man can know God through rational speculation is firmly rejected and Barth argues in a way that makes it clear both why he has been an opponent of exis-tential Christianity and a forerunner, in a certain sense, of the religionless Christianity of Bonhoeffer. Apart from his attacks on religion, his 'Christ-ology' is also emphasized by his commentators. He holds that all life must be centred in Christ for it is through Christ that God reveals himself and 'moves towards' man.

From *Church Dogmatics*, I, pt 2

If it is true that God is God and that as such He is the Lord of man, then it is also true that man is so placed towards Him, that he could know Him. But this is the very truth which is not available to man, before it is told him in revelation. If he really can know God, this capacity rests upon the fact that he really does know Him, because God has offered and manifested Himself to him. The capacity, then, does not rest upon the fact, which is true enough, that man could know Him. Between 'he could' and 'he can' there lies the absolutely decisive 'he cannot', which can be removed and turned into its opposite only by revelation. The truth that God is God and our Lord, and the further

truth that we could know Him as God and Lord, can only come to us
through the truth itself. This 'coming to us' of the truth is revelation.
It does not reach us in a neutral condition, but in an action which stands
to it, as the coming of truth, in a very definite, indeed a determinate
relationship. That is to say, it reaches us as religious men; i.e., it reaches
us in the attempt to know God from our standpoint. It does not reach
us, therefore, in the activity which corresponds to it. The activity which
corresponds to revelation would have to be faith; the recognition of the
self-offering and self-manifestation of God. We need to see that in view
of God all our activity is in vain even in the best life; i.e., that of ourselves we are not in a position to apprehend the truth, to let God be
God our Lord. We need to renounce all attempts even to try to apprehend this truth. We need to be ready and resolved simply to let the
truth be told us and therefore to be apprehended by it. But that is the
very thing for which we are not resolved and ready. The man to whom
the truth has really come will concede that he was not at all ready and
resolved to let it speak to him. The genuine believer will not say that he
came to faith from faith, but – from unbelief, even though the attitude
and activity with which he met revelation, and still meets it, is religion.
For in faith, man's religion as such is shown by revelation to be resistance to it. From the standpoint of revelation religion is clearly seen
to be a human attempt to anticipate what God in His revelation wills to
do and does do. It is the attempted replacement of the divine work by a
human manufacture. The divine reality offered and manifested to us in
revelation is replaced by a concept of God arbitrarily and wilfully
evolved by man.

'Arbitrarily and wilfully' means here by his own means, by his own
human insight and constructiveness and energy. Many different images
of God can be formed once we have engaged in this undertaking, but
their significance is always the same.

The image of God is always that reality of perception or thought in
which man assumes and asserts something unique and ultimate and
decisive either beyond or within his own existence, by which he
believes himself to be posited or at least determined and conditioned.
From the standpoint of revelation, man's religion is simply an assumption and assertion of this kind, and as such it is an activity which contradicts revelation – contradicts it, because it is only through truth that
truth can come to man. If man tries to grasp at truth of himself, he
tries to grasp at it *a priori*. But in that case he does not do what he has to
do when the truth comes to him. He does not believe. If he did, he

would listen; but in religion he talks. If he did, he would accept a gift; but in religion he takes something for himself. If he did, he would let God Himself intercede for God: but in religion he ventures to grasp at God. Because it is a grasping, religion is the contradiction of revelation, the concentrated expression of human un-belief, i.e., an attitude and activity which is directly opposed to faith. It is a feeble but defiant, an arrogant but hopeless, attempt to create something which man could do, but now cannot do, or can do only because and if God Himself creates it for him: the knowledge of the attempt as a harmonious co-operating of man with the revelation of God, as though religion were a kind of outstretched hand which is filled by God in His revelation. Again, we cannot say of the evident religious capacity of man that it is, so to speak, the general form of human knowledge, which acquires its true and proper content in the shape of revelation. On the contrary, we have here an exclusive contradiction. In religion man bolts and bars himself against revelation by providing a substitute, by taking away in advance the very thing which has to be given by God.

23 Bultmann

Whereas the theology of Karl Barth was particularly influential between the two world wars, the New Testament studies of Rudolf Bultmann have received a great deal of attention since the Second World War. Bultmann was born at Wiefelstede in Germany in 1884 and came into particular prominence while holding the chair of New Testament studies at the University of Marburg between 1921 and 1951. From an early date he was deeply impressed by the philosophical ideas of Heidegger (see pp. 115–118) and he is a thinker to whom the term 'Christian existentialist' can be legitimately applied. Indeed, he may be said to emphasize above all the contemporary existential relevance of the Christian gospel.

Bultmann recalls Barth in holding that, in the last analysis, man's relationship with God depends on the Christian message addressed to him as a sinner in need of divine grace. This is the idea of kerygma – God's Word proclaimed to man and soliciting the response of faith. But in order that this message may be clear, and clearly understood, Bultmann introduces the second idea of demythologizing. For him the existential truth to be found in the New Testament is obscured by myth – such things as the Virgin Birth, the Empty Tomb or the 'eschatological myth' according to which the world was shortly to end through divine intervention followed by a final judgement. He therefore regards it as his task (making use of Heideggerian terminology on the way) to reinterpret the mythological discourse of the New Testament in terms that will point up its relevance for contemporary man – its essential kerygma. The close relationship between kerygma and demythologizing is set out in the passage below. This relationship is one of the aspects of Bultmann's writing that has been most widely discussed since there is an obvious danger that thoroughgoing demythologizing might result in the destruction of the kerygmatic element. Bultmann's conception of myth has also given rise to a good deal of debate. There are those who would want to argue that Jungian psychology, for example, suggests the presence of more truth in myths as myths than Bultmann seems prepared to allow.

From *Jesus Christ and Mythology*

The whole conception of the world which is presupposed in the preaching of Jesus as in the New Testament generally is mythological; i.e., the conception of the world as being structured in three storeys, heaven, earth and hell; the conception of the intervention of supernatural powers in the cause of events; and the conception of miracles, especially the conception of the intervention of supernatural powers in the inner life of the soul, the conception that men can be tempted and corrupted by the devil and possessed by evil spirits. This conception of the world we call mythological because it is different from the conception of the world which has been formed and developed by science since its inception in ancient Greece and which has been accepted by all modern men. In this modern conception of the world the cause-and-effect nexus is fundamental. Though modern physical theories take account of chance in the chain of cause and effect in subatomic phenomena, our daily living, purposes and actions are not affected. In any case, modern science does not believe that the course of nature can be interpreted, or, so to speak, perforated, by supernatural powers.

The same is true of the modern study of history, which does not take into account any intervention of God or of the devil or of demons in the course of history. Instead, the course of history is considered to be an unbroken whole, complete in itself, though differing from the course of nature because there are in history spiritual powers which influence the will of persons. Granted that not all historical events are determined by physical necessity and that persons are responsible for their actions, nevertheless nothing happens without rational motivation. Otherwise, responsibility would be dissolved. Of course, there are still many superstitions among modern men, but they are exceptions or even anomalies. Modern men take it for granted that the course of nature and of history, like their own inner life and their practical life, is nowhere interrupted by the intervention of supernatural powers.

Then the question inevitably arises: is it possible that Jesus' preaching of the Kingdom of God still has any importance for modern men and the preaching of the New Testament as a whole is still important for modern men? The preaching of the New Testament proclaims Jesus Christ, not only his preaching of the Kingdom of God but first of all his person, which was mythologized from the very beginnings of earliest Christianity. New Testament scholars are at variance as to whether Jesus himself claimed to be the Messiah, the King of the time of blessedness, whether he believed himself to be the Son of Man who would come on the clouds of heaven. If so, Jesus understood himself in the light of mythology. We need not, at this point, decide one way or the other. At any rate, the early Christian community thus regarded him as a mythological figure. It expected him to return as the Son of Man on the clouds of heaven to bring salvation and damnation as judge of the world. His person is viewed in the light of mythology when he is said to have been begotten of the Holy Spirit and born of a virgin, and this becomes clearer still in Hellenistic Christian communities where he is understood to be the Son of God in a metaphysical sense, a great, pre-existent heavenly being who became man for the sake of our redemption and took on himself suffering, even the suffering of the cross. It is evident that such conceptions are mythological, for they were widespread in the mythologies of Jews and Gentiles and then were transferred to the historical person of Jesus. Particularly the conception of the pre-existent Son of God who descended in human guise into the world to redeem mankind is part of the Gnostic doctrine of redemption, and nobody hesitates to call this doctrine mythological. This raises in an acute form the question: *what is the importance of the preaching of Jesus and of the preaching of the New Testament as a whole for modern man?*

For modern man the mythological conception of the world, the conceptions of eschatology, of redeemer and of redemption, are over and done with. Is it possible to expect that we shall make a sacrifice of understanding, *sacrificium intellectus*, in order to accept what we cannot sincerely consider true – namely because such conceptions are suggested by the Bible? Or ought we to pass over those sayings of the New Testament which contain such mythological conceptions and to select other sayings which are not such stumbling-blocks to modern man? In fact, the preaching of Jesus is not confined to eschatological sayings. He proclaimed also the will of God, which is God's demand, the demand for the good. Jesus demands truthfulness and purity, readiness to sacrifice and to love. He demands that the whole man be obedient to God, and he protests against the delusion that one's duty to God can be fulfilled by obeying certain external commandments. If the ethical demands of Jesus are stumbling-blocks to modern man, then it is to his selfish will, not to his understanding, that they are stumbling-blocks.

What follows from all this? Shall we retain the ethical preaching of Jesus and abandon his eschatological preaching? Shall we reduce his preaching of the Kingdom of God to the so-called social gospel? Or is there a third possibility? We must ask whether the eschatological preaching and the mythological sayings as a whole contain a still deeper meaning which is concealed under the cover of mythology. If that is so, let us abandon the mythological conceptions precisely because we want to retain their deeper meaning. This method of interpretation of the New Testament which tries to recover the deeper meaning behind the mythological conceptions I call *de-mythologizing* – an unsatisfactory word, to be sure. Its aim is not to eliminate the mythological statements but to interpret them.

An objection often heard against the attempt to de-mythologize is that it takes the modern world-view as the criterion of the interpretation of the Scripture and the Christian message and that Scripture and Christian message are not allowed to say anything that is in contradiction with the modern world-view.

It is, of course, true that de-mythologizing takes the modern world-view as a criterion. To de-mythologize is to reject not Scripture, or the Christian message as a whole, but the world-view of Scripture, which is the world-view of a past epoch, which all too often is retained in Christian dogmatics and in the preaching of the Church. To de-mythologize is to deny that the message of Scripture and of the Church is bound to an ancient world-view which is obsolete.

The attempt to de-mythologize begins with this important insight: Christian preaching, in so far as it is preaching of the Word of God by God's command and in his name, does not offer a doctrine which can be accepted either by reason or by a *sacrificium intellectus*. Christian preaching is *kerygma*, that is, a proclamation addressed not to the theoretical reason, but to the hearer as a self. In this manner Paul commends himself to every man's conscience in the sight of God

(II Corinthians 4 : 2). De-mythologizing will make clear this function of preaching as a personal message, and in doing so it will eliminate a false stumbling-block and bring into sharp focus the real stumbling-block, the word of the cross.

Thus it follows that the objection is raised by a mistake, namely, the objection that de-mythologizing dissolves the message into a product of human rational thinking, and that the mystery of God is destroyed by de-mythologizing. Not at all! On the contrary, de-mythologizing makes clear the true meaning of God's mystery. The incomprehensibility of God lies not in the sphere of theoretical thought but in the sphere of personal existence.

24 Bonhoeffer

Dietrich Bonhoeffer (1906–45) was born in Breslau and studied theology at the University of Berlin. From an early stage he was influenced by the writings of Karl Barth whom he later described as 'the first theologian to begin the criticism of religion'. Indeed, there is a direct line of development from Barth's distinction between revelation and religion to Bonhoeffer's own conception of 'religionless' Christianity.

After a mixture of study, teaching and pastoral work which took him to New York and London as well as Berlin, Bonhoeffer was forbidden by the Nazis to teach (1936). He continued, however, to take an active part in the struggle of the German Protestant Church against the régime, publishing the two works by which he was best known during his lifetime: 'The Cost of Discipleship' ('Nachfolge', 1937) and 'Life Together' ('Gemeinsames Leben', 1938). In 1939, while on a lecture tour in America, he took the decision to return to Germany despite the imminence of war. He worked on his 'Ethics', posthumously published in unfinished form in 1949, and was also involved in the Resistance movement within Germany. Eventually he was forbidden to write, lecture or make speeches of any kind, was exiled from Berlin and was finally arrested by the Gestapo in April 1943. Almost exactly two years later, after experience of various prisons (including Buchenwald) he was hanged at Flossenbürg in Bavaria.

The passage below, which contains some characteristic thoughts on the question of religionless Christianity, comes from a letter written from prison in 1944.

From a letter of 30 April 1944 in *Letters and Papers from Prison*

The thing that keeps coming back to me is, what *is* Christianity, and indeed what *is* Christ, for us today? The time when men could be told everything by means of words, whether theological or simply pious, is over, and so is the time of inwardness and conscience, which is to say the time of religion as such. We are proceeding towards a time of no religion at all: men as they are now simply cannot be religious any more. Even those who honestly describe themselves as 'religious' do not in the least act up to it, and so when they say 'religious' they evidently mean something quite different. Our whole nineteen-hundred-year-old Christian preaching and theology rests upon the 'religious premise' of man. What we call Christianity has always been a pattern – perhaps a true pattern – of religion. But if one day it becomes apparent that this *a priori* 'premise' simply does not exist, but was an historical and temporary form of human self-expression, i.e. if we reach the stage of being radically without religion – and I think this is more or less the case already, else how is it, for instance, that this war, unlike any of those before it, is not calling forth any 'religious' reaction? – what does that mean for 'Christianity'?

It means that the linchpin is removed from the whole structure of our Christianity to date, and the only people left for us to light on in the way of 'religion' are a few 'last survivals of the age of chivalry', or else one or two who are intellectually dishonest. Would they be the chosen few? Is it on this dubious group and none other that we are to pounce, in fervour, pique, or indignation, in order to sell them goods we have to offer? Are we to fall upon one or two unhappy people in their weakest moment and force upon them a sort of religious coercion?

If we do not want to do this, if we had finally to put down the western pattern of Christianity as a mere preliminary stage to doing without religion altogether, what situation would result for us, for the Church? How can Christ become the Lord even of those with no religion? If religion is no more than the garment of Christianity – and even that garment has had very different aspects at different periods – then what is a religionless Christianity? Barth, who is the only one to have started on this line of thought, has still not proceeded to its logical conclusion, but has arrived at a positivism of revelation which has nevertheless remained essentially a restoration. For the religionless working man, or indeed, man generally, nothing that makes any real difference is gained by that. The questions needing answers would surely be: What is the significance of a Church (church, parish, preaching, Christian life) in a religionless world? How do we speak of God without religion, i.e. without the temporally-influenced presuppositions of metaphysics, inwardness, and so on? How do we speak (but perhaps we are no longer capable of speaking of such things as we used to) in secular fashion of God? In what way are we in a religionless and secular sense Christians, in what way are we the *Ekklesia*, 'those who are called forth', not conceiving of ourselves religiously as specially favoured, but as wholly belonging to the world? Then Christ is no longer an object of religion, but something quite different, indeed and in truth the Lord of the world. Yet what does that signify? What is the place of worship and prayer in an entire absence of religion? . . . .

The Pauline question whether circumcision is a condition of justification is today, I consider, the question whether religion is a condition of salvation. Freedom from circumcision is at the same time freedom from religion. I often ask myself why a Christian instinct frequently draws me more to the religionless than to the religious, by which I mean not with any intention of evangelizing them, but rather, I might almost say, in 'brotherhood'. While I often shrink with religious people from speaking of God by name – because that Name somehow seems to me here not to ring true, and I strike myself as rather dishonest (it is especially bad when others start talking in religious jargon: then I dry up almost completely and feel somehow oppressed and ill at ease) – with people who have no religion I am able on occasion to speak of God quite openly and as it were naturally. Religious people speak of God when human perception is (often just from laziness) at an end, or human resources fail: it is in fact always the *Deus ex machina* they call to their aid, either for the so-called solving of insoluble problems or as support in human failure – always, that is to say, helping out human weakness or on the borders of human existence. Of necessity, that can only go on until men can, by their own strength, push those borders a little further, so that God becomes superfluous as a *Deus ex machina*. I have come to be doubtful even about talking of 'borders of human existence'. Is even death today, since men are scarcely afraid of it any more, and sin, which they scarcely understand any more, still a genuine borderline? It always seems to me that in talking thus we are only seeking frantically to make room for God. I should like to speak of God not on the borders of life but at its centre, not in weakness but in strength, not, therefore, in man's suffering and death but in his life and prosperity. On the borders it seems to me better to hold our peace and leave the problem unsolved. Belief in the Resurrection is not the solution of the problem of death. The 'beyond' of God is not the beyond of our perceptive faculties. Epistemological theory has nothing to do with the transcendence of God. God is the 'beyond' in the midst of our life. The Church stands not where human powers give out, on the borders, but in the centre of the village.

VI
Modernity and the Arts

Many of the ideas contained in the preceding pages have had an influence, however indirect, on writers, painters and musicians. Sometimes this influence simply amounts to the fact that artists have carried out their work within a general intellectual climate which Marx and Freud, Nietzsche and Dostoevsky, Jung and Buber helped to create. In such cases no specific debt is acknowledged, though historians of ideas may well argue a case for genuine and revealing links. Again, an artist may claim that he has been much impressed, as a man, by a particular thinker (cf. the debt acknowledged by the composer, Michael Tippett, to Jung) and in such a case the consequence for his art may be real without being obviously demonstrable. In a few instances an explicit influence is either actually stated or patently clear, as in the relationships between Freud's ideas and surrealist theory, between Marxism and Brecht's conception of the theatre, between phenomenology and the French 'new novel'.

In the passages on the various arts which follow, examples of all three types of relationship are present. The selection is obviously limited, but I think it is fairly representative. My concern has been to quote artists, not critics, on the arts. Inevitably, there is a certain timelag between the formulation of new ideas by philosophers and the popular 'filtering' of these ideas so that they become part of a general and increasingly accepted intellectual attitude – and hence part of the artist's stock-in-trade. This is why the artists represented are mostly at least a generation younger than the thinkers quoted in earlier sections. At the same time, the volume as a whole has been concerned with modern foundations rather than contemporary trends, so that these artists are, with the exception of Robbe-Grillet, either dead or elderly. All of them affect our current thinking about the arts whether in terms of abstraction in painting, 'truth to the material' in sculpture, total theatre, the decline of the novel based on nineteenth-century assumptions about man and society or the general flight from sentimental and 'inspirational' interpretations of artistic activity.

FURTHER READING

A number of the passages quoted below, together with others on similar subjects, can be found in H. M. Block and H. Salinger, *The Creative Vision: Modern European Writers on their Art*, New York, Grove Press, 1960; R. Ellmann and C. Feidelson, eds, *The Modern Tradition*, New York, Oxford University Press, 1965; R. Phelps, ed., *Twentieth-Century Culture: the Breaking Up*, New York, Braziller, 1965; R. L. Herbert, ed., *Modern Artists on Art*, Englewood Cliffs, N.J., Prentice-Hall (Spectrum Books), 1964; J. Scully, ed., *Modern Poets on Modern Poetry*, Collins (Fontana), 1966.

25 Rimbaud (1854–91)

From a letter of 15 May 1871 to Paul Demeny

Romanticism has never been properly judged. Who was there to judge it? The Critics!! The Romantics? who proved so clearly that the song is very seldom the work, that is to say, the idea sung and intended by the singer.

For *I* is someone else. If brass wakes up a trumpet, it is not its fault. To me this is obvious: I witness the unfolding of my own thought: I watch it, I listen to it: I make a stroke of the bow: the symphony begins to stir in the depths, or springs on to the stage.

If the old fools had not discovered only the false significance of the Ego, we should not now be having to sweep away those millions of skeletons which, since time immemorial, have been piling up the fruits of their one-eyed intellects, and claiming themselves to be the authors of them!

In Greece, I say, verses and lyres give rhythm to action. After that, music and rhymes are a game, a pastime. The curious are charmed with the study of this past: many of them delight in reviving these antiquities – that's their affair. Universal mind has always thrown out its ideas naturally; men would pick up a part of these fruits of the brain: they acted through them, they wrote books through them: and so things went on, since man did not work on himself, either not yet being awake, or not yet in the fullness of the great dream. Writers, civil servants: author, creator, poet, *that* man never existed!

The first study for a man who wants to be a poet is the knowledge of himself, complete. He looks for his soul, inspects it, puts it to the test, learns it. As soon as he knows it, he must cultivate it! It seems simple: in every brain a natural development takes place; so many *egoists* proclaim themselves authors; there are plenty of others who attribute their intellectual progress to themselves! – But the soul has to be made monstrous, that's the point: after the fashion of the *comprachicos*, if you like! Imagine a man planting and cultivating warts on his face.

I say that one must be a *seer*, make oneself a *seer*.

The poet makes himself a *seer* by a long, prodigious, and rational *disordering* of *all the senses*. Every form of love, of suffering, of madness; he searches himself, he consumes all the poisons in him, and keeps only their quintessences. This is an unspeakable torture during which he needs all his faith and superhuman strength, and during which he becomes the great patient, the great criminal, the great accursed – and the great learned one! – among men. – For he arrives at the *unknown*. Because he has cultivated his own soul – which was rich to begin with – more than any other man! He reaches the unknown, and even if, crazed, he ends up by losing the understanding of his visions, at least he has seen them! Let him die charging through those unutterable, unnameable things: other horrible workers will come; they will begin from the horizons where he has succumbed! . . . .

– To continue:

So, then, the poet really is the thief of fire.

He is responsible for humanity, even for the *animals*; he must see to it that his inventions can be smelt, felt, heard. If what he brings back from *down there* has form, he brings forth form; if it is formless, he brings forth formlessness. A language has to be found – for that matter, every word being an idea, the time of the universal language will come! One has to be an academician – deader than a fossil – to finish a dictionary of any language. Weak-minded people, beginning by *thinking about* the first letter of the alphabet, would soon rush into madness!

This [new] language would be of the soul, for the soul, containing everything, smells, sounds, colours; thought latching on to thought and pulling. The poet would define the amount of the unknown awakening in the universal soul in his own time: he would produce more than the formulation of his thought or the measurement *of his march towards Progress*! An enormity who has become normal, absorbed by everyone, he would really be a *multiplier of progress*!

This future will, as you see, be materialistic – Always filled with

Number and *Harmony*, these poems will be made to endure. Essentially it will be Greek poetry again, in a way.

Eternal art will have its function, since poets are citizens. Poetry will no longer rhyme with action; *it will be ahead of it!*

Poets like this will exist! When the unending servitude of woman is broken, when she lives by and for herself, when man – hitherto abominable – has given her her freedom, she too will be a poet! Woman will discover part of the unknown! Will her world of ideas be different from ours? She will discover things strange and unfathomable, repulsive and delicious. We shall take them unto ourselves, we shall understand them.

Meanwhile let us ask the *poet* for the *new* – in ideas and in forms.

26 Mondrian (1872–1944)

From the essay, 'Plastic Art and Pure Plastic Art', 1937

It must be obvious that if one evokes in the spectator the sensation of, say, the sunlight or moonlight, of joy or sadness, or any other determinate sensation, one has not succeeded in establishing universal beauty, one is not purely abstract.

As for surrealism, we must recognize that it deepens feeling and thought, but since this deepening is limited by individualism it cannot reach the foundation, the universal. So long as it remains in the realm of dreams, which are only a rearrangement of the events of life, it cannot touch true reality. Through a different composition of the events of life, it may remove their ordinary course but it cannot purify them. Even the intention of freeing life from its conventions and from everything which is harmful to the true life can be found in surrealist literature. Non-figurative art is fully in agreement with this intention but it achieves its purpose; it frees its plastic means and its art from all particularity. The names, however, of these tendencies, are only indications of their conceptions; it is the realization which matters. With the exception of non-figurative art, there seems to have been a lack of realization of the fact that it is possible to express oneself profoundly and humanely by plastics alone, that is, by employing a neutral plastic means without the risk of falling into decoration or ornament. Yet all the world knows that even a single line can arouse emotion. But although one sees – and this is the artist's fault – few non-figurative works which live by virtue of their dynamic rhythm and their execution, figurative art is no better in this respect. In general, people have not realized that one can express our very essence through neutral constructive elements; that is to say, we can express the essence of art. The essence of art of course is not often sought. As a rule, individualist human nature is so predominant, that the expression of the essence of art through a rhythm of lines, colours, and relationships appears insufficient. Recently, even a great artist has declared that 'complete indifference to the subject leads to an incomplete form of art'.

But everybody agrees that art is only a problem of plastics. What good then is a subject? It is to be understood that one would need a subject to expound something named 'Spiritual riches, human sentiments and thoughts'. Obviously, all this is individual and needs particular forms. But at the root of these sentiments and thoughts there is one thought and one sentiment: these do not easily define themselves and have no need of analogous forms in which to express themselves. It is here that neutral plastic means are demanded.

For pure art then, the subject can never be an additional value, it is the line, the colour, and their relations which must 'bring into play the whole sensual and intellectual register of the inner life . . .,' not the subject. Both in abstract art and in naturalistic art colour expresses itself 'in accordance with the form by which it is determined', and in all art it is the artist's task to make forms and colours living and capable of arousing emotion. If he makes art into an 'algebraic equation' that is no argument against the art, it only proves that he is not an artist.

If all art has demonstrated that to establish the force, tension and movement of the forms, and the intensity of the colours of reality, it is necessary that these should be purified and transformed; if all art has purified and transformed and is still purifying and transforming these forms of reality and their mutual relations, if all art is thus a continually deepening process: why then stop halfway? If all art aims at expressing universal beauty, why establish an individualist expression? Why then not continue the sublime work of the cubists? That would not be a continuation of the same tendency, but on the contrary, *a complete break-away from it and all that has existed before it.* That would only be going along the same road that we have already travelled.

Since cubist art is still fundamentally naturalistic, the break which pure plastic art has caused consists in becoming abstract instead of naturalistic in essence. While in cubism, from a naturalistic foundation, there sprang forcibly the use of plastic means, still half object, half abstract, the abstract basis of pure plastic art must result in the use of purely abstract plastic means.

In removing completely from the work all objects, 'the world is not separated from the spirit', but is on the contrary *put into a balanced opposition* with the spirit, since the one and the other are purified. This creates a perfect unity between the two opposites. There are, however, many who imagine that they are too fond of life, particular reality, to be able to suppress figuration, and for that reason they still use in their work the object or figurative fragments which indicate its character. Nevertheless, one is well aware of the fact that in art one cannot hope to represent in the image things as they are, nor even as they manifest themselves in all their living brilliance. The impressionists, divisionists, and pointillists have already recognized that. There are some today who, recognizing the weakness and limitation of the image, attempt to create a work of art through the objects themselves, often by composing them in a more or less transformed manner. This clearly cannot lead to an expression of their content nor of their true character. One can more or less remove the conventional appearance of things (surrealism), but they continue nevertheless to show their particular character and to arouse in us individual emotions. To love things in reality is to love them profoundly; it is to see them as a microcosmos in the macrocosmos. *Only in this way can one achieve a universal expression of reality.* Precisely on account of its profound love for things, non-figurative art does not aim at rendering them in their particular appearance.

Precisely by its existence non-figurative art shows that 'art' *continues always on its true road*. It shows that 'art' is *not the expression of the appearance of reality such as we see it, nor of the life which we live*, but that *it is the expression of true reality and true life . . . indefinable but realizable in plastics.*

27 Apollinaire (1880–1918)

From *The Cubist Painters*, 1913

Many new painters limit themselves to pictures which have no real subjects. And the titles which we find in the catalogues are like proper names, which designate men without characterizing them.

There are men named Stout who are in fact quite thin, and others named White who are very dark; well now, I have seen pictures entitled *Solitude* containing many human figures.

In the cases in question, the artists even condescend at times to use vaguely explanatory words such as *Portrait, Landscape, Still-life*; however, many young painters use as a title only the very general term *Painting.*

These painters, while they still look at nature, no longer imitate it, and carefully avoid any representation of natural scenes which they may have observed, and then reconstructed from preliminary studies.

Real resemblance no longer has any importance, since everything is sacrificed by the artist to truth, to the necessities of a higher nature whose existence he assumes, but does not lay bare. The subject has little or no importance any more.

Generally speaking, modern art repudiates most of the techniques of pleasing devised by the great artists of the past.

While the goal of painting is today, as always, the pleasure of the eye, the art-lover is henceforth asked to expect delights other than those which looking at natural objects can easily provide.

Thus we are moving towards an entirely new art which will stand, with respect to painting as envisaged heretofore, as music stands to literature.

It will be pure painting, just as music is pure literature.

The music-lover experiences, in listening to a concert, a joy of a different order from the joy given by natural sounds, such as the murmur of the brook, the uproar of a torrent, the whistling of the wind in a forest, or the harmonies of human speech based on reason rather than on aesthetics.

In the same way the new painters will provide their admirers with artistic sensations by concentrating exclusively on the problem of creating harmony with unequal lights.

Everybody knows the story told by Pliny about Apelles and Protogenes. It clearly illustrates the aesthetic pleasure resulting solely from the contradictory harmonies referred to above.

Apelles landed, one day, on the Isle of Rhodes, and went to see the work of Protogenes, who lived there. Protogenes was not in the studio when Apelles arrived. An old woman was there, looking after a large canvas which the painter had prepared. Instead of leaving his name, Apelles drew on the canvas a line so subtle that nothing happier could be conceived.

Returning, Protogenes saw the line, recognized the hand of Apelles, and drew on the latter's line another line of another colour, one even more subtle, so that it seemed as if there were three lines.

Apelles came back the next day, and again did not find his man; the subtlety of the line which he drew this time caused Protogenes to despair. The sketch aroused for many years the admiration of connoisseurs, who contemplated it with as much pleasure as if it had depicted gods and goddesses, instead of almost invisible lines.

The secret aim of the young painters of the extremist schools is to produce pure painting. Theirs is an entirely new plastic art. It is still in its beginnings, and is not yet as abstract as it would like to be. Most of the new painters depend a good deal on mathematics, without knowing it; but they have not yet abandoned nature, which they still question patiently, hoping to learn the right answers to the questions raised by life.

A man like Picasso studies an object as a surgeon dissects a cadaver.

This art of pure painting, if it succeeds in freeing itself from the art of the past, will not necessarily cause the latter to disappear; the development of music has not brought in its train the abandonment of the various genres of literature, nor has the acridity of tobacco replaced the savouriness of food.

The new artists have been violently attacked for their preoccupation with geometry. Yet geometrical figures are the essence of drawing. Geometry, the science of space, its dimensions and relations, has always determined the norms and rules of painting.

Until now, the three dimensions of Euclid's geometry were sufficient to the restiveness felt by great artists yearning for the infinite.

The new painters do not propose, any more than did their predecessors, to be geometers. But it may be said that geometry is to the plastic arts what grammar is to the art of the writer. Today, scientists no longer limit themselves to the three dimensions of Euclid. The painters have been led quite naturally, one might say by intuition, to preoccupy themselves with the new possibilities of spatial measurement which, in the language of the modern studios, are designated by the term: the fourth dimension.

Regarded from the plastic point of view, the fourth dimension appears to spring from the three known dimensions: it represents the immensity of space eternalizing itself in all directions at any given moment. It is space itself, the dimension of the infinite; the fourth dimension endows objects with plasticity. It gives the object its right proportions on the whole, whereas in Greek art, for instance, a somewhat mechanical rhythm constantly destroys the proportions.

Greek art had a purely human conception of beauty. It took man as the measure of perfection. But the art of the new painters takes the infinite universe as its ideal, and it is to this ideal that we owe a new norm of the perfect, one which permits the painter to proportion objects in accordance with the degree of plasticity he desires them to have.

Nietzsche divined the possibility of such an art:

'O divine Dionysius, why pull my ears?' Ariadne asks her philosophical lover in one of the celebrated dialogues on the Isle of Naxos. 'I find something pleasant and delightful in your ears, Ariadne; why are they not even longer?'

Nietzsche, in relating this anecdote, puts in the mouth of Dionysius an implied condemnation of all Greek art.

Finally, I must point out that the fourth dimension – this utopian expression should be analyzed and explained, so that nothing more than historical interest may be attached to it – has come to stand for the aspirations and premonitions of the many young artists who contemplate Egyptian, negro, and oceanic sculptures, meditate on various scientific works, and live in the anticipation of a sublime art.

Wishing to attain the proportions of the ideal, to be no longer limited to the human, the young painters offer us works which are more cerebral than sensual. They discard more and more the old art of optical illusion and local proportion, in order to express the grandeur of metaphysical forms. This is why contemporary art, even if it does not directly stem from specific religious beliefs, nonetheless possesses some of the characteristics of great, that is to say, religious art.

28 Picasso (b. 1881)

From the essay entitled 'Statement by Picasso', 1923

We all know that art is not truth. Art is a lie that makes us realize truth, at least the truth that is given us to understand. The artist must know the manner whereby to convince others of the truthfulness of his lies. If he only shows in his work that he has searched, and re-searched, for the way to put over his lies, he would never accomplish anything.

The idea of research has often made painting go astray, and made the artist lose himself in mental lucubrations. Perhaps this has been the principal fault of modern art. The spirit of research has poisoned those who have not fully understood all the positive and conclusive elements in modern art and has made them attempt to paint the invisible and, therefore, the unpaintable.

They speak of naturalism in opposition to modern painting. I would like to know if anyone has ever seen a natural work of art. Nature and art, being two different things, cannot be the same thing. Through art we express our conception of what nature is not.

Velasquez left us his idea of the people of his epoch. Undoubtedly they were different from what he painted them, but we cannot conceive a Philip IV in any other way than the one Velasquez painted. Rubens also made a portrait of the same king and in Rubens' portrait he seems to be quite another person. We believe in the one painted by Velasquez, for he convinces us by his right of might.

From the painters of the origins, the primitives, whose work is obviously different from nature, down to those artists who, like David, Ingres and even Bourguereau, believed in painting nature as it is, art has always been art and not nature. And from the point of view of art there are no concrete or abstract forms, but only forms which are more or less convincing lies. That those lies are necessary to our mental selves is beyond any doubt, as it is through them that we form our esthetic point of view of life.

Cubism is no different from any other school of painting. The same principles and the same elements are common to all. The fact that for a long time cubism has not been understood and that even today there are people who cannot see anything in it, means nothing. I do not read English, an English book is a blank book to me. This does not mean that the English language does not exist, and why should I blame anybody else but myself if I cannot understand what I know nothing about?

I also often hear the word evolution. Repeatedly I am asked to explain how my painting evolved. To me there is no past or future in art. If a work of art cannot live always in the present it must not be considered at all. The art of the Greeks, of the Egyptians, of the great painters who lived in other times, is not an art of the past; perhaps it is more alive today than it ever was. Art does not evolve by itself, the ideas of people change and with them their mode of expression. When I hear people speak of the evolution of an artist, it seems to me that they are considering him standing between two mirrors that face each other and reproduce his image an infinite number of times, and that they contemplate the successive images of one mirror as his past, and the images of the other mirror as his future, while his real image is taken as his present. They do not consider that they all are the same images in different planes.

Variation does not mean evolution. If an artist varies his mode of expression this only means that he has changed his manner of thinking, and in changing, it might be for the better or it might be for the worse.

The several manners I have used in my art must not be considered as an evolution, or as steps toward an unknown ideal of painting. All I have ever made was made for the present and with the hope that it will always remain in the present. I have never taken into consideration the spirit of research. When I have found something to express, I have done it without thinking of the past or of the future. I do not believe I have used radically different elements in the different manners I have used in painting. If the subjects I have wanted to express have suggested different ways of expression I have never hesitated to adopt them. I have never made trials nor experiments. Whenever I had something to say, I have said it in the manner in which I have felt it ought to be said. Different motives inevitably require different methods of expression. This does not imply either evolution or progress, but an adaptation of the idea one wants to express and the means to express that idea.

Arts of transition do not exist. In the chronological history of art there are periods which are more positive, more complete than others. This means that there are periods in which there are better artists than in others. If the history of art could be graphically represented, as in a chart used by a nurse to mark the changes of temperature of her patient, the same silhouettes of mountains would be shown, proving that in art there is no ascendant progress, but that it follows certain ups and downs that might occur at any time. The same occurs with the work of an individual artist.

Many think that cubism is an art of transition, an experiment which is to bring ulterior results. Those who think that way have not understood it. Cubism is not either a seed or a foetus, but an art dealing primarily with forms, and when a form is realized it is there to live its own life. A mineral substance, having geometric formation, is not made so for transitory purposes, it is to remain what it is and will always have its own form. But if we are to apply the law of evolution and transformism to art, then we have to admit that all art is transitory. On the contrary, art does not enter into these philosophic absolutisms. If cubism is an art of transition I am sure that the only thing that will come out of it is another form of cubism.

Mathematics, trigonometry, chemistry, psychoanalysis, music, and whatnot, have been related to cubism to give it an easier interpretation. All this has been pure literature, not to say nonsense, which brought bad results, blinding people with theories.

Cubism has kept itself within the limits and limitations of painting, never pretending to go beyond it. Drawing, design and colour are understood and practiced in cubism in the same spirit and manner that they are understood and practiced in all other schools. Our subjects might be different, as we have introduced into painting objects and forms that were formerly ignored. We have kept our eyes open to our surroundings, and also our brains.

We give to form and colour all their individual significance, as far as we can see it; in our subjects we keep the joy of discovery, the pleasure of the unexpected; our subject itself must be a source of interest. But of what use is it to say what we do when everybody can see it if he wants to?

29 Stravinsky (b. 1882)

From *Poetics of Music*, 1939

We are living at a time when the status of man is undergoing profound upheavals. Modern man is progressively losing his understanding of values and his sense of proportions. This failure to understand essential realities is extremely serious. It leads us infallibly to the violation of the fundamental laws of human equilibrium. In the domain of music, the consequences of this misunderstanding are these: on one hand there is a tendency to turn the mind away from what I shall call the higher mathematics of music in order to degrade music to servile employ- ment, and to vulgarize it by adapting it to the requirements of an elementary utilitarianism – as we shall soon see on examining Soviet music. On the other hand, since the mind itself is ailing, the music of our time, and particularly the music that calls itself and believes itself *pure*, carries within it the symptoms of a pathologic blemish and spreads the germs of a new original sin. The old original sin was chiefly a sin of knowledge; the new original sin, if I may speak in these terms, is first and foremost a sin of non-acknowledgement – a refusal to acknowledge the truth and the laws that proceed therefrom, laws that we have called fundamental. What then is the truth in the domain of music? And what are its repercussions on creative activity?

Let us not forget that it is written: 'Spiritus ubi vult spirat' (St John, 3 : 8). What we must retain in this proposition is above all the word WILL. The Spirit is thus endowed with the capacity of willing. The principle of speculative volition is a fact.

Now it is just this fact that is too often disputed. People question the direction that the wind of the Spirit is taking, not the rightness of the artisan's work. In so doing, whatever may be your feelings about ontology or whatever your own philosophy and beliefs may be, you must admit that you are making an attack on the very freedom of the spirit – whether you begin this large word with a capital or not. If a believer in Christian philosophy, you would then also have to refuse to accept the idea of the Holy Spirit. If an agnostic or atheist, you would have to do nothing less than refuse to be a *free-thinker* . . . .

It should be noted that there is never any dispute when the listener takes pleasure in the work he hears. The least informed of music-lovers readily clings to the periphery of a work; it pleases him for reasons that are most often entirely foreign to the essence of music. This pleasure is enough for him and calls for no justification. But if it happens that the music displeases him, our music-lover will ask you for an explanation of his discomfiture. He will demand that we explain something that is in its essence ineffable.

By its fruit we judge the tree. Judge the tree by its fruit then, and do not meddle with the roots. Function justifies an organ, no matter how strange the organ may appear in the eyes of those who are not accustomed to see it functioning. Snobbish circles are cluttered with persons who, like one of Montesquieu's characters, wonder how one can possibly be a Persian. They make me think unfailingly of the story of the peasant who, on seeing a dromedary in the zoo for the first time, examines it at length, shakes his head and, turning to leave, says, to the great delight of those present: 'It isn't true.'

It is through the unhampered play of its functions, then, that a work is revealed and justified. We are free to accept or reject this play, but no one has the right to question the fact of its existence. To judge, dispute, and criticize the principle of speculative volition which is at the origin of all creation is thus manifestly useless. In the pure state, music is free speculation. Artists of all epochs have unceasingly testified to this concept. For myself, I see no reason for not trying to do as they did. Since I myself was created, I cannot help having the desire to create. What sets this desire in motion, and what can I do to make it productive?

The study of the creative process is an extremely delicate one. In truth it is impossible to observe the inner workings of this process from the outside. It is futile to try and follow its successive phases in someone else's work. It is likewise very difficult to observe one's self. Yet it is only by enlisting the aid of introspection that I may have any chance at all of guiding you in this essentially fluctuating matter.

Most music-lovers believe that what sets the composer's creative imagination in motion is a certain emotive disturbance generally designated by the name of *inspiration*.

I have no thought of denying to inspiration the outstanding role that has developed upon it in the generative process we are studying; I simply maintain that inspiration is in no way a prescribed condition of the creative act, but rather a manifestation that is chronologically secondary.

Inspiration, art, artist – so many words, hazy at least, that keep us from seeing clearly in a field where everything is balance and calculation through which the breath of the speculative spirit blows. It is afterwards, and only afterwards, that the emotive disturbance which is at the root of inspiration may arise – an emotive disturbance about which people talk so indelicately by conferring upon it a meaning that is shocking to us and that compromises the term itself. Is it not clear that this emotion is merely a reaction on the part of the creator grappling with that unknown entity which is still only the object of his creating and which is to become a work of art? Step by step, link by link, it will be granted him to discover the work. It is this chain of discoveries, as well as each individual discovery, that give rise to the emotion – an almost physiological reflex, like that of the appetite causing a flow of saliva – this emotion which invariably follows closely the phases of the creative process.

All creation presupposes at its origin a sort of appetite that is brought on by the foretaste of discovery. This foretaste of the creative act accompanies the intuitive grasp of an unknown entity already possessed but not yet intelligible, an entity that will not take definite shape except by the action of a constantly vigilant technique.

This appetite that is aroused in me at the mere thought of putting in order musical elements that have attracted my attention is not at all a fortuitous thing like inspiration, but as habitual and periodic, if not as constant, as a natural need.

This premonition of an obligation, this foretaste of a pleasure, this conditioned reflex, as a modern physiologist would say, shows clearly that it is the idea of discovery and hard work that attracts me.

The very act of putting my work on paper, of, as we say, kneading the dough, is for me inseparable from the pleasure of creation. So far as I am concerned, I cannot separate the spiritual effort from the psychological and physical effort; they confront me on the same level and do not present a hierarchy.

The word *artist* which, as it is most generally understood today, bestows on its bearer the highest intellectual prestige, the privilege of being accepted as a pure mind – this pretentious term is in my view entirely incompatible with the role of the *homo faber*.

At this point it should be remembered that, whatever field of endeavour has fallen to our lot, if it is true that we are *intellectuals*, we are called upon not to cogitate, but to perform.

The philosopher Jacques Maritain reminds us that in the mighty structure of medieval civilization, the artist held only the rank of an artisan. 'And his individualism was forbidden any sort of anarchic development, because a natural social discipline imposed certain limitative conditions upon him from without.' It was the Renaissance that invented the artist, distinguished him from the artisan and began to exalt the former at the expense of the latter.

At the outset the name artist was given only to the Masters of Arts: philosophers, alchemists, magicians; but painters, sculptors, musicians, and poets had the right to be qualified only as artisans.

> Plying divers implements,
> The subtle artizan implants
> Life in marble, copper, bronze,

says the poet Du Bellay. And Montaigne enumerates in his *Essays* the 'painters, poets and other artizans'. And even in the seventeenth century, La Fontaine hails a painter with the name of *artisan* and draws a sharp rebuke from an ill-tempered critic who might have been the ancestor of most of our present-day critics.

The idea of work to be done is for me so closely bound up with the idea of the arranging of materials and of the pleasure that the actual doing of the work affords us that, should the impossible happen and my work suddenly be given to me in a perfectly completed form, I should be embarrassed and nonplussed by it, as by a hoax.

We have a duty towards music, namely, to invent it.

30 André Breton (b. 1896)

From *What is Surrealism?*, 1934

In an article, 'Enter the Mediums', published in *Littérature*, 1922, reprinted in *Les Pas Perdus*, 1924, and subsequently in the *Surrealist Manifesto*, I explained the circumstance that had originally put us, my friends and myself, on the track of the surrealist activity we still follow and for which we are hopeful of gaining ever more numerous new adherents in order to extend it further than we have so far succeeded in doing. It reads:

'It was in 1919, in complete solitude and at the approach of sleep, that my attention was arrested by sentences more or less complete, which became perceptible to my mind without my being able to discover (even by very meticulous analysis) any possible previous volitional effort. One evening in particular, as I was about to fall asleep, I became aware of a sentence articulated clearly to a point excluding all possibility of alteration and stripped of all quality of vocal sound; a curious sort of sentence which came to me bearing – in sober truth – not a trace of any relation whatever to any incidents I may at that time have been involved in; an insistent sentence, it seemed to me, a sentence I might say, that *knocked at the window*. I was prepared to pay no further attention to it when the organic character of the sentence detained me. I was really bewildered. Unfortunately, I am unable to remember the exact sentence at this distance, but it ran approximately like this: 'A man is cut in half by the window.' What made it plainer was the fact that it was accompanied by a feeble visual representation of a man in the process of walking, but cloven, at half his height, by a window perpendicular to the axis of his body. Definitely, there was the form, re-erected against space, of a man leaning out of a window. But the window following the man's locomotion, I understood that I was dealing with an image of great rarity. Instantly the idea came to me to use it as material for poetic construction. I had no sooner invested it with that quality, than it had given place to a succession of all but intermittent sentences which left me no less astonished, but in a state, I would say, of extreme detachment.

'Preoccupied as I still was at that time with Freud, and familiar with his methods of investigation, which I had practised occasionally upon the sick during the War, I resolved to obtain from myself what one

seeks to obtain from patients, namely a monologue poured out as
rapidly as possible, over which the subject's critical faculty has no
control – the subject himself throwing reticence to the winds – and
which as much as possible represents *spoken thought*. It seemed and
still seems to me that the speed of thought is no greater than that of
words, and hence does not exceed the flow of either tongue or pen. It
was in such circumstances that, together with Philippe Soupault,
whom I had told about my first ideas on the subject, I began to cover
sheets of paper with writing, feeling a praiseworthy contempt for
whatever the literary result might be. Ease of achievement brought
about the rest. By the end of the first day of the experiment we were
able to read to one another about fifty pages obtained in this manner
and to compare the results we had achieved. The likeness was on the
whole striking. There were similar faults of construction, the same
hesitant manner, and also, in both cases, an illusion of extraordinary
verve, much emotion, a considerable assortment of images of a quality
such as we should never have been able to obtain in the normal way of
writing, a very special sense of the picturesque, and, here and there, a
few pieces of out and out buffoonery. The only differences which our
two texts presented appeared to me to be due essentially to our respective temperaments, Soupault's being less static than mine, and, if he will
allow me to make this slight criticism, to his having scattered about at
the top of certain pages – doubtlessly in a spirit of mystification –
various words under the guise of titles. I must give him credit, on the
other hand, for having always forcibly opposed the least correction of
any passage that did not seem to me to be quite the thing. In that he
was most certainly right.

'It is of course difficult in these cases to appreciate at their just value
the various elements in the result obtained; one may even say that it is
entirely impossible to appreciate them at a first reading. To you who
may be writing them, these elements are, in appearance, *as strange as to
anyone else*, and you are yourself naturally distrustful of them. Poetically
speaking, they are distinguished chiefly by a very high degree of
immediate absurdity, the peculiar quality of that absurdity being, on close
examination, their yielding to whatever is most admissible and legitimate in the world: divulgation of a given number of facts and pro-
perties on the whole not less objectionable than the others.'

The word 'surrealism' having thereupon become descriptive of the
generalizable undertaking to which we had devoted ourselves, I thought
it indispensable, in 1924, to define this word once and for all:

'SURREALISM, n. Pure psychic automatism, by which it is intended to express, verbally, in writing, or by other means, the real process of thought. Thought's dictation, in the absence of all control exercised by the reason and outside all aesthetic or moral preoccupations.'

31 Brecht (1898–1956)

From the essay 'A Little Private Tuition for my friend Max Gorelik', 1944

The modern playwright's (or scene designer's) relations with his audience are far more complicated than a tradesman's with his customers. But even the customer isn't always right; he by no means represents a final unalterable phenomenon that has been fully explored. Certain habits and appetites can be induced in him artificially; sometimes it is just a matter of establishing their presence. The farmer was not aware throughout the centuries of his need or potential need for a Ford car. The rapid social and economic development of our period alters the audience swiftly and radically, demanding and facilitating ever new modes of thought, feeling and behaviour. And a new class is standing, *Hannibal ante portas*, outside the doors of the theatre.

The sharpening of the class struggle has engendered such conflicts of interest in our audience that it is no longer in a position to react to art spontaneously and unanimously. In consequence the artist cannot take spontaneous success as a valid criterion of his work. Nor can he blindly admit the oppressed classes as a court of first instance, for their taste and their instincts are oppressed as well.

In times such as these the artist is driven to do what pleases himself, assuming hopefully that he represents the perfect spectator. He needn't land up in an ivory tower so long as he is really concerned to take part in the struggle of the oppressed, to find out their interests and represent them and develop his art on their behalf. But even an ivory tower is a better place to sit in nowadays than a Hollywood villa.

It leads to a lot of confusion when people hope to put across certain truths by wrapping them up and coating them with sugar. This is much the same as trying to raise the drug traffic to a higher moral plane by introducing the truth to its victims; they cannot recognize it in the first place and are certainly incapable of remembering it once they have sobered up.

Hollywood's and Broadway's methods of manufacturing certain excitements and emotions may possibly be artistic, but their only use is to offset the fearful boredom induced in any audience by the endless repetition of falsehoods and stupidities. This technique was developed and is used in order to stimulate interest in things and ideas that are not in the interest of the audience.

The theatre of our parasitic bourgeoisie has a quite specific effect on the nerves, which can in no way be treated as equivalent to the artistic experience of a more vital period. It 'conjures up' the illusion that it is reflecting real-life incidents with a view to achieving more or less primitive shock effects or hazily defined sentimental moods which in fact are to be consumed as substitutes for the missing spiritual experiences of a crippled and cataleptic audience. One only has to take a brief look to see that every one of these results can also be achieved by utterly distorted reflections of real life. Many artists have indeed come to believe that this up-to-date 'artistic experience' can *only* be the produce of such distorted reflections.

Against that it has to be remembered that one can feel a natural interest in certain incidents between people quite independently of the artistic sphere. This natural interest can be made use of by art. There is also such a thing as a spontaneous interest in art itself; that is, in the capacity to reflect real life and to do so in a fantastic, personal, individual way, that of the artist in question. Here we have an autonomous excitement that doesn't have to be manufactured, concerning what happens in reality and how the artist expresses it.

The conventional theatre can only be defended by using plainly reactionary phrases like 'the theatre never changes' and 'the play's the thing'. By such means the notion of drama is restricted to the parasitic bourgeoisie and its rotten plays. Jove's thunderbolts in the tiny hands of Louis B. Mayer. Take the element of conflict in Elizabethan plays, complex, shifting, largely impersonal, never soluble, and then see what has been made of it today, whether in contemporary plays or in contemporary renderings of the Elizabethans. Compare the part played by empathy then and now. What a contradictory, complicated and intermittent operation it was in Shakespeare's theatre! What they offer us nowadays as the 'eternal laws of the theatre' are the exceedingly present-day laws decreed by L. B. Mayer and the Theater Guild.

A certain amount of confusion about the non-aristotelian drama was due to the identification of 'scientific drama' with the 'drama of a scientific age'. The boundaries between art and science are not absolutely immutable; art's tasks can be taken over by science and science's by art, and yet the epic theatre still remains a theatre. That is to say that the theatre remains theatre even while becoming epic.

It is only the opponents of the new drama, the champions of the 'eternal laws of the theatre', who suppose that in renouncing the empathy process the modern theatre is renouncing the emotions. All the modern theatre is doing is to discard an outworn, decrepit, subjective sphere of the emotions and pave the way for the new, manifold, socially productive emotions of a new age.

The modern theatre mustn't be judged by its success in satisfying the audience's habits but by its success in transforming them. It needs to be questioned not about its degree of conformity with the 'eternal laws of the theatre' but about its ability to master the rules governing the great social processes of our age; not about whether it manages to interest the spectator in buying a ticket – i.e. in the theatre itself – but about whether it manages to interest him in the world.

32 Henry Moore (b. 1898)

From the essay, 'The Sculptor's Aims', 1934

Each sculptor through his past experience, through observation of natural laws, through criticism of his own work and other sculpture, through his character and psychological make-up, and according to his stage of development, finds that certain qualities in sculpture become of fundamental importance to him. For me these qualities are:

Truth to material. Every material has its own individual qualities. It is only when the sculptor works direct, when there is an active relationship with his material, that the material can take its part in the shaping of an idea. Stone, for example, is hard and concentrated and should not be falsified to look like soft flesh – it should not be forced beyond its constructive build to a point of weakness. It should keep its hard tense stoniness.

Full three-dimensional realization. Complete sculptural expression is form in its full spatial reality.

Only to make relief shapes on the surface of the block is to forego the full power of expression of sculpture. When the sculptor understands his material, has a knowledge of its possibilities and its constructive build, it is possible to keep within its limitations and yet turn an inert block into a composition which has a full form existence, with masses of varied size and section conceived in their air-surrounded entirety, stressing and straining, thrusting and opposing each other in spatial relationship – being static, in the sense that the centre of gravity lies within the base (and does not seem to be falling over or moving off its base) – and yet having an alert dynamic tension between its parts.

Sculpture fully in the round has no two points of view alike. The desire for form completely realized is connected with asymmetry. For a symmetrical mass being the same from both sides cannot have more than half the number of different points of view possessed by a non-symmetrical mass.

Asymmetry is connected also with the desire for the organic (which I have) rather than the geometric.

Organic forms, though they may be symmetrical in their main disposition, in their reaction to environment, growth, and gravity, lose their perfect symmetry.

Observation of natural objects. The observation of nature is part of an artist's life, it enlarges his form-knowledge, keeps him fresh and from working only by formula, and feeds inspiration.

The human figure is what interests me most deeply, but I have found principles of form and rhythm from the study of natural objects such as pebbles, rocks, bones, trees, plants, etc.

Pebbles and rocks show nature's way of working stone. Smooth, sea-worn pebbles show the wearing away, rubbed treatment of stone and principles of asymmetry.

Rocks show the hacked, hewn treatment of stone, and have a jagged nervous block rhythm.

Bones have marvellous structural strength and hard tenseness of form, subtle transition of one shape into the next, and great variety in section.

Trees (tree trunks) show principles of growth and strength of joints, with easy passing of one section into the next. They give the ideal for wood sculpture, upward twisting movement.

Shells show nature's hard but hollow form (metal sculpture) and have a wonderful completeness of single shape.

There is in nature a limitless variety of shapes and rhythms (and the telescope and microscope have enlarged the field) from which the sculptor can enlarge his form-knowledge experience.

But beside formal qualities there are qualities of vision and expression:

Vision and expression. My aim in work is to combine as intensely as possible the abstract principles of sculpture along with the realization of my idea.

All art is an abstraction to some degree (in sculpture the material alone forces one away from pure representation and toward abstraction).

Abstract qualities of design are essential to the value of a work, but to me of equal importance is the psychological, human element. If both abstract and human elements are welded together in a work, it must have a fuller, deeper meaning.

Vitality and power of expression. For me a work must first have a vitality of its own. I do not mean a reflection of the vitality of life; of movement, physical action, frisking, dancing figures, and so on, but that a work can have in it a pent-up energy, an intense life of its own, independent of the object it may represent. When a work has this powerful vitality we do not connect the word Beauty with it.

Beauty, in the later Greek or Renaissance sense, is not the aim in my sculpture.

Between beauty of expression and power of expression there is a difference of function. The first aims at pleasing the senses, the second has a spiritual vitality which for me is more moving and goes deeper than the senses.

Because a work does not aim at reproducing natural appearances it is not, therefore, an escape from life – but may be a penetration into reality, not a sedative or drug, not just the exercise of good taste, the provision of pleasant shapes and colours in a pleasing combination, not a decoration to life, but an expression of the significance of life, a stimulation to greater effort in living.

33 Auden (b. 1907)

From *The Dyer's Hand*, 1963

In my daydream College for Bards, the curriculum would be as follows:

1) In addition to English, at least one ancient language, probably Greek or Hebrew, and two modern languages would be required.
2) Thousands of lines of poetry in these languages would be learned by heart.

3) The library would contain no books of literary criticism, and the only critical exercise required of students would be the writing of parodies.

4) Courses in prosody, rhetoric and comparative philology would be required of all students, and every student would have to select three courses out of courses in mathematics, natural history, geology, meteorology, archaeology, mythology, liturgics, cooking.

5) Every student would be required to look after a domestic animal and cultivate a garden plot.

A poet has not only to educate himself as a poet, he has also to consider how he is going to earn his living. Ideally, he should have a job which does not in any way involve the manipulation of words. At one time, children training to become rabbis were also taught some skilled manual trade, and if only they knew their child was going to become a poet, the best thing parents could do would be to get him at an early age into some Craft Trades Union. Unfortunately, they cannot know this in advance, and, except in very rare cases, by the time he is twenty-one, the only nonliterary job for which a poet-to-be is qualified is unskilled manual labour. In earning his living, the average poet has to choose between being a translator, a teacher, a literary journalist or a writer of advertising copy and, of these, all but the first can be directly detrimental to his poetry, and even translation does not free him from leading a too exclusively literary life.

There are four aspects of our present *Weltanschauung* which have made an artistic vocation more difficult than it used to be.

1) *The loss of belief in the eternity of the physical universe.* The possibility of becoming an artist, a maker of things which shall outlast the maker's life, might never have occurred to man, had he not had before his eyes, in contrast to the transitoriness of human life, a universe of things, earth, ocean, sky, sun, moon, stars, etc., which appeared to be everlasting and unchanging.

Physics, geology and biology have now replaced this everlasting universe with a picture of nature as a process in which nothing is now what it was or what it will be. Today, Christian and Atheist alike are eschatologically minded. It is difficult for a modern artist to believe he can make an enduring object when he has no model of endurance to go by; he is more tempted than his predecessors to abandon the search for perfection as a waste of time and be content with sketches and improvisations.

2) *The loss of belief in the significance and reality of sensory phenomena.* This loss has been progressive since Luther, who denied any intelligible relation between subjective Faith and objective Works, and Descartes, with his doctrine of primary and secondary qualities. Hitherto, the traditional conception of the phenomenal world had been one of sacramental analogies; what the senses perceived was an outward and visible sign of the inward and invisible, but both were believed to be real and valuable. Modern science has destroyed our faith in the naïve observation of our senses: we cannot, it tells us, ever know what the physical universe is *really* like; we can only hold whatever subjective notion is appropriate to the particular human purpose we have in view.

This destroys the traditional conception of *art* as *mimesis*, for there is no longer a nature 'out there' to be truly or falsely imitated; all an artist can be *true* to are his subjective sensations and feelings. The change in attitude is already to be seen in Blake's remark that some people see the sun as a round golden disc the size of a guinea but that he sees it as a host crying Holy, Holy, Holy. What is significant about this is that Blake, like the Newtonians he hated, accepts a division between the physical and the spiritual, but, in opposition to them, regards the material universe as the abode of Satan, and so attaches no value to what his physical eye sees.

3) *The loss of belief in a norm of human nature which will always require the same kind of man-fabricated world to be at home in.* Until the Industrial Revolution, the way in which men lived changed so slowly that any man, thinking of his great-grandchildren, could imagine them as people living the same kind of life with the same kinds of needs and satisfactions as himself. Technology, with its ever-accelerating transformation of man's way of living, has made it impossible for us to imagine what life will be like even twenty years from now.

Further, until recently, men knew and cared little about cultures far removed from their own in time or space; by human nature, they meant the kind of behaviour exhibited in their own culture. Anthropology and archaeology have destroyed this provincial notion; we know that human nature is so plastic that it can exhibit varieties of behaviour which, in the animal kingdom, could only be exhibited by different species.

The artist, therefore, no longer has any assurance, when he makes something, that even the next generation will find it enjoyable or comprehensible.

He cannot help desiring an immediate success, with all the danger to his integrity which that implies.

Further, the fact that we now have at our disposal the arts of all ages and cultures, has completely changed the meaning of the word tradition. It no longer means a way of working handed down from one generation to the next; a sense of tradition now means a consciousness of the whole of the past as present, yet at the same time as a structured whole the parts of which are related in terms of before and after. Originality no longer means a slight modification in the style of one's immediate predecessors; it means a capacity to find in any work of any date or place a clue to finding one's authentic voice. The burden of choice and selection is put squarely upon the shoulders of each individual poet and it is a heavy one.

4) *The disappearance of the Public Realm as the sphere of revelatory personal deeds.* To the Greeks the Private Realm was the sphere of life ruled by the necessity of sustaining life, and the Public Realm the sphere of freedom where a man could disclose himself to others. Today, the significance of the terms private and public has been reversed; public life is the necessary impersonal life, the place where a man fulfills his social function, and it is in his private life that he is free to be his personal self.

In consequence the arts, literature in particular, have lost their traditional principal human subject, the man of action, the doer of public deeds.

34 Robbe-Grillet (b. 1922)

From *Towards a New Novel*, 1956

At first sight it hardly seems reasonable to think that an entirely *new* literature might one day – now, for instance – be possible. There have been many attempts, during the last thirty or more years, to get the art of fiction out of its rut, but they have only, at best, resulted in isolated works. And – as we are often told – none of these works, whatever its interest, has won the support of a public comparable to that of the bourgeois novel. The only conception of the novel that is current today is, in fact, that of Balzac.

It would not even be difficult to go back as far as Madame de la Fayette. For even in those days the same sacrosanct psychological

analysis constituted the basis of all prose: it presided over the conception of a book, the description of its characters and the development of
its plot. Ever since, a 'good' novel has always been the study of a passion – or of conflicting passions, or of the absence of passion – in a given
environment. Most of our contemporary traditional novelists – those
whom the consumers actually approve of, that is – could copy long
passages from *The Princess of Cleves* or from *Old Goriot* without arousing the suspicions of the vast public that devours their products. They
would merely need to alter an occasional figure of speech, break up a
construction or two, give an indication of the particular character of
each by a word here or there, a daring metaphor, a turn of phrase. . . .
But they all admit, though they see nothing extraordinary about it, that
the things that constitute their major preoccupations, as writers, date
back several centuries. . . .

. . . if the standards of the past are used to measure the present, they
are also used to construct it. The writer himself, however much he
craves independence, is part of a mental civilization and a literature
which can only be those of the past. It is impossible for him to escape,
from one day to the next, this tradition of which he is the issue. Sometimes, even, the elements he has tried hardest to combat seem, on the
contrary, to blossom more vigorously than ever in the very work in
which he thought he had dealt them a mortal blow. And he will be
congratulated, of course, and with relief, on having cultivated them so
zealously.

Thus the specialists of the novel (whether novelists, or critics, or
over-assiduous readers) will no doubt be the ones who will have the
greatest difficulty in getting themselves out of the rut.

Even the least conditioned observer can't manage to see the world
around him with an unprejudiced eye. Let us make it quite clear before
we go any further that we are not here concerned with that naïve preoccupation with objectivity which so amuses the analysts of the
(subjective) soul. Objectivity, in the current meaning of the term – a
completely impersonal way of looking at things – is only too obviously
a chimera. But it is *liberty* which ought at least to be possible – but isn't,
either. Cultural fringes (bits of psychology, ethics, metaphysics, etc.)
are all the time being attached to things and making them seem less
strange, more comprehensive, more reassuring. Sometimes the
camouflage is total: a gesture is effaced from our minds and its place
taken by the emotions that are supposed to have given rise to it; we
remember a landscape as being 'austere', or 'calm', without being able

to describe a single line of it, or any of its principle elements. Even if we immediately think: 'But that's literature,' we don't try to rebel. We are used to this literature (the word has become perjorative) functioning like a screen, made of pieces of differently coloured glass, which splits our field of perception up into small, easily assimilable squares.

And if something resists this systematic arrangement, if some element in the world breaks the glass without finding any place in the interpretative screen, we can still make use of the convenient category of the absurd, which will absorb this irritating remainder.

But the world is neither meaningful nor absurd. It quite simply *is*. And that, in any case, is what is most remarkable about it. And suddenly this obvious fact strikes us with a force against which we are powerless. At one stroke the whole wonderful structure collapses: by opening our eyes unexpectedly we have experienced once too often the shock of this obstinate reality whose resistance we had been claiming to have broken down. All around us, defying our pack of animistic or domesticating adjectives, things *are there*. Their surface is smooth, clear and intact, without false glamour, without transparency. The whole of our literature has not yet managed even to begin to penetrate them, to alter their slightest curve.

The vast number of filmed novels that encumber our screens enables us to relive this curious experience as often as we like. The cinema, which is also heir to the psychological and naturalistic tradition, in most cases merely aims at transposing a story into pictures: it simply tries to impose on the spectator, by means of some well-chosen scenes, the meaning that the more leisurely comments in the book have for the reader. But what is always happening is that the filmed story drags us out of our comfortable state of mind and into the world it shows us, and with a violence we would look for in vain in the corresponding written text, whether novel or scenario.

Everyone can perceive the nature of the change that has taken place. In the original novel the objects and gestures that support the plot disappear completely and leave room only for their meaning: the vacant chair was only an absence of an expectation, the hand placed on the shoulder was only a sign of sympathy, the bars on the windows were only the impossibility of getting out. ... But now we *see* the chair, the movement of the hand, the shape of the bars. Their meaning remains obvious, but instead of monopolizing our attention it seems just like one more attribute; one too many, even, because what reaches us, what persists in our memory, what appears as essential and incapable of being reduced to vague mental ideas, is the gestures *per se*, the objects, the movements and the shapes, to which the picture has restored at one stroke (and unintentionally) their *reality*.

It may seem odd that these fragments of basic reality, which the filmed story cannot help unwittingly offering us, should make such an impression on us when identical scenes in day to day life would not suffice to free us from our blindness. It seems, in fact, as if the conventions of photography (the two dimensions, the black and white, the frame, the difference in scale between the foreground and the background) all help to liberate us from our own conventions. The slightly unusual appearance of this reproduction-world reveals to us, at the same time, the *unusual* character of the world around us; it too is unusual in so far as it refuses to submit to our habitual ways of understanding and to our notions of order.

And so we should try to construct a solider, more immediate world to take the place of this universe of 'meanings' (psychological, social, functional meanings). So that the first impact of objects and gestures should be that of their *presence*, and that this presence should then continue to dominate, taking precedence over any explanatory theory which would attempt to imprison them in some system of reference, whether it be sentimental, sociological, Freudian, metaphysical, or any other.

In the construction of future novels, gestures and objects will be *there*, before they are *something*; and they will still be there afterwards, hard, unalterable, ever-present, and apparently quite indifferent to their own meaning, which meaning tries in vain to reduce them to the precarious role of utensils, to a temporary and shameful fabric which has form only by kind permission of a superior human truth that has chosen it as a means of self-expression, after which it immediately reconsigns this embarrassing auxiliary to oblivion.

But from now on, on the contrary, objects will gradually lose their instability and their secrets, they will forego their false mystery, and that suspect inner life that an essayist has called 'the romantic heart of things'. They will no longer be the vague reflection of the vague soul of the hero, the image of his torments, the shadow of his desires. Or rather, if it does still happen that things are used for a moment as a support for human passions, it will only be temporarily, and they will only be making a more or less derisive show of accepting the tyranny of meanings, the better to indicate how far they remain alien to man.

As for the characters in the novel, they will be able to contain a multiplicity of possible interpretations; they will be open to every sort of comment to suit every sort of prejudice, whether psychological, psychiatric, religious or political. People will soon perceive their indifference to these so-called riches. Whereas the traditional hero is always being got at, cornered, destroyed, by the author's suggested interpretations, for ever being pushed into an intangible and unstable *elsewhere*, which gets more and more vague and remote, the future hero will on the contrary remain *there*. While it will be the comments that remain elsewhere; when the hero's presence is indisputable they will seem useless, superfluous, and even dishonest.

Acknowledgements

We are grateful to the following for permission to reproduce copyright material:

George Allen & Unwin Ltd for an extract from *Ideas: General Introduction to Pure Phenomenology* by Husserl; George Allen & Unwin Ltd and Alfred A. Knopf Inc for an extract from *The Decline of the West* by Oswald Spengler, copyright © 1926, 1928 by Alfred A. Knopf Inc; George Allen & Unwin Ltd and Liveright Publishing Corporation for an extract from *Introductory Lectures on Psycho-Analysis* by Freud, copyright © 1963 by Joan Rivere; Basil Blackwell & Mott Ltd for an extract from *Existentialism* by Martin Heidegger; Basil Blackwell & Mott Ltd and Harper & Row, Publishers Inc for an extract from *Being and Time* by Martin Heidegger, translated by John Macquarrie and Edward Robinson, copyright © 1962 by S.C.M. Press; Calder & Boyars Ltd and Grove Press Inc for an extract from *Towards A New Novel* by Alain Robbe-Grillet, translated by Barbara Wright; T. & T. Clark Publishers for an extract from *Church Dogmatics, Volume 1, Part 2* by Barth; T. & T. Clark and Charles Scribner's Sons for an extract from *I and Thou* by Martin Buber; Collins Publishers Ltd and Harper & Row Inc for an extract from *The Present Age* by Kierkegaard and an extract from *The Future of Man* by Pierre Teilhard de Chardin, translated by Norman Denny, copyright © 1959 by Editions du Seuil, copyright 1964 in the English translation by Collins and Harper & Row Inc; Doubleday & Co Inc for extracts from *The Birth of Tragedy and The Genealogy of Morals* by Friedrich Nietzsche, translated by Francis Golffing, copyright © 1956 by Doubleday & Co; Dover Publications Inc for an extract from *The Autobiography of Charles Darwin & Selected Letters* edited by Francis Darwin; Faber & Faber Ltd for an extract from *What is Surrealism* by Breton, translated by D. Gascoyne; Faber & Faber Ltd and Random House Inc for an extract from *The Dyer's Hand and Other Essays* by W. H. Auden, copyright © 1962 by W. H. Auden; authors agents, Trinity College Cambridge, and Macmillan & Co Ltd for extracts from *Psyche's Task, The Golden Bough* and *Garnered Sheaves* by Sir James Frazer; Harvard University Press for an extract from *Poetics of Music* by Igor Stravinsky, copyright © 1947 by the President and Fellows of Harvard College; Hogarth Press Ltd, Sigmund Freud Copyrights Ltd, Mrs. Alix Strachy and (1)

Liveright Publishing Corporation for an extract from *Five Lectures on Psychoanalysis*, (2) Basic Books Inc for an extract from *Studies in Hysteria* edited by Ernest Jones, and Hogarth Press and Alfred A. Knopf Inc for an extract from *Moses and Monotheism* translated by James Strachey; Hogarth Press and W. Norton & Co Inc for an extract from *An Outline of Psychoanalysis* translated by Strachey, copyright © 1949 by W. Norton & Co Inc, all from *The Complete Psychological Works of Sigmund Freud*; Houghton Mifflin Co Inc for an extract from 'Contrite Consciousness' from *The Phenomenology of Mind* translated by Josiah Royce; Hutchinson & Co Ltd and Houghton Mifflin Co Inc for an extract from *Mein Kampf* by Adolf Hitler; The Macmillan Co Inc for extracts from *The Modern World: 1848 to the Present World* edited by Hans Kohn, copyright © 1944 by Hans Kohn; Methuen & Co Ltd and Hill and Wang Inc Publishers for an extract from *Brecht on Theatre* by Bertolt Brecht, translated by John Willett, copyright © 1957, 1963 and 1964 by Suhrkamp Verlag, Frankfurt am Main. Translation and notes © 1964 by John Willett; Methuen & Co Ltd, Literary Masterworks Inc and Editions Gallimard for an extract from *Being and Nothingness* by Jean-Paul Sartre, (French title L'Etre et le Neant) © 1943 by Editions Gallimard; Methuen & Co Ltd and Les Editions Nagel for an extract from *Existentialism and Humanism* by Jean-Paul Sartre, translated by Philip Mairet; The Museum of Modern Art for an extract 'Statement by Picasso: 1923' from *Picasso: Fifty Years of His Art* by Alfred H. Barr Junior, copyright © 1946 by The Museum of Modern Art; Oxford University Press Inc for extracts from *From Max Weber: Essays in Sociology* edited and translated by H. H. Gerth and C. Wright Mills, copyright © 1946 by Oxford University Press; The Pall Mall Press Ltd and Frederick A. Praeger Inc for extracts from *Vilfredo Pareto: Sociological Writings* edited by S. E. Finer; Penguin Books Ltd for extracts from *Selected Verse* by Rimbaud and *The Brothers Karamazov* by Fyodor Dostoyevsky; Penguin Books Ltd and Harcourt, Brace & World Inc for an extract from *Marx on Economics* by R. Freedman; Philosopical Library, Publishers for an extract from *Encyclopedia of Philosophy* by Hegel, translated by G. E. Mueller; Princeton University Press Inc. and the American Scandinavian Foundation for extracts from *Concluding Unscientific Postscript* by Soren Kierkegaard, translated by D. F. Swenson and Walter Lowrie; Princeton University Press Inc for an extract from *Fear and Trembling* and *The Sickness Unto Death* by S. Kierkegaard, translated by Walter Lowrie, and for an extract from *A Kierkegaard Anthology* edited by Robert

Bretall, copyright © 1947 by Princeton University Press; author for an extract from an article by Henry Moore from *Unit One* edited by Herbert Read; Routledge & Kegan Paul Ltd and Harcourt, Brace & World Inc for extracts from *Modern Man in Search of a Soul* by Carl Jung; Routledge & Kegan Paul Ltd and Princeton University Press for extracts from 'Archetypes and the Collective Unconscious' from *Collected Works of C. J. Jung* edited by G. Alder, M. Fordham and H. Read, translated by R. F. C. Hull, copyright © 1959 by the Bollingen Foundation, and for extracts from *Suicide* by Durkheim; Routledge & Kegan Paul Ltd and The Macmillan Co Inc for an extract from *Between Man and Man* by Martin Buber, copyright © 1965 by The Macmillan Co; S.C.M. Press Ltd and Charles Scribner's Sons Inc for extracts from *Jesus Christ and Mythology* by Rudolf Bultmann, copyright © 1958 by R. Bultmann; S.C.M. Press Ltd and The Macmillan Co Inc for extracts from *Letters and Papers from Prison* by Bonhoeffer; edited by E. Bethge, copyright © 1953 by Macmillan © 1967 S.C.M. Press; Charles Scribner's Sons Inc for extracts from *Hegel Selections* edited by J. Loewenberg, copyright © 1929, renewed 1957 by Charles Scribner's Sons; The Viking Press Inc for an extract from *The Portable Nietzsche* translated and edited by Walter Kaufmann, copyright © 1954 by The Viking Press, and an extract from *The New Art, The New Life: The Culture of Pure Relationships and Other Essays* by Piet Mondrian, ed. H. Holtzman and M. James, British publishers Thames & Hudson; C. A. Watts & Co Ltd for extracts from *Karl Marx: Selected Writings* by T. B. Bottomore and M. Rubel; George Wittenborn Inc for an extract from *The Cubist Painters* by Apollinaire, translated by Lionel Abel (Documents of Modern Art – Volume 1).

We have been unable to contact the American copyright owners of *Suicide* and *The Rules of Sociological Method* by Durkheim and would appreciate any information that would enable us to do so.

Index